Phantom Variati

Phantom Variations

The Adaptations of Gaston Leroux's
Phantom of the Opera,
1925 to the Present

Ann C. Hall

McFarland & Company, Inc., Publishers
Jefferson, North Carolina, and London

LIBRARY OF CONGRESS CATALOGUING-IN-PUBLICATION DATA

Hall, Ann C., 1959–
    Phantom variations : the adaptations of Gaston Leroux's
Phantom of the opera, 1925 to the present / Ann C. Hall.
        p.   cm.
    Includes bibliographical references and index.

    ISBN 978-0-7864-4265-2
    softcover : 50# alkaline paper ∞

    1. Leroux, Gaston, 1868–1927. Fantôme de l'Opéra.
2. Leroux, Gaston, 1868–1927 — Film and video adaptations.
3. Leroux, Gaston, 1868–1927 — Adaptations.   4. Horror
tales — Film and video adaptations.   I. Title
PQ2623.E6F233   2009
843'.912 — dc22   2009012730

British Library cataloguing data are available

Cover photograph ©2009 Shutterstock

Manufactured in the United States of America

McFarland & Company, Inc., Publishers
  Box 611, Jefferson, North Carolina 28640
  www.mcfarlandpub.com

To Geoffrey C. Nelson

Acknowledgments

I would like to thank the public television station in Cleveland, Ohio, for its horror film series aired during the late seventies. While babysitting, I learned about classic horror films such as *The Phantom of the Opera*. Later, Steve Watt reintroduced me to the Phantom through Arthur Kopit's musical version, and this book came out of a paper that I wrote on that version. I would also like to thank Ohio Dominican University for the sabbatical leave to begin my work on this book many years ago. Also, to Katherine Burkman, who read a number of drafts and versions of this piece, my greatest thanks. To Mardia Bishop, who read a later version, much thanks and appreciation throughout the process. Of course, I cannot forget my family, particularly my children, Sarah and Zach Nelson, who watched a good number of film versions with me and offered their own takes on some of these versions. And to Geoff Nelson, who helped me hone ideas, find versions and variations, and who always hears the music of the night.

Table of Contents

Introduction:
The Skull Beneath the Skin

> The Phantom of the Opera existed. He was not, as was believed
> for a long time, a creature imagined by artists; a superstition of
> directors; a droll creation of the excitable minds of young women
> in the corps de ballet, their mothers, or the box attendants, the
> cloak room employees or the doorkeeper.
> — Gaston Leroux's Preface to *The Phantom of the Opera*

Thanks to Andrew Lloyd Webber's *Phantom of the Opera* (1986), audiences across the globe know about the existence of the Phantom. Transported by the music, the setting, and the story, millions have entered the dark underworld of the Paris Opera House where Erik, otherwise known as the Phantom, lives, loves, and perhaps dies. Lloyd Webber's talents as a musician and the haunting lyrics by Charles Hart and Richard Stilgoe recreate a creature whose story was envisioned nearly ninety years earlier by the popular French writer and newspaper reporter, Gaston Leroux. Lloyd Webber, Hart and Stilgoe, of course, are not the only artists to adapt *Phantom*. From 1910 to the present day, the story has fascinated many writers, audiences, and cultures. The claim made by Gaston Leroux's narrator in the preface to his novel eerily anticipates the independent life his creation continues to enjoy since his appearance in novel form. The variations are endless. He exists in numerous genres: films, novels, short stories, musicals, dramas, television series, cartoons, children's literature, and adult fantasy. He exists in order to be loved by a mother. He exists in order to be abandoned by a mother. He exists during the *fin de siècle* of two centuries. He exists in simple versions, and he exists in stage versions so lavish they put many spectacular films to shame.

What spell does the Phantom cast over generations?

This book is an attempt to answer that question by examining the themes and variations on the original *Phantom of the Opera*.

Several others have tried to explain the "Phantom phenomenon." For some, the popularity of the original novel grew out of the ravages of the French Revolution: having experienced the terrors of the era, the French reading public in particular demanded more, horrific details in the guise of the gothic novels and thrillers that were popular in the 19th century, paving the way for *The Phantom*. And while this is a compelling explanation of the explosion of interest in the other thrillers that Leroux and his contemporaries produced, it does not fully explain *The Phantom*, since it was not particularly popular upon its release in Paris.

Others argue that the story mimics the Freudian unconscious, a popular approach for many horror works such as Bram Stoker's *Dracula*, since it explains why audiences would want to see or sit through gore, bloodshed, or terror. In the case of *The Phantom*, moreover, the argument is particularly compelling as a result of the theme of masking and unmasking. In essence, the narrative is a symbolic representation of the Freudian world, the manifest content, which is socially acceptable, disguising the grotesque desires of the latent content, in this case the distorted face of Erik. Jungian interpretations, too, would uncover the face beneath the mask, and argue that while the mask is necessary for us all, it is essential not to become the mask, which apparently Erik desires to do but, thanks to Christine's unveiling, cannot.

Such strategies diminish the narrative that most people presume they enjoy. Bruno Bettelheim's *The Uses of Enchantment*, for example, addresses the popularity and unconscious content of fairy tales, in this case cultural myths and legends. While many such readings are valid and important, this approach for a work like Leroux's *Phantom of the Opera* tends to dismiss the crafting of the author and the very variations that we so enjoy. In its extreme, such psychological interpretation makes all the variations one story, without honoring the differences among them, the unique additions, deletions, or alterations that captivate many readers and audiences.

Still other readers argue that the Phantom represents not only the unconscious but the repressed — in this case, those repressed by the society. Erik then becomes a symbol for the marginalized, the deformed, the poor, and the dispossessed by the culture. The entire work does not appeal to our tendency to root for underdogs, but rather, serves as yet another monolithic narrative of the manner in which society represses the ugly, the distorted, and the needy in order to create a world that is none of these, a world of art, success, and beauty. But like all repressed entities, whether cultural or personal manifestations of the unconscious, there is a return of the repressed. We can never ignore the Phantom.[1]

Monolithic statements about the versions seem to erode the individual works' unique characteristics, and yet there must be something about the narrative that transcends or invigorates the particulars of the various works. What the works require is a kind of double vision, a dual nature, very similar to the dual nature of the narrative's main character. Honor the differences among the versions, examine the theme that seems to unite them, assess the attraction of the foundational story, while simultaneously enjoying the aberrations and examining their effects on the narrative. I realize the irony of these statements — criticizing monolithic statements by making a monolithic statement that challenges monolithic interpretations. But this is precisely what is needed in order to appreciate the variations on the theme of *Phantom of the Opera.* To take the irony further, by examining *The Phantom of the Opera* and its variations from a fresh perspective, it becomes clear that the narrative, in all its variations, encourages viewers to avoid monolithic interpretations and encourages them to think more deeply, to see more deeply, to look beyond the mask, to forgo the day and its emphasis on sight, and to hear, truly hear, to listen to the "music of the night."

At its very essence, the story, the narrative, the plot, challenges traditional distinctions between truth and fiction. Commonly labeled "gothic fiction" or a "spectacular story, film or musical," *The Phantom of the Opera's* very fantastical elements in its original form and its variations — that is, all of the structures and forms that help make it fictional — in fact enable *The Phantom* and its variations to reflect reality better than what we would describe as "realistic" representations.[2] That is, because *The Phantom* is so spectacular, it actually appears more realistic than it would without the fantastical elements. How? Surprising as it may seem, this unbelievable story about a disfigured psychopathic stalker who is not only a gifted musician, but independently wealthy, a world traveler, and a sometime architect, who falls in love with his protégé only to have his heart broken by her decision to return to a conventional and domestic relationship with a previous lover, not only reflects a reality, but a reality that we all, across cultures and time periods, understand. It is a spectacular tale about identity, of ourselves and others, of appearances, and of deception, and these matters are common to all, both within the Opera House and outside the Phantom's lair.

To enable readers and viewers to more readily identify with these matters and to underscore the narrative's ultimate purpose — to challenge readers and viewers to think, see, and listen more attentively — nothing is as it seems in the Phantom's world; there is a dark side and light side to everything and everyone. The Opera House itself is a world of illusion and unrealities, and many of the characters are multi-faceted, as they are in life. There are no cardboard notices to identify one person as a "villain" and another as a "do-gooder."

If there were one word to characterize the story's world, it would have to be "dualistic." Everything is divided; everyone is tortured. Erik, of course, is the classic tortured artist, and we are drawn to the "artist's double nature: a haunted figure at once exalted and disfigured by his genius, eternally isolated from other men" (Byrd xiv–xv). And though some versions depict his beloved, Christine, as a mere victim, the more interesting and successful versions offer her a choice as well: the conventional family life or a life of art in Erik's underground lair.

Music itself has a dual nature not just in this story but in history as well. One need only remember Tolstoy's *Kreutzer Sonata* (1890), for example, in which a husband is driven to murder as a result of his jealousy toward his wife's music partner and their work together on the Beethoven piece. From Chinese philosophers to Christian philosophers to Baptist ministers, music's ambivalent nature is highlighted: it transcends the limits of space and time, transporting us to the heavenly heights, but it can lead us into the temptations of hell (Dolar 17) as surely as Circe's song, which brought destruction to the Greek travelers who were lured to her shore in Homer's *Odyssey*.

But it is music's uncontrollable or ethereal quality that finally unites Erik and Christine in ways that seem more erotic than physical expression. In all versions, for instance, the couple connects on the basis of sound, not sight; they unite via breath, not body, thereby giving their romance an "otherworldly" quality. Such passion, moreover, once again forces us to question our overreliance on the visual. In the world of the Phantom, it is not love at first sight, but love at first song.

In the end, Christine, like us, returns to the "normal" world, the world of appearances and tradition. Once she has made her desires clear, it is now the Phantom's turn to choose: he can either force Christine to marry him in order to save Raoul, or let her go with the man she has chosen. In the end, most of the Phantoms, including Leroux's, sacrifice their desires for a woman's and honor her choice. As will be clear from the discussion of the various versions, this sacrifice is the true aphrodisiac of most Phantom narratives: women's desires are honored and upheld, no matter how conventional. It is this moment that earns the Phantom narrative its audience's loyalty, not the unseen "happily ever after" promised to Christine by her conventional Raoul. More importantly, the Phantom-artist's dual nature is presented positively. While the world sees Erik as a freak, a monster, less than human, the real secret to the underworld is his compassion and sacrifice. Clearly, things are not what they seem.

Fin de Siècle versus Belle Époque

Tellingly, the cultural and historical milieu in which Leroux wrote the original story is also characterized by its dualism. Though the novel was published in 1910, it is set during the turn of the century, and its author was a product of his end-of-the-century. Like our own turn of the century, Leroux's was characterized by contradictions. The period itself is referred to by mutually exclusive terms, the *fin de siècle*, the end of the century and old ways and mores, and the *la belle époque*, the beautiful era, which ushered in new life, art, and culture. There were those who saw the cultural change as corrupt and those who saw the change as positive, a "step towards transcending the stifling mediocrities of everyday convention" (Showalter 15).

Two paintings by two artists of the time illustrate the contradictions of the age, and both are readily available online through various image-search engines: Pierre–August Renoir's *Dance at Bougival*, 1883, held by the Museum of Fine Arts, Boston, and Henri de Toulouse-Lautrec's *La Goulue Arriving at the Moulin Rouge with Two Women*, 1892, held by the Museum of Modern Art. Both document the period's social nature, but the Renoir is decidedly more optimistic, while the Lautrec is fraught with anxiety. In the Renoir, the young girl, appropriately covered from head to toe, participates in a courtship ritual, dancing. There are chaperones, and one could easily see her bending her face to receive the kiss her partner so clearly wishes to give her. She is, after all, wearing a brilliant red hat. She is not entirely without feeling. The Lautrec, however, creates one of the period's great "monster" women, a harpy-like creature of indistinct sexuality, indecently dressed, smoking, being escorted, not "chaperoned," by two females, one whose face is half out of frame, the other whose face looks like that of a mannequin. Both paintings suggest sexuality but from very different perspectives. As Asti Hustvedt observes:

> The vulgar application of Darwin to human society placed women near the bottom of the evolutionary ladder, where they could easily fall off and degenerate even further. At the same time, medical theories of sexual difference constructed femininity as inherently diseased. The root of a woman's problems was her reproductive system.... Just being a woman was a dangerous, pathological condition [18].

In the Renoir, there is hope; in the Lautrec, despair in the house of pleasure. In the Renoir, there is life. In the Lautrec, there is a skull beneath the flesh — a phantom.

Charles Darwin's theories challenged not only social hierarchies but inspired stories about "freaks of nature," creatures who did not quite evolve or who were devolving: "Monsters, criminals, savages, prostitutes, syphilitics, hysterics, alcoholics, drug addicts, sexual deviants, madmen, and idiots preoccupied writers of all kinds: naturalists and decadents, doctors and philosophers" (Hustevedt 10–11). The Phantom's situation also highlighted the concerns over race, immigrants, and foreign influences — outsiders adulterating pure classes and cultures, as noted by Eugen Weber's magnificent study of turn-of-the century France. And from a less exclusive perspective, the move towards equality had its own dark side: standardization and homogeneity, a society without individuals, only automatons (Hustevedt 15).

And while there are certainly a number of differences between the nineteenth century and the twenty-first, the question of individuality and identity, equality, race relations, and others remain. The position of women has improved in most first-world countries, but the questions of equity and equality persist. In the aftermath of the World Trade Center attack, the role of foreigners has also become complicated. The natural and physical sciences continue to raise just as many issues as they solve. Stem-cell research, reproductive practices, genetic coding and determinism, as well as a persistent distrust in the conclusions of Charles Darwin demonstrate that we may have more in common with our nineteenth-century ancestors than we would care to admit.

On a very practical level, advances in science have enhanced our ability to change our faces, our shapes, and our looks, but the ramifications of such shape-shifting are still being discovered and discussed. For example, the first face transplant took place, appropriately for the purposes of this study, in France in November of 2005. And while the ability to transplant faces had been available to scientists for some time, the ethical ramifications were a consideration. The transplant, for instance, necessitates that the donor's heart be still beating when the face is removed. Further, the face is not the face of either the recipient or the donor, but instead, a "hybrid," and psychologists were concerned about the effects of this reality on the recipient. The mask may be new, but it is a mask just the same ("Woman Has First Face Transplant"). In this way, the Phantom and all its variations have as much to teach us about the "skull beneath the skin" as Gaston Leroux's audiences one hundred years ago.

Gaston Leroux

Gaston's Leroux's life, career and writings mimic the dualism of his age and indicate that while he was certainly a popular author, his themes were serious reflections on the concerns of his day and ours. For example, he was acutely aware of the dual nature of his age and of humanity. Through a successful career as a journalist, he witnessed many of the era's important events first-hand. Born 6 May 1868 in a country house, he was well-educated as a boy, finally landing in law school in Paris. As is the case with many writers, his parents encouraged him to find a stable career, even though he was already having some minor success with his poetry and other writings. When his parents died in 1889, Leroux's new-found freedom was enhanced by a large inheritance.

Though he had always been "tormented by the demon of literature" (Byrd viii), he had only written a few pieces before this time. Once he ran out of money, he began writing for newspapers, where his intuition and nose for stories were legendary (Byrd x). He reported on the Dreyfus Affair, a trial in which Alfred Dreyfus, the only Jewish member of a military team, was accused of treason. Subsequent documents revealed the accusations as ridiculous, but the courts and the military persisted in their persecution of Dreyfus, largely motivated by anti–Semitism. In classic military style, Dreyfus was found guilty during a second trial in 1899, but he was then pardoned by the French president and reinstated into the military with honors. As Leroux wrote, "This moment ... will be a date in the history of justice and future school children will be no more able to ignore it than they would the battle of Actium or that of the crowning of Charlemagne" (qtd. in Wolf 8). And he was correct.

One of the reasons for his success was that he "had the knack for getting on with people, no matter how high or low their station" (Perry 24), a characteristic that seems to have been required during this period characterized by fluctuating social hierarchies. Success and subterfuge characterized Leroux's journalistic career. His numerous escapades included one in which he posed as a prison anthropologist, a deception that brought down the wrath of many legal minds and journalists but eventually saved the life of an innocent man.

Ends justifying the means seems to have been Leroux's motto for most everything in life, including women. Early in his journalistic career he married Marie Lefranc, but the marriage was not a happy one. The two were ill-suited, and Leroux was prone to infidelities on the road and at home in Paris. Then Leroux met Jeanne Cayatte in 1902, the love of his life. As Leonard Wolf notes, it "was the beginning of an enthusiastic courtship which, since Marie Lefranc continued to refuse Leroux a divorce, ended for him and Jeanne Cayatte in that irregular relationship that in France has the name *concubinage*" (11). In other words, Leroux was leading a double life, married to Lefranc, but living with and fathering children with Cayatte until Lefranc's death in 1917.

During this time, Leroux wrote fictional stories, but it was not until 1907 that his most famous work up to that time was published, *The Mystery of the Yellow Room*. In it, a young woman is attacked and left for dead in a room that seems completely sealed. A young detective, Joseph Rouletabille, arrives on the scene. As we learn throughout the story, the young Rouletabille, whose name figuratively means "one who goes his own way" (Byrd ix), has been abandoned by his own mother and grew up on the streets. In the sequel to this story, *The Perfume of the Lady in Black* (1908), Rouletabille meets Gaston Leroux, the newspaperman, and sells him a newspaper. The generous Leroux gives him a big tip because, he says, they are in the same business, and this money helps the young Rouletabille set up a real business as a shoe shiner, and ultimately leads him to detective work. According to *The New York Times* book review, *The Mystery of the Yellow Room* was a great success: "Horrors accumulate. The most famous of the detectives of Paris is put on that famous case, and he is foiled by Rouletabille, who displays such superhuman sagacity that even the most modest writer for the press feels reflected glory" ("A Book of Mysteries"). And of the sequel, *The Perfume of the Lady in Black, The New York Times* is even more praiseworthy because of "the machinations of as villainous a villain as ever sprang, fully armed for villainy, out of an author's brain, whereby he seeks to wreak destruction upon the happiness of the couple with whose marriage the story begins" ("A Detective Story"). Without going into great detail here about these two works, it is clear that many of the themes that appear in *Phantom* also appear here: the loss of the mother, the threat of the supernatural which in fact turns out to be the handiwork of a villain, and the relationship between the classes.

Other short stories illustrate Leroux's odd and macabre sense of humor. In "A Terrible Tale," for example, the narrator meets with four old "sea dogs" who share their stories of sea adventures with him. In one story, Captain Alban explains how he lost his arm. In his youth, he happened upon a mysterious occurrence, odd comings and goings in a neighboring house with a beautiful mistress. Determined to find out what was going on, the man entered the house, where he met an old acquaintance who was nothing more than a "bust," having lost his arms and legs. The legless and armless man then went on to explain how he had become such a creature. As it turns out, he and his friends, and his lovely wife, the mistress of the house, were shipwrecked, and as is often the case, they were at sea for many days, hungry. Rather than killing and feeding on one person, the group decided to eat part of one another. Coincidentally, one of the men was a doctor, so his limbs were left intact in order that he might perform the surgery. The woman, as lovely and loved as she was, was also left intact. As more and more men lost their arms, she also began to serve them. They were rescued "a month" later, but "the frightful part of it was that these people retained a taste for human flesh"

(32), and so once a year, they reunited for a "special meal." In this case, it was Captain Alban's arm.

Leroux, however, was most popular in France for his Chéri-Bibi stories, tales of a Robin Hood–style adventurer. In *Missing Men* (1923), one of Cheri's old friends grieves over Cheri's death, but soon meets another man, a French noble. As he gets to know this man, he suddenly supposes that the man could be Cheri. He remembers a man named Kanaka who had been accused of stealing flesh from live victims. Initially, he presumes, as in the "Terrible Tale," that the flesh may have been consumed in an act of cannibalism, but then realizes that it has been used for plastic surgery:

> Good Heavens, it was possible for people's faces to be altered in that way.... Not forgetting that if it were possible, it would not have been very difficult since Cheri-Bibi and the Marquis's heads in length, breadth and shape were pretty well of the same dimensions.... But how had the Kanaka managed with the nose ... to place the Marquis's Bourgon nose on Cheri-Bibi's face? He must have removed Cheri-Bibi's nose and grafted that of the Marquis on his face. What a piece of work! What a piece of work! [25].

Again, the parallels between these stories and the *Phantom* are also clear. Identity shifts; appearances deceive; women are sometimes saints, sometimes sinners; and there is always some game afoot. But most importantly, his other works also emphasize the sometimes tantalizing, sometimes horrifying lessons found in *The Phantom*—to look deeply, consider, and reflect, to avoid easy answers based upon superficial evidence.

A dramatic writer who frequently announced the end of a book by shooting a gun out the family home's window (Wolf 17), Leroux also confessed that his ideas came to him in dreams, from the unconscious, the divided nature of the self. Such admissions clearly fuel the Freudian interpretations of his work and the thrillers he and others like him wrote. Leroux, however, admitted that *The Phantom* came to him as a result of a tour of the Opera House: "In those labyrinthine cellars and the mysterious subterranean lake which was visible through iron grilles in the floor only if a torch was lit to pierce the blackness, there was an atmosphere that seemed to demand that a yarn be told" (qtd. in Perry 28).

When *Phantom* appeared, it received only lukewarm success. *The New York Times* review faulted Leroux for making Erik a man: "if we are introduced to a ghost, let him be a ghost to the end no less.... There is a far cry, however, from the author's thrilling 'Mystery of the Yellow Room'" ("An Opera-House Phantom"). Clearly, the reviewers missed the challenging nature of the book: to create a story that asked us to do more than look for ghosts.

The book would have lapsed into obscurity if it were not for the film version starring Lon Chaney in 1925. In 1919, Leroux had established his own film company, and in 1922, he met with Carl Laemmle, the president of Universal Pictures, and gave him a copy of *Phantom of the Opera*. The rest is history: "Leroux lived long enough to enjoy the renewed fame the film brought him in his last years" (Perry 31). Peter Haining reports events differently, saying the film "did little for the man who had created the original story. Gaston Leroux was ill at his Paris home at the time the picture was being made in Hollywood and played no part in its creation" (Foreword 9). He died in 1927 and was buried in Nice, one of his favorite cities. Called the "eternal reporter" in his obituary in *The New York Times*, Leroux was praised for his "weird mystery tales," his reporting, and his travels throughout the world. Quoting a French critic who had written about Leroux years earlier, the *Times* honored Leroux with the critic's following words:

> To be a reporter means to hold in one's grasp a piece of life, to feel it tremble when it comes in contact with one's fingers: it means to give it life or to blow it out with one's own breath, to clothe it or lay it bare. To do that, treasures of fine feeling are needed. M. Gaston Leroux is in possession of them, and he joins them to an imagination which is all his own ["Gaston Leroux Dies"].

Leroux's own commitment to reportage, life, and truth at all costs suggests at the very least that he was interested in doing more than telling a ghost story, and thankfully for the rest of us and the veritable Phantom industry, he did.

The reason for the appeal is simple: the original, as well as the subsequent versions, all require that audiences read beyond the surface of things, to look deeper, and even to abandon the power of the eye, the spectacular, the very essence of what we see in favor of the "music of the night," sounds which transcend the limits of the visual. In this way, the audience is engaged, searching, and wondering, just as the characters search and wonder.

And in the end, Leroux succeeds through his narrative and its subsequent incarnations to educate audiences on the fine art of interpretation. The first chapter of this book examines the ways in which the Leroux novel accomplishes this task, teaching us to examine our preconceptions and perceptions more closely. The second chapter moves to the film versions which sprang up not long after the appearance of Leroux's novel and certainly during his lifetime. In some cases, the camera, the new technology of the age, co-opts the narrative as a means to highlight its own importance and power, but in other instances, the narrative triumphs by reminding viewers once again that they should not place their blind faith in the new motion picture images, the spectacle of film.

Interestingly, the novel and its variations seem to serve as harbingers of new technology throughout most of their history. In order to highlight the changing dynamics of the entertainment industry, the third chapter includes the musical and stage versions, versions which followed the first film versions. And the fourth chapter includes various novels and other versions of the famous tale. As will become clear throughout the book, *The Phantom* not only speaks to audiences and encourages them to view entertainment differently, but the entire chronology of the novel and its various incarnations demonstrates a strange and shifting relationship among various art forms: novel to film to theatre to film to novel and film again. These wildly shifting genres and treatments not only illustrate the incredible popularity of *The Phantom* story, but also demonstrate the narrative's flexibility — its ability to change and withstand permutation. All ages, all genres, all peoples, it appears, hope to capture the "music of the night."

CHAPTER 1

Masking and Unmasking: Gaston Leroux's Original *Phantom of the Opera* (1910)

Any true Parisian has learned to hide his grief under a mask of joy, or his innermost delight with a look of melancholy or indifference.

— Gaston Leroux's *Phantom of the Opera*

After watching, hearing, or reading some of the various versions of *Phantom of the Opera,* it is perhaps a great pleasure for some readers to experience the original version. And one of the first noticeable characteristics of the work is Leroux's dry, sardonic narration and humor. It is a delight, and many versions struggle to reproduce it, and oftentimes fail.

Another characteristic that is apparent very early on is the novel's penchant for polarities, dualities, the "doubleness" of life. Perhaps inspired by his age, an age of contradictions, perhaps inspired by his own bifurcated married life, perhaps dissatisfied with his earlier novel, *The Double Life of Theophraste Longuet* (1902), Gaston Leroux not only underscores the existence of double lives in his major characters and even the setting of *Phantom of the Opera,* but he also shows us that this dualism or this ambiguity characterizes all of humankind. It becomes very clear early on in the novel that Erik is not the only one wearing a mask. There is a double life, another side to all of us, a public and a private face, a good and bad side.

And Leroux does not limit this ambiguous representation to characters. Leroux highlights what may be obvious to some, but not all — ideologies, belief systems, and institutions are multifaceted as well. While Erik and Christine struggle with their rational and passionate sides in light and darkness, the Paris Opera House serves as a monument to the division between art and life, wealth and poverty, culture and chaos. Above ground the Opera House represents beauty, form, function, order, and perfection — below, the homeless, ugly, defiled, poor, and mad. Through these dualities, Leroux's novel provides us with many opportunities to read between the lines and below the surface, to enter the underworld, to interpret. In the end, his novel becomes an extensive lesson in interpretation, analysis, and detective work, complete with musical score. There is more to life than meets the eye — again, there is the "music of the night" which Leroux takes great pleasure in masking and unmasking throughout his novel.

Narrative Perspective

Before entering the narrative, the story and plot line of the novel, it is important to understand the important role of the narrator in the series of events, a role that is frequently overlooked. The narrative begins conventionally enough, with the narrator reporting on the claims regarding the Opera Ghost. He does what good reporters do and what good readers should do — he digs for information, in his case, through newspapers, books, interviews, and journals, otherwise known as "reportage." On the one hand, this material creates the illusion of reality in much the same way that other fantastical stories create verisimilitude: Bram Stoker's *Dracula* (1897) or Henry James's *Turn of the Screw* (1898), for example. Like these authors, by using materials that generally constitute "real" research, Leroux creates the illusion of credibility for his fantastic tale.

Simultaneously, however, this strategy blurs distinctions between real and unreal (Hogel, *Undergrounds* 32–39). That is, Leroux concocts "real" evidence to create fiction, thereby calling both into question. What is real? What is fabrication? What is fiction? Given Leroux's sense of humor in this and other works, it is also tempting to conclude that Leroux uses this reportage to educate his readers on the fine art of critical thinking and reading, in effect saying through this reportage, this fabricated fantasy, "Don't trust everything you read, no matter how factual it appears. All of this material is concocted in order to tell a realistic ghost story." The narrator's most important sources, *Memoirs of a Director*, for example, not only look like "real" books, but the narrator even includes a brief review, in the appropriate "reviewer tone," describing it as "a lightweight work of the too-skeptical M. Moncharmin" (22).[3] It is, of course, a complete concoction created by the sardonic Leroux (Wolf 22). In this way, not only are the situations and plot of the novel ambiguous, but the narrative itself is double-edged, a realistic fabrication that actually presents life realistically through its fantastical tale.

The role of the narrator is also suspect. Readers of Leroux would know that he had muddied the narrative waters before, casting himself as a character in *The Perfume of the Lady in Black* (1908). Like an Alfred Hitchcock cameo, Leroux in this novel buys a newspaper from a boy and tips him mightily, thereby enabling the young man to use the money to become one of the most famous detectives in both the fictional and the real France. That boy, of course, is none other than Joseph Rouletabille, Leroux's most popular detective and character. To conclude that Leroux is having a bit of fun here or elsewhere is fine; to conclude that he is blurring the boundaries between the real and the imagined is also clear; but to conclude that Leroux is the narrator is dangerous. Still, such conclusions persist even in modern editions of the novel.[4] In some ways, readers who equate Leroux with his novel are doing exactly what the novel teaches readers to avoid, to assume that what we are being told is true, that the speaker and the author are one and same, that they have our best interests at heart by presenting factual information. In this way, the "facts," though clearly fabricated, seduce us to "suspend disbelief" and judgment. But the novel's entire purpose is to encourage its readers to analyze, question, and become our own literary and life detectives.

The Paris Opera House

The setting, the Paris Opera House, also perpetuates the novel's illusory veracity. It is, of course, a real and important building in France — so important, in fact, that George Perry begins his *The Complete Phantom of the Opera* with a discussion of the building, not the novel or its author. Leroux, of course, was inspired to write *Phantom* by the Opera House.

But since he references the Opera House so specifically, the implied argument in the novel reflects a common practice in urban legends — no matter how unbelievable the tale, there is always something in the legend to tie it to a real place, person, or occurrence to give the legend its veracity. In Leroux's case, given the existence of this real and imposing work of architecture, we must be in a "real" story.

The history of the Paris Opera House underscores the theme of duality and ambivalence articulated by the novel as well. The Opera House is a beautiful work of art created through oppression, turmoil, political unrest, and in spite of a multitude of natural difficulties. According to George Perry's *The Complete Phantom of the Opera*, the nephew of Napoleon Bonaparte, Napoleon III, was interested in creating the Opera House because he was attacked on his way to the opera one evening in 1858. He decided, as supreme rulers are wont to do, that he would build his own Opera House and thereby avoid using the ones other people used. He enlisted the help of Baron Haussmann, "a city planner of genius," who not only laid the foundation for the modern city of Paris, creating a beauty which beckons to all today, but who was also given "draconian powers of demolition" (Perry 8). Again, ambiguity in art and construction. A young Charles Garnier won the architect competition, perhaps as a result of his diplomatic response to the Empress's question regarding the style his model embodied. His response: "The Napoleon III style, ma'am" (Perry 10).

Garnier's diplomacy and/or political bravado brought him no luck when excavations began on the site: "An underground stream running through the site which had the effect of turning the soil into mud, making it unstable for the laying of foundations," was discovered (Perry 10). Undeterred, the crew installed pumps to remove the water. When the foundation was finished, the water was reintroduced and the lake under the Opera House was created and persists to this day. When the water level is lowered, people can tour the underground reservoir in a boat, but this is done only sporadically while foundations are inspected.

The Opera House was "conceived not merely for performances on stage but as a setting for grand state occasions, for galas and balls, festivals and feasts. It was to be a palace both for culture and society, a gathering point for the new middle classes where they could parade and show off their finery" (Perry 11). These fine expectations, however, were challenged by both natural and political causes. The excavations, of course, displaced homes and other buildings, and the hydraulic pumping left many without water.

The Franco–Prussian War (1870–71) brought an end to Napoleon III's reign, and brought about yet another revolutionary period in French history, the fourth since the Reign of Terror. The working classes once again took control of the government, this time called the "Commune of Paris" (Perry 12). At this point the Opera house became a true servant to the community, serving as a warehouse for supplies, while the French attempted to defend themselves from the Prussians. A national guard force arose, the Communards, and used the Opera House's basements as prisons. Such a building, then, is ripe for haunting or at least a story about a haunting. Leroux, moreover, uses the violent past to underscore the story's credibility. The cadaver that he thinks is that of the Phantom of the Opera, the bones that begin his search and his discovery of the legend of the Opera Ghost, cannot be mistaken for one of the wretched who died during the Commune because, he tells us, they are buried in a different part of the Opera's underworld (26).

With political unrest subsiding, the Opera House finally opened in 1875 but not without problems. The opening night offered selections from Delibes's ballet *Le Source* and an aria from Meyerbeer's *Les Huguenots*, but the musicians felt that the orchestra was too cramped, so in "a modest form of industrial action in protest ... played so softly that they were almost inaudible" (Perry 14). In 1896, the famous chandelier fell and killed a woman, an event which Leroux also incorporated into his story, once again underscoring the veracity of his wildly fantastic tale. The Opera House still stands today, and it is a monument to French arts, a "worldly cathedral of civilization" (Theophile Gautier qtd. in Perry 21). At the same time, however, the Opera House was built for all, particularly the growing middle class. As Andras Batta reminds us, "Apart from the Budapest opera house, which was built on the Paris model (1884), there is scarcely another such theatre in the world described by the elegant term of 'palace.' But the Palais Garnier was never the property of kings or princes; it is a palace of the bourgeoisie" (192). Again, there is a paradox that reflects the dualism of the novel and its age, a palace for the middle, not ruling, class.

Choosing to write a fictional book about operas and the Opera House also challenges conventional generic distinctions and to some, ordinary common sense. How can we read about opera? The entire project seems ill-fated, much like Oscar Wilde's *Salome* (1893), which places one of the most seductive dances in the Western canon under the control of opera singers, who are notoriously rotund and immobile. But both Wilde and Leroux succeed in their experiments, blending art forms and blurring distinctions.

Further, in the case of *The Phantom of the Opera*, the operas mentioned are decidedly French, perhaps playing to the original audience's experience with French operas and music. Leroux's readership, it might be supposed, had a running mental soundtrack of these operas, in much the same way today's generation might have clear understandings when a riff from the Rolling Stones' "I Can't Get No Satisfaction" is mentioned in a Stephen King novel.

The predominance of French operas, moreover, might not only be a case of Leroux's nationalism, but the tendency might also be used as a kind of encouragement to others to familiarize themselves with French work. The French composer Charles Gounod, who had died in 1893, several years before the Leroux novel, for example, has three or four operas mentioned, one of which, *Polyeucte* (1878) is an obscure work that few would have seen.[5] The Italians are decidedly underrepresented, and Wagner is absent completely because France was a "staunch bastion of anti–German protectionism" (Hogle, *Undergrounds* 21).

Though there are many operas mentioned in the novel, Gounod's *Faust* (1859), based upon German author Johann Wolfgang Goethe's narrative, plays a significant role in the novel both practically and symbolically. And there are many similarities between the Faust myth and Erik's story. Through Erik makes no deal with the devil, he has some extraordinary talents that remove him from the commonplace and ordinary, and like Gounod's Faust, he, too, longs for a beloved. In the case of the opera, it is Marguerite, and in the case of the novel, it is Christine. Like Faust, Erik is devilish, an outcast, set to seduce the young Christine, not through wealth as in the Goethe story, but through music and perhaps the promise of success and fame. Further, Marguerite and Christine both violate conventional female stereotypes. Marguerite is not virtue personified, and she is not condemned for her sins. Instead, she is like Mary Magdalene who has desire, sins, but is redeemed. And while Christine's virtue is unquestioned, as we shall see later, she has spent a good deal of time on the dark side, but in the end, chooses a life in the secular light.

Trilby

Before moving to the Leroux novel in earnest, it is impossible to overlook the widely popular serialized novel by George du Maurier, *Trilby* (1894). Young women at the mercy of dastardly men was a common theme during the nineteenth century, but no one better than George du Maurier, Daphne du Maurier's grandfather, represented the theme, with his melodramatic interaction between the beloved Trilby and evil Svengali. The novel, like many works of the era, notably Coventry Pattimore's lengthy poem *The Angel in the House* (1854), idealizes the self-sacrificing and obedient woman of the late nineteenth century. Such self-sacrifice was rampant in literature, from Charles Dickens to Charlotte Bronte. In *Trilby*, which is also set in Paris, a young English student comes to the bohemian city, and, with his friends, meets a young woman named Trilby. Trilby is good-hearted and beautiful, but she has been on the streets, and though she is pure, she is not a member of the appropriate class, so Trilby dutifully ends the affair after her beloved's mother asks her to do so.

At the heart of this story is the Jewish Svengali, an evil man whose ethnicity reflects the anti–Semitism which was as "French as croissants" (Weber 130). After the heroine rejects her beloved for duty's sake, Svengali enslaves Trilby. While under his hypnotic power, Trilby has a hauntingly beautiful voice. In the end, the young men rescue Trilby from Svengali, who has been forcing her to perform on stage. It is too late, of course, and Trilby — exhausted and perhaps sexually depleted — dies, surrounded by her adoring male friends. Throughout the story Trilby's desires are repressed; she loves a young man, but she will not violate social conventions to fulfill her desire. She does not even choose to partner with Svengali; she merely falls limply under his power. In the end, Trilby dies, leaving a beautiful corpse upon which the men may gaze, a precursor to Disney's Sleeping Beauty. The men overcome Svengali, and the world is safe once more. No ambivalence here. The good are good and the bad are bad — and ultimately punished.

The Leroux Novel

Leroux clearly borrows from the Trilby motif, but he departs from its simplistic and melodramatic characterization and conclusion. In a very symbolic way, Leroux's novel begins not with spectacle, a picture of Christine or Erik or, in the case of the du Maurier novel, Trilby and the boys, but with breath and sound. There are rumors of an Opera Ghost, as well as the "voice over" of the narrator. In this way, we are forced to remember that there is more going on in the Opera House, than meets the eye.

The novel begins with the narrator defending the veracity of his fantastic tale. He, like many, was interested in the myth of the Phantom, and he began researching, cataloguing references in documents, but nothing substantial could be found. One day, as luck would have it, he was introduced to the Persian, who reportedly knew the Phantom personally and possessed letters to substantiate the claim. The narrator double-checked his source, who was found to be sound. Also, and again as luck would have it, when the opera attempted to bury several phonographic records of great opera singers in the basement of the Opera House, they found a cadaver, and this cadaver, argues the narrator, is without a doubt the missing Phantom because he "had the administrator touch this evidence with his own two hands" (26).

Quickly, too, the novel establishes the narrator's sarcasm and cynicism. He reports, but he also comments. We are being led to certain facts and occurrences, but there are some moments he cannot help but comment. He notes, for example, that the famed dancer Sorelli is so beautiful that one reporter wrote: "When she raises her arms and leans forward to begin a pirouette, accenting thereby the outline of her bosom, and causing the hips of this delicious woman to sway, she appears to be in a tableau so lascivious that it could drive a man to blow his brains out" (33). Leroux's narrator adds to this report, assuring us that the dancer had no brains herself, "but no one reproached her for that" (33). Later, when Joseph Buquet's body is found, the police rule the incident a "*natural suicide*" (36). The narrator's italics imply the question, "Is there an unnatural suicide?" And still later in the opening scenes of the novel, the narrator notes that one of the new opera house owners wrote such voluminous memoirs that "one has a right to wonder if he had the time to devote himself to the Opera beyond giving an account of what transpired" (61). By embedding these jibes and subjective comments in what is supposed to be a journalistic report on the legend of the Phantom of the Opera, Leroux illustrates that reportage is often biased, and by placing the comments in the hands of a fictional narrator, Leroux may make social commentary without fear — he is not making the comments; the narrator is. Clearly, we are in a different world from that of the melo-dramatic *Trilby*.

The narrator, moreover, tends to be cruelest to those who pretend to be what they are not — his comments on the diva, Carlotta, are per-haps the most scathing because she pretends to be, in this case, ironi-cally, an opera singer. As the narrator notes, "Carlotta had neither heart nor soul. She was nothing more than an instrument ... [like] your voice whose marvel it is that it sings indifferently and with the same perfec-tion of the sublimity of love, or of the most abysmal debauchery" (110–111). He continues, losing all sense of objectivity, noting that "when I think of all the pettiness and vile behavior that Christine Daaé had to endure at that time from Carlotta, I can't restrain my anger" (111). As the novel progress, the narrator's judgments clearly criticize those who wear masks to deceive as hypocrites, while those who wear masks for self-pro-tection or art, do not receive his approbation.

Consequently, the narrator refrains from cynical commentary when discussing the characters that make up the novel's love triangle. Raoul, Erik, and Christine escape his sarcasm and criticism, even when they make flawed choices. In this way, the novel allows us to make up our own minds about the love triangle, if not the politics of opera, music, and police investigations. In fact, the love triangle serves as the novel's "final exam" regarding its lessons on interpretation and critical analysis. Educated in the ways of duplicity, social expectations, and pretensions, Leroux's readers must draw their own conclusions regarding the ending of the novel.

The novel begins with the sale of the Opera House, the rumors of the Opera Ghost and the death of Joseph Buquet. In addition, since the new Opera House has new owners, so there is change afoot and, as is usually the case, gossip. To compound the volatile atmosphere, Chris-tine Daaé, a veritable nobody, has sung at a celebration for the new own-ers and made her mark as a competitor for the place of lead singer. As the impish young Meg Giry mentions off-handedly, "Not six months ago, she was singing like a cow" (39). Now, however, Christine's voice triumphs, and the narrator waxes poetic: there was no one in attendance "who did not thrill to the melody of her seraphic voice, who did not feel their souls fly, together with hers, over the tomb of the lovers of Verona" (41–42). As a matter of fact, it is the result of this performance and the narrator's good fortune to be in attendance that prompts his investigation into the life and loves of Christine Daaé. On this night, he is taken with her voice, and he has decided to investigate her disappearance and the rumors regarding the Opera Ghost.

In order to avoid the criticism of bias, the narrator, like all good researchers, quotes a reviewer who describes Christine's transformation: "To understand what had happened to Daaé, *one would need to imagine that she had fallen in love for the first time* [Leroux's italics]" (42). Or, if not that, it may be a "pact with the devil," because: "Anyone who has not heard Christine sing the final trio from *Faust* does not know *Faust*: that exaltation of voice, that sacred intoxication of the pure soul could not be surpassed" (43). Conveniently, the "review" succinctly illustrates the two opposing forces of the novel, music in general, and Christine's conundrum regarding Erik. As the review illustrates, only two mutually exclusive elements provoke such passion: evil and hate, or good and love. As the rest of the novel demonstrates, however, passion of this kind is rarely quantifiable or rational.

Before we learn the secret to Christine's success, the novel introduces Raoul, a young man whose complexion and temperament are more akin to that of a "young woman's" (45) than a dashing hero of a gothic romance. When he first appears, the narrator describes him in great detail, offering more information to support the fact that he is one of the unlikeliest heroes: "He seemed to have just emerged from the pampering hands of the women who raised him — his sisters and the old aunt. From that purely feminine education he retained a candied manner and charm which nothing until now had been able to tarnish" (45). It is for precisely this reason that his older brother, the philanderer Phillipe, brings Raoul to Paris: "It was not too good to be too good" (45).

Once again, the novel blurs the distinctions between extremes, in this case, good and evil behavior. Though Raoul is clearly the hero, he is not quite complete, not quite mature enough. He is too good, lacking "a dark side."[6] He must experience life's ambiguities and contradictions before he is a fully formed hero capable of rescuing Christine from the underworld and returning her to the "real" world of light, reason, opera, and domesticity. Raoul's goodness and overdeveloped feminine qualities must meet the reality of sin, passion, death, and masculine violence. He is unable to save or possess Christine until he learns to interpret, to analyze. Ultimately, he emerges victorious, perhaps more human than a stereotypical unblemished hero. But as we shall see later, Erik's passion and darkness must be tempered as well.

Ironically, Leroux introduces the audience to the Phantom, not through Christine, but through Raoul. Thanks to an invitation from Christine, Raoul attends her famous performance and later goes backstage to congratulate her on her triumphant debut. As we learn later, the two are childhood friends who had strong feelings for one another in their youth but were too young and too ill-suited in terms of class to respond to these nascent romantic stirrings. Anxious to congratulate his long-lost friend and love, Raoul hopes to meet Christine, but cannot. In an agitated state following her performance, she secludes herself in her room and asks Raoul to come another day. Perhaps in the hope of catching Christine as she leaves, perhaps to demonstrate his earnestness regarding Christine, Raoul waits in the hallway outside of her dressing room when he hears a man's voice coming from Christine's room.

Like us, he listens in, and he hears a man demand, "Christine, you must love me." Again, like Christine's first meeting with the Phantom, Raoul's and ours is through voice, not sight. Christine defends herself, saying, "How can you say that to me? To me, who sings only for you" (49). She underscores her words by saying that she has given him her soul through song (50). Clearly, the two have an extraordinary relationship, one that transcends physical limitations and exists on some incredible spiritual level. Almost as if to confirm this interpretation, the Phantom says that when Christine sang "the angels wept" (50).

The comment also highlights the differentiation of styles, between an artist and a technician. The narrator, for example, notes that Carlotta, the diva:

> had neither heart nor soul. She was nothing more than an instrument. A marvelous instrument certainly... . But no one could say to Carlotta what Rossini said to Krauss after she had sung "Dark Forests" for him in German, "You sing with your soul, dear girl, and your soul is beautiful" [110].

Thanks to the Phantom, Christine has such a voice.

From Raoul's perspective, however, Christine's angelic and soulful voice might be hiding the heart of a whore, and throughout the early stages of the novel, Raoul wrestles with the characteristic stereotypes of female behavior: women are either Madonnas or whores. On one side of the door,

Christine is an angel; on the other, a double-dealing, cheating woman. The irony, of course, is that when Raoul enters the dressing room after Christine's departure, there is no one in the dressing room. In this way, the novel undercuts such female stereotypes: the distinctions are illusory.

When Raoul and Christine finally meet, they do so, at Christine's request, at her father's grave. We learn that Raoul and Christine were children together and that her father was a remarkable musician. Upon his death, however, Christine and Raoul were separated, with only a brief meeting on the beach when they were early adolescents and during which Raoul rescued a scarf for Christine. The symbolism of the scene is difficult to miss: upon the grave is life, and in the case of Christine and Raoul, love as well.

Christine, moreover, initiates contact with Raoul two times, clearly unprecedented at the time. But again, the novel protects Christine, for as we later learn, Christine is only trying to protect Raoul from the hot-tempered Phantom. Christine hopes that she can discourage Raoul's affections and keep the Phantom happy. Of course, this strategy backfires, for Raoul and she fall in love more deeply, and the Phantom spies on their trysts, which fuels his anger.

At the tomb, Raoul's desires are clear. Christine hesitates. She finally confesses that she has an "angel of music" who is jealous and who would not like her meeting with Raoul. Raoul laughs, and the two separate again. During the breach, Raoul attempts to come to some conclusions about Christine, but he cannot. Confronted by both woman and girl, both friend and professional opera star, both victim and victimizer, Raoul ends up "thinking less about Christine herself than 'around' her, and that 'around' was so diffuse, so vague, so ungraspable that he experienced a very strange and agonizing malaise" (93). Christine violates simple conventions regarding female behavior and expectations, and Raoul, who is still "too good," who has not made his descent into the underworld, cannot fathom her ambiguity.

Ironically, this ambiguity and distance codify the couple's relationship and very nearly literally solidify Raoul. He returns to Christine's residence, sees her leaving once again, and follows her. She returns to her father's grave, and Raoul, overcome by the Phantom, lies on the father's tomb, nearly freezing to death. Raoul, who wants clear, irrefutable evidence about life and love, is nearly frozen to death by the amorphous Phantom.

Through notes from a "police interview," Raoul admits that he followed Christine to the gravesite, but then began to hear music from some invisible source. Appropriately, the music is the "Resurrection of Lazarus," a story that demonstrates that the dead rise, perhaps indicating that both Christine's father and the Phantom have found new life. Christine ecstatically responds to the music, while Raoul himself, the paragon of virtue and reason, resists, but admits that he "did not know just where my imagination might have gone nor where it would have stopped" (96), but then the music ceases and suddenly a number of skulls roll to Raoul's feet. He sees a shadow and pursues the creature, thinking it "Satan himself," but he is overcome and remembers nothing else from that night (97). In this great macabre scene, Leroux clearly establishes not only Raoul's vulnerability, but Erik's power, the power of music, which blurs distinctions between reality and illusion, love and death, life and destruction, truth and fiction.[7]

To underscore this point, the scene precedes the famous chandelier incident which not only establishes Erik's great power and the new Opera owners' lack of imagination, but also illustrates the fate that awaits those who care too much about appearances, as well as the Phantom's enemies. While Raoul and Christine romp through the graveyard, the new Opera owners fire Madame Giry. Having received a request for payment from the Phantom through Madame Giry, the new owners conclude that it is Madame Giry who is extorting them, and so fire her. They hire a woman who knows nothing of opera or the arts and who attends the opera for the first time. She is the only one killed by the falling chandelier, and her "funeral oration" is simple: "200,000 kilos land on a concierge's head" (122). Those who do not interpret, who do not appreciate art, are punished.

From this point on, Christine goes missing, and Raoul, desperate to find her, confronts Madame Valerius, her guardian, about Christine and her whereabouts. Valerius tells Raoul that Christine is with the "angel of music." She informs Raoul that Christine may never marry because the "angel of music" forbids such alliances. Still trapped in his dual expectations regarding female behavior, Raoul asks the question outright: "Is Christine still virtuous?" (128). Madame Valerius's shock at the question itself proves Christine's purity. Despite these reassurances, Raoul feels betrayed: "How could he have believed in so much innocence, so much purity?" (129).

Raoul's torment clearly stems from his simplistic expectations and assumptions regarding femininity: "There was nothing colder or deader than his heart. He had loved an angel and now he despised a woman" (131). He wonders how anyone could have the eyes of a child, but the soul of a "courtesan" (131). Raoul's discomfort here is his "dark night of the soul" brought about by the fact that he is faced with a real woman, not an idealized or romantic stereotype. Clearly part of his maturation process is to see women in a multifaceted, not simplistic way. Women are neither angels or whores, mothers or lovers. They are like us all, and Raoul learns about this more complicated representation of femininity, along with many readers, perhaps, thanks to the Leroux novel. When Christine's letter arrives inviting Raoul to the masked ball, his decision to attend symbolizes his movement, at least, towards a more complex reading of femininity and existence. A masked ball, of course, is about both appearances and deception, fiction and truth. His decision to enter the chaotic world reflects his growing maturity and critical perspective.

Tellingly, the masquerade serves as the setting for his meeting with Christine and her "confession" regarding her relationship with the Phantom. And while the actual confession takes place above the streets of Paris, removed from the masked ball, and under the statue of Apollo, the god of both music and truth, Christine's story represents her conflicting views regarding both men, music, and life. Her feelings are as chaotic as the masked ball. The novel establishes her virtue early on, but her desires clearly reflect a more complicated representation of a damsel in distress. Christine admits to an incredibly intimate relationship with the Phantom that transcends physical contact. As she admits to Raoul:

> But above all the Voice taught me secret of combining chest sounds with the soprano voice. Finally, all of that was enclosed within the sacred fire of inspiration. It awakened within me an ardent, insatiable, and sublime life force. The virtue of the Voice was that, by making itself heard, it elevated me to its own level and linked me in its own superb flight. Its soul lived in my mouth, breathing harmony [164].

Unlike her predecessor, Trilby, Christine is aware of the hypnotic power of the "voice," her Phantom-Svengali. And such awareness brings both pleasure and pain. She loves being united to him, but she fears a loss of self. She enjoys the musical passions, but they result in compassion which causes her to empathize with Erik's pain and suffering.

Raoul, perhaps as a result of his participation in the masked ball, makes a remarkably insightful observation, one that may have been impossible for him earlier in the novel:

> And why so much talk? You must love him. All that fear and terror. All that is love of the most delectable kind. The kind one doesn't admit ... . The kind that makes you shiver when you think about it. Just imagine, a man who lives in an underground palace [173].

To a certain degree, Raoul has articulated one of the many reasons for the Phantom narrative's popularity: his mystery and his otherness. His singularity makes him all the more alluring. Like Christine, we are fascinated by the "music of the night," as well as the face behind the mask.

Christine's response is also enlightening:

> How can I hate him, Raoul? ... I am forced to recall that, if he is neither Phantom nor genie nor an angel, he is still the Voice. Because he sings. And I listen — and I stay ... . My dear, there is a virtue in music that can make you feel that nothing of the external world exists except those sounds that strike the heart. Forgotten was my bizarre adventure. Only the voice existed, and intoxicated, I followed its harmonious voyage; I was one with Orpheus' flock [174].

Erik and Christine's relationship transcends words, time, space; it is otherworldly, unfettered by the usual physical limitations.

The reference to the Orpheus-Eurydice myth is also telling. In the myth, Orpheus, as a result of his musical prowess, is permitted the unthinkable, the opportunity to enter the underworld in order to retrieve his wife Eurydice. In the context of the Leroux novel, it is important to note the one interdiction: Orpheus cannot look back at his wife. The spectacular renders the contract null and void. Orpheus, at the last moment, does so, and he loses his wife to the underworld. The reason Orpheus looks back is open to many interpretations. In a modern update, Mary Zimmerman suggests that Eurydice has forgotten Orpheus, so she is unwilling to return from the underworld. Orpheus must turn around to persuade her to come, but it is too late. Such sentiments resonate here in Christine's retelling. She has entered the underworld, and though she has not passed through the river of forgetfulness, there is something very compelling about this world.

And in some ways, she embodies both Orpheus and Eurydice in this novel, for she descends into the otherworld, but it is she who violates that one rule of the darkness. She wishes to see, to participate in spectacle rather than sound. She violates the god of the underworld's one rule — she removes his mask. For some, the unveiling, combined with the couple's already established extraordinary intimacy, might symbolize sexuality. But given the emphasis on sound in the underworld, it is more likely that Christine, who has been carried away by their singing once again, resorts to the traditions of the upper-world, the world of sight and spectacle. Of course, she does not see a whole and complete face; instead, she sees disfigurement, incompletion, and she responds with horror, and in some film versions, a "silent scream." With the visual and the aural opposed to one another, distortion, chaos, confusion results when the two attempt to become one.

Such symbolism is worth discussing at this point, particularly its placement in a novel devoted to opera. As many have argued, the relationship between opera, between voice and word, has been a longstanding and tense one. And some have personified the relationship between film and theater as one of an "inferiority complex," since film did not have sound at its origin though theater did.[8] The voice is supposedly the truest, earliest instrument of communication, but the word transcends many of the limits imposed by the voice. At the same time the word is also very limited; it is restricted to certain forms, and it is limited by its rules. The voice, too, is capable of violating such rules and restrictions. It can travel, sometimes beyond physical boundaries, as we have seen in this work. Of course, today's Internet and electronic devices make words much less reliant on physical media such as paper.

At the time of the novel's authorship and throughout most of civilized history, however, the word was characterized by a certain rigidity, while the voice was characterized by its flexibility. In the end, Christine, like all of us, needs both. And what the novel appears to be saying at this important moment is that the visual is not supreme; spectacle is not all. There is a force that transcends the page, that lurks in the corner, that has its own power and methods. According to Madlen Dolar:

> The voice offered the illusion that one could get immediate access to an unalloyed presence, an origin not tarnished by externality, a firm rock against the elusive interplay of signs, which are anyway surrogates by their very nature and always point to an absence [12].

Furthermore, Dolar continues, the voice has a revolutionary component to it — it is untamable and outside the realm of the law, sometimes characterized as female:

There exists a different metaphysical history of voice, where the voice, far from being the safeguard of presence, is considered dangerous, threatening, and possibly ruinous.... [In one of the earliest commentaries on music] the Chinese emperor Chun, advises that music, in particular the voice, shouldn't stray from the words, which endow it with sense; as soon as it departs from its textual anchorage, the voice becomes senseless and threatening, all the more so because of its seductive and intoxicating powers. Furthermore, the voice beyond sense is self-evidently equated with femininity, whereas the text, the instance of signification, is in this simple paradigmatic opposition on the side of masculinity [16–17].

The voice, while beautiful, is also subversive in the same way that women, though beautiful, may be subversive. The voice transports all to heaven, but it is created here, as Leroux so astutely points out, by the devilish Phantom.

Christine, too, violates social norms and expectations regarding femininity in a significant way when she enters the Phantom's underworld. In addition to her initiating contact with Raoul, Christine's desires, both physical and professional, do not coincide with the expectations of proper young women at the time. The only other example of a successful woman on stage is the diva Carlotta, who is the object of ridicule because she is vain and untalented. Christine is innocent, beautiful, and onstage. But her performances leave her prey to the objectifying gaze of audiences, so to a certain extent, when Erik abducts her from the stage, he rescues her from a stereotypical female role, that of "object of desire," a thing to be viewed. Furthermore, while the novel may remove her from the stage, she is not silenced. It is her story, her narrative, her voice that tells us about Erik and the underworld, a world beyond spectacle. And while it is true that she ultimately chooses Raoul and the domestic life in the upper world, the novel clearly empowers her and makes the choice hers, rather than a passive acceptance of the inevitable heterosexual conclusion of femininity.

In his other works, *The Mystery of the Yellow Room* (1907), *The Perfume of the Lady in Black* (1909), and *Missing Men* (1923), Leroux defends women whom society ostracizes. *The Mystery* and *The Perfume* are about one woman, Madame Strangerson, who has been misled by an evil man who marries her and then abuses her, frequently reappearing at the most inopportune moments to harass her and make her life miserable — when she is about to be engaged, since she thinks the man dead, and when she is about to be married, because the character was supposedly killed off in the first installment. In the case of *Missing Men*, the fallen woman is, in fact, loyal to her true love, Cheri-Bibi. And he, in a very complex plot and disguise sequence, ultimately reveals himself to her, defending her against the attacks of the town gossips. There may be men who haunt these women and remind them of their bad judgment, but Leroux's narrators are always there to defend these fallen women and to show, once again, that things are not what they seem. A marginal female can be true to her true love, children, and family. Here, too, the novel painstakingly defends Christine's passion, ambition, and conflicting desires. Christine lives to tell her story, escapes unpunished, and finally chooses the man she wishes to love and marry.

During Christine's great confession, of course, lurks Erik listening. He discovers that Christine loves Raoul and pities him, and he acts accordingly, like a male monster. He becomes enraged, plots another abduction, and sharpens his instruments of torture. His abduction is a success, and Raoul must rescue his love from the underworld. Interestingly, during the height of suspense and action in the novel, Leroux makes it clear that the newspapers who report on this crisis have no idea about the facts of the case and Raoul's relationship to Christine (191–192). They misunderstand the couple's love, and presume that his brother may have something to do with the entire mess.

With Christine's disappearance, Raoul sets out to rescue her. Luckily for him, he meets the Persian, who offers a great deal of detail to the narrator about the entire incident. As it turns out, Erik and the Persian know each other fairly well. Erik spent time in Persia, being educated in the fine arts of torture and sexual deviance. Through the Persian we learn that Erik has been mistreated as a child and as an adult in the Persian court, where Erik learned to indulge his worst instincts. In addition to providing information, the Persian serves many purposes. He shows us that Erik is simultaneously victim and victimizer, but his willingness to help Raoul underscores the novel's theme regarding superficial judgments. The Persian, a foreigner, is actually helpful, not a threat, a departure from the ethnocentrism rampant in Europe at the time of the novel's publication.

Classifying or characterizing Erik is just as dangerous. He is powerful and vulnerable, homicidal and provincial. He attempts to kill Raoul and the Persian in a number of exotic ways — dehydration in a desert room created by mirrors, drowning, and later gunpowder — and he torments Christine mercilessly, tricking her regarding her choice of men — but he also tells Christine his true goal: he longs to be "normal," like everyone else:

> I want to have a quiet apartment, with ordinary doors and windows, and an honest wife, like the rest of the world. You should be able to understand that, Christine, and I shouldn't have to keep repeating it. A wife, like the rest of the world. A wife whom I would love, and with whom I could take Sunday walks, and whom I would amuse all week long. Ah, you would never be bored with me [287].

Lurking beneath this artistic Phantom and his grand passions is the desire for a middle-class domestic life, a life that would help him be like "everyone else." Unfortunately, both he and society are unable to attain this goal. He is too passionate, too prone to rage, nearly killing the object of his love. He cannot control himself in order to gain his goal. He loses all sense of proportion, in the end making even his music, his life's sustenance, demonic and discordant.

Ultimately, Christine's willingness to sacrifice herself, as well as her ability to love, saves all of the characters in the novel. She tenderly kisses the Phantom without his mask, revealing her ability to love the disfigured and incomplete, literally accepting incompleteness, ambiguity, and disfigurement as part of love and life. It is at this moment that Erik is transformed and perhaps gains the insight he could have used to obtain Christine's love in the first place. But like many tragic awakenings, this one comes too late. As the Phantom tells the Persian: "I'm telling you I still love her, daroga, because love is killing me. If you knew how beautiful she was when she let me kiss her, alive, as she had sworn on her eternal soul. It was the first time ... the first time, do you hear, that I kissed a woman. Yes, alive. I kissed her alive, and she was as beautiful as any dead woman" (316). Leonard Wolf notes that the reference to necrophilia is unusual not only following on the heels of his desire for the typical, middle-class marriage, but also because we have heard nothing about Erik's necrophiliac tendencies in the novel before (316). More importantly, however, is the fact that Erik has changed as a result of his contact with Christine. He has finally experienced unconditional love and compassion, and he learns as a result. This love makes him better, and he releases Christine and Raoul, allowing them to have their lives fulfilled. Erik, too, has embraced ambiguity — he loves without possessing the object of his desire.

Almost as if to test our understanding of the novel and its themes regarding ambiguity, superficial interpretations, and dualities, the narrator concludes with a series of questions regarding Erik, a character whom we see as much more complicated than he was when the novel began:

> Is he to be pitied? Is he to be cursed? He wanted only to be some-one, like everyone else. But he was too ugly! And he was required to hide his genius or else play tricks with it. Had he had ordinary features, he would have been one of the noblest members of the human race! He had a heart capacious enough to contain the whole world, but he had, finally, to content himself with a cellar. Certainly, we must pity the Phantom of the Opera! [329].

As a result of his change, we are asked to "reread" the Phantom, both novel and character, in order to make sure the lessons presented are learned, to remind all that Erik's remains are from "no ordinary skeleton" (329). Given the subsequent versions of the narrative, the narrator has his wish fulfilled. The skeleton, Erik, attains immortality through the various revisions and reinterpretations of his story throughout history and across a myriad of genres.

CHAPTER 2

Darkness Made Visible:
The Phantom on Film

I think we loved each other like the damned, trying to forget in
the embrace of love a lost paradise.
— Gaston Leroux's "The Mystery of the Four Husbands"

The film versions of Gaston Leroux's *Phantom of the Opera* present
challenges to even the most astute filmmakers and screenwriters. The
1925 version sought to film a book about opera on the silent screen. And
very few films capture Leroux's satiric wit. Frequently, the characters
become stereotypes, caricatures, rather than fully realized creations. Erik's
complicated nature also frequently eludes moviemakers, as does Christine's ambivalence regarding the world of light and the world of darkness presented to her by the Phantom. Instead, many of the films opt for
villains and heroines.

To some degree, these difficulties accompany every screen adaptation. Screenwriters must determine how closely they follow the literary
original, and a close adaptation does not always guarantee success. As a
matter of fact, some of the more successful adaptations of literature to
film have taken great liberties with their originals.[9] In the case of *The
Phantom*, however, there is the added burden of the novel's theme — the
challenge the novel makes to spectacle, the world of light and sight, the
very components that make film possible. Given the fact that film is a
predominantly visual medium, it comes as no surprise that the adaptation of the novel to the film might falter at times. But in some of the
more successful films, the films use cinematic technology which privi-
leges spectacle in order to highlight its limits as well as its power.

Film itself is based upon an illusion. When viewing a film, for example, most audiences presume that they are seeing "reality" in such a way that supersedes the written word, the still image, and the musical composition. The film image looks so much like life that we are lulled into a sense of security when viewing even the most extraordinary of images. In truth, however, our ability to watch films is the result of something called the "persistence of vision," the brain's ability to retain an image while the eye captures a subsequent image, which leads us to "see" the motion in motion picture photography. When we view a film, then, we are, in fact, spending most of our time in the dark, not watching images at all.

This paradox is reflected in Gaston Leroux's own *Phantom*. That is, his novel and some of his other writings underscore the limits of spectacle, showing readers that the eye does not always see clearly, and the reality readers frequently experience through reportage, newspapers, and nonfiction can be just as easily manipulated and manufactured as fiction. It should also come as no surprise to learn that Leroux himself was interested in film, and in "1919 he formed a film company ... called Cineromans ... but after a disagreement with the literary director of Cineromans in 1922, Leroux lost interest in films" (Perry 28). The details of the disagreement matter less than the disagreement itself: the literary and the visual are at odds. With film in its early stages, motion picture companies looked not only for established scripts that would gain audience attention, but also those classic scripts that would provide film, a new genre, greater artistic and aesthetic respect. "Highbrow" titles such as the works of William Shakespeare or historical dramas such as *Queen Elizabeth* (1912) starring Sarah Bernhardt helped film overcome its humble beginnings. Film, of course, began as a science but very quickly became popular as an oddity, a sideshow attraction, through the nickelodeons where turnover was high, audiences decidedly lowbrow, and the finer questions of art and production value were discouraged. By adapting literary classics, film tried to establish its credibility as a valid and important art form.

The film industry also needed cash to survive, so in many cases, film companies, like Universal, churned out films quickly, saving their resources for one or two what they called "jewels" per year. As it happens, the 1925 *Phantom* was Universal's "jewel" of that production season, following closely behind the extremely popular *Hunchback of Notre*

Dame. In this way, the horror film and the literary classic were wed, but for the most part, the horror films presented by filmmakers served to fund the more serious works. New Line Cinema, for example, owes much of its success to Freddy Krueger and *The Nightmare on Elm Street* series.

The various film versions of *The Phantom* also reflect the changing history and development of film. The 1925 version reflects the silent screen era. And by 1943, production quality, sound, artistic settings, and color were earning filmmakers Oscars. Later, *The Phantom* is served up as a popular horror genre, with directors and movie houses apparently feeling an obligation to offer their particular rendition of the famous Leroux story. Britain's Hammer Films offers a version of the Leroux classic, but it deviates from its own formula, presenting not the blood, cleavage, and Christopher Lee menu many audiences still crave, but a more sedate, more domestic *Phantom.* New Line Cinema creates its version starring Robert Englund, otherwise known as Freddy Krueger to *Nightmare on Elm Street* fans. And there is even a rock music version, which looks very similar to the cult classic *The Rocky Horror Picture Show* (1975), directed by none other than Brian De Palma.

In some cases, the film's backstories have as much drama as the film itself, but all the film versions of *The Phantom* give audiences an opportunity to examine their roles as spectators in challenging and new ways. As the privileged spectator afforded by film, audiences are challenged to see what this powerful position entails. We, like Christine, hope to get at the truth in the story, and sometimes this search leads to suffering, and sometimes this search leads to discovery, and sometimes this search leads to nothing. The Leroux story continues to challenge us as film viewers, not only to see but to interpret. Through spectacle, the films challenge us to interrogate the very spectacles we view.

Defining the Phantom: Lon Chaney's *Phantom of the Opera* (1925)

There is evidence of several film versions of *The Phantom* prior to 1920. Philip Riley reports a 1915 "unauthorized" version called *The Phantom of the Violin* that has "disappeared" (34). And there is also evidence of a 1916 German film version of *The Phantom of the Opera*, but it is virtually unknown in this country and very difficult to find. The director,

Ernst Matray, however, later has a tenuous connection with the 1943 *Phantom*. Born in Hungary, Matray worked in Max Reinhart's theater, established himself as a choreographer and director, and then came to Hollywood, like many European artists of his day, and choreographed a number of films throughout the forties and fifties. Many of these were the films starring "America's Sweethearts," Nelson Eddy and Jeannette MacDonald, whose backstage romances fuel the backstories of the 1943 film version of *Phantom of the Opera*, starring Nelson Eddy, Claude Rains, and Susanna Foster, not Jeanette MacDonald.

There can be no doubt, however, that when *Phantom of the Opera* is mentioned in the context of film, the image that springs to mind is Lon Chaney's portrayal in the 1925 film. His is the role by which all others are measured, the standard for all Phantoms throughout the ages and throughout subsequent genres. His is the performance that rescues the film from the numerous problems that plagued the production both onscreen and off.

Leroux's basic plot remains, but some important details are either overlooked completely or changed to such an extent that the themes developed in the novel are no longer present in the film. Specifically, the film lacks Leroux's social commentary, and his sardonic sense of humor is transformed into slapstick through a vaudevillian performance by Universal's fairly well-known Hungarian actor, Snitz Edwards. More importantly, not only is Christine presented as a complete victim, but Erik is presented as "criminally insane," an escaped lunatic, no longer a victim of Nature's arbitrary cruelty. Admittedly, Erik has tutored Christine and enables her to get to the stage, through a threat to the diva Carlotta, but once Christine meets Raoul and is abducted by the Phantom, she has no feelings for him at all, no understanding of his suffering and pain. In a word, the characters become stereotypes — Erik becomes the evil villain, and Christine becomes the innocent, female victim. It is only through the work of Lon Chaney that any sympathy for Erik remains; it is his performance, not the script, which elicits our compassion. As *Photoplay* commented, "In spite of the horror of his role, Lon Chaney wins, at times, sympathy" (qtd. in Blake, *Lon Chaney* 137). And the discrepancy between the script and the performance may have also influenced the mixed reviews the film garnered upon its opening (Blake, *Lon Chaney* 137–38). There is still, of course, the distinction between the world of light and the world of darkness, but in this case, Erik's underworld, as defined by the script, is clearly evil, and Christine's participation involuntary. He is the villain to her victim. These difficulties, however, did not interfere with the film's success.

Jerrold Hogle argues that the film appeals to audiences as a result of the historical period. Following World War I, many men returned home deformed both physically and emotionally. Comparing *Phantom* to the German horror classic *The Cabinet of Dr. Caligari* (1919), he notes that the

> scenes and characters, we can now conclude, are anguished cultural reactions to World War I, partly to how that conflict produced half-dead and "disfigured bodies," partly to how it led to extensive mental illness, and partly to how men had been turned to automatons.... Chaney's Erik incarnates all those levels and the fears about them in one contradictory being [*Undergrounds* 139].

Truly, the effects of the war cannot be overestimated. Writers such as Wilfred Owen, Virginia Woolf, and Ernest Hemingway all struggled with the realities of this large-scale war.

But the film succeeds well beyond its historical period, appealing to more common themes. Like it or not, the deformed, the maimed, the physically handicapped, and even the mentally ill, sell. They are always a popular draw in the entertainment industry. Tellingly, many film stars and directors had their start in freak shows and traveling circus acts. *Dracula* (1931) director Tod Browning worked in carnivals and freak shows prior to his film career, and his film *Freaks* (1932), about these sideshow characters, still haunts and disturbs audiences.

Chaney's own career illustrates this penchant for the unusual. *The Hunchback of Notre Dame* (1923), with the deformed but kind Quasimodo, established his career and propelled him to the starring role of *Phantom*. Oscar Wilde noted of his performance that, Chaney "was exactly what a hunchback ought to be ... a sort of human gargoyle who looked as though he climbed down the front of the cathedral of Notre Dame" (121). Prior to that performance, he played a man who had his legs amputated in error only to become a sociopath in *The Penalty* (1919). In *A Blind Bargain* (1923), Chaney doubles his freakishness by playing both a mad scientist and his crippled assistant.

Leroux's writing career, too, underscores the idea that freaks fascinate. Many of his characters and stories revolve around mutilations, as in "A Terrible Tale" (1925), the story of a shipwrecked group who grow to like the taste of human flesh they eat while waiting to be rescued. And Leroux's own popular fictional hero, Cheri-Bibi, is noted for his ability to transform his appearance through fantastical plastic surgeries.

In this way, the 1925 film succeeds because it plays on the audience's desire to see the unusual, to participate in spectacle, not just work out the horrors of war. Ian Conrich goes so far as to argue that "cinema was a successful alternative cultural site for the development of the sideshow" (50). The fact that Erik is criminally insane makes him more freak than symbol for modern existential angst.

The film, moreover, is important as a result of its self-reflexivity. It is, in many ways, as I will show throughout the rest of the chapter, a film about film, a film about spectacle and the very process of watching, viewing, and perceiving. It is not about the love triangle articulated in the Leroux novel or the difficulties with deformity; instead, it is a propaganda film for film. With little psychological or philosophical tension, the film relies on events, spectacle, and the very act of filmmaking to propel the narrative forward. The film succeeds upon very different grounds from the novel by highlighting the visual pleasures and opportunities the new motion picture camera can provide for audiences. From the gory to the glory, the camera presents all. Perhaps as a result of the metacinematic emphasis, the film continues in the Leroux tradition, almost in spite of the script and the difficulties of production, for it, too, like the novel, shows in very dramatic ways the importance of interpreting visual information carefully.

The film production's backstory is as dank, dark, and mysterious as the Phantom's underground lair beneath the Paris Opera House. Incredible conflicts over power, money, and studio control lurk beneath the 1925 film. Combine that with the founding of the studio which produced it, Universal, and the entire production takes on epic or mythic proportions. Universal's history is an American fairy tale starring a German immigrant, Carl Laemmle, who originally intended to start a grocery store, but when he saw the crowds around the nickelodeon, as well as the entertainment's ability to keep the crowds, and by association, the money, coming, was hooked. Off he went with his great family in tow to start Universal Pictures.[10] As far as the *Phantom* goes, its inception serves as a metaphor for the Laemmle method — use what you have, invite the family, and make a movie. The project began, innocently enough, with a vacation. According to Carl Laemmle in an interview prior to the opening of *Phantom,* he discovered the novel during a visit to Gaston Leroux, who was running a French film studio and mentioned his book to the U.S. studio head: "I remember buying a copy and sitting up all night to read it. It is a marvelously interesting story, just jammed with love interest and one of the most mysterious plots I have ever come across" (qtd. in Riley 46). Others note that it was Universal's new head of production, Irving Thalberg, who knew of the book as a child and promoted the idea to Laemmle (Riley 34). Whatever the case, according to Mark Vieira, the achievement was the result of three Universal employees: "Irving Thalberg, Lon Chaney, and Tod Browning" (9). And while Browning did not participate in *Phantom's* production, the Chaney film laid the groundwork for their later work together.

Further, Universal Studios was undergoing challenging times. Carl Laemmle was notorious for hiring family members, and in some cases, these relatives were not fiscally responsible. Mark Vieira's description of the hiring of Irving Thalberg hints at the kind of world Laemmle created at Universal City:

> Only a mogul as expansive, eccentric, and nepotistic as Laemmle could make a self-educated nineteen-year-old "general manager in charge of production" ... Universal was concerned with quantity, not quality, sometimes releasing two hundred films a year.... Thalberg's sense of dramatic construction improved Universal's output and increased profits, which then allowed him the luxury of prestige productions such as Erich von Stroheim's *Foolish Wives.* It also gave him the power to fire Stroheim from another film when the extravagant director became intractable [10].

Due to disagreements, including the firing of von Stroheim, Thalberg left Universal during the production of *The Phantom.* He went to work for Metro-Goldwyn-Mayer, leaving Universal with what Laemmle said privately was a film that would cost "a million dollars ... with a freak as the main character" (qtd. in Riley 40).

Rupert Julian, "a fixture on the Universal lot" (Blake, *Thousand* 156) and former actor, replaced von Stroheim in an early film, so he was the "heir apparent" director on the Universal lot. He did not, however, earn the respect of cast and crew. Many thought he spent more time on his hair and dress than on actual directing. Cast and crew ridiculed Julian about his past job as a barber, sometimes calling out, "a shave and a cut!" or "next" to infuriate their self-important director (MacQueen). In another story, Charles Van Enger, the cameraman for the film, relates that Julian basically tried to shoot the chandelier scene in the dark. Rather than fight the pompous director, Van Enger merely put the darkest filter over the eyeglass of the camera, so Julian thought he got what he wanted, and Van Enger saved the film (qtd. in Blake, *Lon Chaney* 134).

The hostility between Chaney and Julian became legendary. Chaney was so upset with the director that he did not speak to him directly: "Camerman Charles van Enger acted as an intermediary between the two, relaying Julian's direction to Lon and returning Lon's usual reply: 'Tell him to go to hell'" (Blake, *Thousand* 157).[11] According to Scott Mac-Queen, if there were auteurs for this film, they were Chaney and artist Ben Carre, who served as a consultant to the film. When a version was shown to Universal representatives, including Laemmle, Julian was fired because the pace of the film was "too slow" (Perry 50). In order to pick up the pace, the mob scene was added and developed by Edward Sedgewick (Perry 50). The studio then previewed the film, and the audiences "felt there was too much suspense" (Blake, *Thousand* 159). In what can only be an example to the old saying "Too many cooks spoil the broth," these comments were taken to heart, and comic relief scenes were added, scenes which neither reflect Leroux's satire nor Chaney's passionate performance. Another preview revealed that the new comic subplot "made no sense" (Blake, *Thousand* 160), so most of the scenes were removed. They do, however, illustrate a certain kind of vaudevillian performance popular at the time, so in some ways, though the scenes do nothing for the plot or the underlying themes of the film, they do illustrate a transitional moment between the stage and the film. And what clearly may have worked on the stage no longer works in the same way in the film. A new set of title cards was created for the silent film, and the film was released. In all, there are five versions of the film, with the script by Elliot Clawson and Raymond Schrock making the final film version seen today. Sound was added in 1929, with dialogue written by Ernest Laemmle and a musical score which included selections from Gounod's *Faust*, but without the voice of Chaney.

For Michael Blake, "We are left with a mediocre melodrama that holds up today solely due to Chaney's riveting performance" (*Thousand* 161). There is no doubt that Chaney's performance is key to the film. Born in 1883 to deaf parents, Chaney developed the ability to mimic, perform, and understand the disabled, which helped him create many memorable characters. He, too, was a Universal fixture, but it is not until Thalberg that his talents were utilized to their full ability. With *The Blind Bargain* (1922), he earned his "man of a thousand faces" title and a large following of fans. Mark Vieira summarizes Chaney's abilities and popularity with this anecdote: "Director Marshal Neillan expressed popular sentiment when a fellow partygoer was about to squish a spider: 'Don't step on it! It might be Lon Chaney'" (9). With *The Hunchback* Chaney's star power was golden, so he was the only choice for *The Phantom*. The trouble arose, of course, when the script was under construction, and Chaney understood the Leroux script better than his director.

While Chaney was the only choice for the role of Erik, the search for his leading lady was another story. Many stars were considered, so why Mary Philbin? In yet another classic Laemmle story, Philbin had come to California as a result of a contest she had won in Chicago. According to Philip Riley, Erik von Stroheim promised to cast her in a lead role, but when she appeared in Hollywood, the role had disappeared. Thanks to her good friend, a niece of Carl Laemmle, she was given more acting opportunities, particularly with Von Stroheim as director (50–51). While this story may be of passing interest to film historians, Mary's story symbolizes the dreams films perpetuated for young women in America at the time. She was "discovered." Underneath her "ordinary exterior" was a star. In "Anytown USA" Hollywood could uncover, unveil, unmask stars, ironically performers who played many roles, thereby creating a virtual hall of mirrors regarding identity, fame, and film. Finally, Mary had little talent, and according to MacQueen, her inexperience enervated other cast members. In the end, her acting career was short-lived.

Despite these tremendous difficulties, the 1925 *Phantom* succeeds to a certain extent. It is one of the first horror films, one which still establishes Universal's contributions to the horror film genre, and Chaney's performance is difficult to ignore. Further, if viewed as a propaganda film about film, the 1925 *Phantom* highlights many innovations and film's power. Carl Laemmle, in a radio interview, basically says as much, as he tries to defend his film and his studio from rumors of failure, following Thalberg's departure:

> I am making *Phantom of the Opera* for music-lovers and movie fans throughout the world.... Five thousand people are now engaged in its making, so you can imagine its magnitude.... All the life of the

> opera singer — the great Opera Ball — all the glitter and excitement
> of the presentation of the opera — all this I am putting on the screen
> ... a group of well-known musicians ... are going to arrange a musi-
> cal score.... When this picture reaches the screen, the public will
> have full opportunity of realizing what great strides have been taken
> in motion picture production and musical presentation [Riley 46].

In a classic illustration of the battle film had to prove itself to highbrow
audiences, Laemmle tried to persuade the Metropolitan Opera to per-
mit him to show the film in their performance space, but given the time's
own culture wars, the Met declined the opportunity (Riley 195). Given
the sumptuous and highly touted opening of the film, Laemmle did not
take the rejection too hard, and like many moguls of his day proved the
high society wrong by creating an art form that endures.[12]

The film itself opens with a glowing title and an appropriate nod
in the direction of Gaston Leroux's authorship. The pride of place in the
film opening, however, is reserved for the words, A Universal Production ... by Universal Pictures Corp. Laemmle's home and studio. The
camera lingers on these words, which are highlighted by a static background. The earlier titles were underscored by the Phantom-figure, not
Chaney, moving behind the titles, creeping through the underground of
the Paris Opera house. Such an announcement is important because it
highlights the importance of not only film but the newly-created American film. Universal City "was a magical land that existed outside of reality. It had its own mayor and city council, fire department, post office,
power plants, street department, chicken ranch, mountains, rivers, a
miniature desert, drill grounds big enough for 10,000 troops, rocky western backgrounds, and many acres of sound stages and back lot sets"
(Riley 55).

The construction of the Paris Opera House on the California set
was one of the most astounding feats of movie construction in history.
It was "the first steel and concrete stage ever built in Hollywood" (Blake,
Chaney 134), and it has served as a set for many other films including
the 1943 remake of *Phantom of the Opera*. *Life* said that if Laemmle had
spent his time and money reconstructing Europe rather than the Paris
Opera House for this film, "there would be no trace of the Great War
left" (qtd. in Skal 67). The set still stands today.

Like the Leroux novel, the opening title emphasizes the dual nature
of art and beauty: "Sanctuary of song lovers, The Paris Opera House,

rising nobly over medical torture chambers, hidden dungeons, long forgotten." Unlike in the novel, however, the ugliness below is not the price of the beauty above, but rather serves as a threat to art, order, domestic happiness, and society. The external, the "seen," must be protected from "unseen" forces. Here, the music of the night menaces and threatens social conventions. The underworld is not a haven from social expectations and judgments as it is for Erik in the Leroux novel.

To highlight this conclusion, the film moves quickly to an impressive cinematic view of the Opera House, both inside and outside. It is spectacular: the external structure dwarfs passersby, and the grand staircase is filled with casts of thousands, women in gowns and jewels, men in indeterminate military garb. During these opening scenes, the camera takes its audiences to one of the great temples of "high art," the Paris Opera House. Thanks to the camera, we have the best seats in the house, and if we have never seen the opera or ballet before, we can do so at a fraction of the cost. The camera's power is undeniable, and the opening scenes of this film underscore its power. The sumptuousness of the opera house, the ballet, and the people inspire awe and wonder.

The camera, however, is not only useful for bringing grand spectacle. It also presents the most private and intimate moments of individuals, virtually invisible intimate moments. We see, for example, a profession of love, again one of the most intimate and personal moments of human life. To further underscore the point, Christine hesitates. The camera shows Raoul's humiliation and Christine's confusion. Unlike the novel and later versions in which Christine is genuinely interested in a career on stage as an opera singer, in this version she explains to Raoul that she is "inexplicably" drawn to song and stage, indicating the she has no will of her own; perhaps she is under the Svengali-like power of this Phantom.

Later, when Christine and Raoul meet high above the city of Paris, under the stature of Apollo, we are also privy to their professions of love, as well as the spectacle of Paris. Clearly, the film demonstrates the camera's prowess on macroscopic and microscopic levels. It offers grand spectacle, provides travel to exotic locations, and represents mystery, even the complexities of the human heart.

It is all available to us, even the underground caverns of the Paris Opera House, which are some of the best scenes in the film, with and without Chaney. In one scene, for example, a relatively minor character,

Florin, works, while a black cat crosses the steps near him, casting a gloomy shadow in the black and white film environment. In another, ballerinas flit while their shadows appear brilliantly black against the wall. And when Florin and the ballerinas discuss the Phantom, the ballerinas pirouette uncontrollably, reflecting their fear in the only way they know how — through dance. As a matter of fact, "over 250 dancers from the Chicago, Metropolitan, and other opera companies were brought to the studio for the dance numbers that were supervised by noted dance producer Ernest Belcher" (Blake, *Chaney* 134). This film offered spectacle of the highest order. Even Joseph Buquet, who will soon be hanged, works on the head of a prop, John the Baptist in *Salome,* offering an eerie symbolic foreshadowing of his own mortality. Even a walking tour of the Opera House backstage could not provide these fantastic visuals, visuals that rely upon the interplay of light and darkness, visuals that only the new invention, the camera, can now provide.

As in the novel, thanks to the Phantom's intervention, Christine is the newest opera singer to tackle the role of Marguerite in *Faust.* For Philip Riley, "Erik is Faust turned inside out — or sideways" (22), with Faust, following his pact with the devil, being the handsome young man with the hideous interior, while Leroux's Erik had the hideous exterior and a compassionate interior. Again, it is only thanks to Chaney's performance that any sympathy towards Erik is elicited, as he grows increasingly maniacal as the film progresses.

The focus on opera here serves a less thematic and more practical purpose than the novel. *Faust* is an opera that most might recognize, if not the Gounod version, then the story itself, so audiences would be familiar with the highbrow culture the film invoked, even though they themselves were not members of this elite, intellectual class. And in many ways, this lowbrow appreciation for a highbrow art form expressed in what was then considered a lowbrow art form illustrates the appeal of *The Phantom.* People appreciate its opera because it is not really opera but a form of opera they may relate to or identify with in palatable ways. In other words, *Phantom of the Opera* is frequently opera for non-opera lovers, and this point will become clear in the discussion of the Andrew Lloyd Webber version some fifty years later. In the case of this film, the cinematic strategies help further the comparison between Mephistopheles and Erik, by juxtaposing scenes that illustrate that the characters are both demonic.

During one of these scenes, the chandelier falls, again spectacularly so, and Erik abducts Christine. In some of the most beautiful scenes in the film, he leads her to his lair. Trilby-like, she follows, crossing the underground waters of the Opera House, a modern-day River Lethe. When she awakens, however, she has not forgotten her past and her life. She needs to know the identity of her abductor, but Erik warns her not to try to find out. She consents momentarily, but drawn by Erik's music, she enters and watches him play his organ. Overcome with curiosity, she removes his mask.

She, of course, is surprised by the horror she uncovers. Almost as if to excuse or ignore the absence of a scream because of the film's lack of sound, the film presents Christine blocking her mouth with her fist, presenting a visual image of a silent scream, perhaps more frightening than a sound. The script describes her reaction as a collection of inarticulate sobs, heaving tears, beyond words (Riley 102). It is the Phantom who speaks, berating her and abusing her and his own ugliness with his words: "Feast your eyes. Glut your soul on my cursed ugliness." As Blake notes, "we see all [his] strength and self-confidence shatter" in this scene (*Thousand* 162). Like Pandora, Christine's curiosity has certainly brought her the truth about the Phantom, but given Chaney's performance, it's clear that her need to "see" has also brought about a great deal of suffering and danger. She has gone too far, perhaps the camera has gone too far as well. It would appear that the film punishes her desire for greater visual pleasure. She has wanted too much, taken the visual curiosity too far.

In one of the greatest moments in film history, Chaney's artistry is revealed. As Michael Blake notes, Chaney "strove to come as close to the novel's description of the Phantom as possible" (*Lon Chaney* 132). And his work succeeded. His work "is still considered by motion picture make-up artists as one of the truly classic make-up creations in film history" (*Lon Chaney* 134). Ironically, in order to demonstrate the Phantom's lack of control, his role as the object of speculation, something-to-be-looked-at, Chaney had to control every detail of his face, literally reshaping his own face into a visage of monstrosity.[13]

With his secret revealed, the Phantom, who has lost control, reestablishes control over his own looks by creating a spectacle of himself. He appears at the masked ball dressed as the "Red Death," complete with a colorized entrance, using the new two-color Technicolor process. He is completely spectacle. His connection to the other revelers is severed. He is not like all the other masked people of Paris, as was the case in the Leroux novel. As in his unmasking, spectacle here establishes power, not egalitarian relationships. That is, the film's camera makes the audience similar: everyone sees what the camera shows. In the Phantom's unmasking and the masked ball, however, the spectacle highlights difference — the Phantom is different from everyone else. But unlike the past sense, the Phantom's mask, his costume, his celebration of death, makes him control the spectacle. He is the center of attention, colored red to highlight his power.

Following his performance at the masqued ball and the realization that Christine will not love him because she loves Raoul, Erik abducts her once again. Raoul and the Persian pursue, and in some equally memorable scenes, Erik disguises himself further by submerging himself under water and laying traps for those who wish to rescue Christine. Once again, he is in charge of what is seen and not seen.

And yet, Christine's Pandora-like curiosity is what has been motivating this film, as well as the film industry, and so, while the Phantom is momentarily successful in punishing her, in the end, it is he who is punished. As in the novel, he attempts to kill Raoul and the Persian through a series of extremes, heat and thirst, and then later, near drowning. Ultimately, Christine, in a very feminine and victim-like way, manages to thwart his attempts kill Raoul and the Persian are thwarted, as are his plans to blow up the Opera House. In this film, we learn that Erik has escaped from an institution for the criminally insane, so he is no longer Leroux's victim of nature, a poor deformed creature, a temperamental, misunderstood, but ultimately gifted artist.

His crime, then, is his attempt to blur distinctions between light and darkness, good and evil, spectator and spectacle, distinctions that the nascent film technology depends upon. In addition to the practical requirements of filmmaking, there were social considerations as well, considerations which led to the Hays Code in 1930, which not only clearly understood the power of the new film technology but also its effects on its viewers. As noted in the introduction to the "rules," "Motion picture producers recognize the high trust and confidence which have been placed in them by the people of the world and which have made motion pictures a universal form of entertainment. They recognize their responsibility to the public because of this trust and because entertainment and art are important influences in the life of a nation." Of course, the code goes on to censor films rigidly, "prohibiting and the presentation of crimes in such a way as to throw sympathy with the crime as against law and justice or to inspire others with a desire for imitation" ("Hays Code"). The code, of course, did not merely reflect the morals and sentiments of 1930. Rather it was the culmination of years of work by groups to restrict the representation of particular acts on film, a new genre that seemed to perpetuate immorality in a new and perhaps more effective way. By taking the law into his own hands, the Phantom, then, blurred the divisions between good and evil, and consequently, had to be punished.

Perhaps most importantly, however, is his attempt to control the film. He wields power over the camera without realizing that the camera works both ways — he can use and be used by the camera. The camera is everywhere. Privacy, secrecy, are gone. And when he tries to control Christine's desire for seeing the truth, he commits the film's ultimate sin. Despite his subsequent successes at controlling the camera, he cannot escape this sin. He must be punished for his unwillingness to participate in the spectacle by being part of the spectacle.

The final mob scene portrays Erik as a terrorist, not an outcast artist, but a madman intent on destroying all that is good and beautiful in life. He does not experience love in any way, as in the novel. He does not sacrifice his Christine for her happiness. He is simply greedy, selfish, and most of all, disrespectful of spectacle. He is pushed into the river by an angry mob, friends and neighbors of one of his early victims, Joseph Buquet. Clearly, the class content is difficult to miss, but the Hays Code and its predecessors did not discourage class propaganda. The workers of the world unite to save the aristocrats, as embodied by Christine, Raoul, and the Opera House, from the evil underworld creature who hoped to overreach and steal an aristocrat's girl. Erik is dead, the ugliness removed. The Opera House and its art stand. Audiences are happy. They need no longer gaze upon the evil death's-head Chaney created.

Given the incredible departures from the Leroux story, it may come as a surprise that Leroux actually enjoyed the film, which brought him more fame in his old age. He even liked the ending because, he did not see the scene as a conclusion or one that may or may not have represented his novel. Rather, he, like many writers after him, saw an opportunity for a sequel. Consequently, and thanks to the success of the film, he began working on a sequel which included Erik's survival in the icy waters and his later stalking of Christine and Raoul (Riley 287). The idea never made it to film or page.

Such changes from the original make the film a challenge for those who appreciate the novel, but it will not be the last time that the complexities of the novel are lost on adaptors. At the same time, the adaptations present their own narratives and points of view. Here, for example, the film is a testimony to Hollywood's infancy, the horror genre's dynamic nature, back-lot politics, the emphasis on the visual, and the historical position of the new cinematic technology. Through the power of the camera, which ultimately destroys Erik, and Chaney's performance, the film is ultimately one of the most memorable films in movie history, a film that simultaneously celebrates and cautions against the new film medium's ability to show us all.

The Feminist Phantom: Claude Rains's *Phantom of the Opera* (1943)

While the 1925 film struggled with its soundlessness, script, and an early color process, the 1943 film version of *Phantom of the Opera* has it all: sound, color, and a very popular cast. What is so striking about the film, however, is how successful the film is given the departures it takes from the novel. Unlike the 1925 version, the variations on the *Phantom* theme work in this film. Gone are the atmospheric underground gondola rides of the 1925 version; gone is the spectacular makeup and performance of Lon Chaney, and surprisingly, gone is the narrative's focus on the Phantom. Praised by some, hated by others, the 1943 version uses the Gaston Leroux tale as a pretext for creating a new work of art, not merely a retelling for film. As memorable as the 1925 version with Lon Chaney is, this 1943 version is noteworthy for its creative adaptation of the novel. And given the difficulties associated with the Chaney film, it is no wonder that this narrative succeeds where the 1925 version did not. This adaptation does what many cannot: it creates another, unique work of art based on its source novel, the hallmark of a great adaptation. At the same time, some of the thematic concerns remain, the differentiation between light and darkness, good and evil, and the cautionary advice regarding critical viewing. And like the 1925 version, a great backstory haunts the film's production.

Here, the Phantom becomes Erique Claudin, played by Claude Rains, who turns out to be not the lover, but the father of Christine Dubois, played by Susanna Foster. There is no shortage of romance, however, since two lovers appear: the usual Raoul, played by Edgar Barrier, and a new addition, a dashing baritone, Anatole Garron, played by Nelson Eddy. The addition of Eddy as a competitor creates a number of comic scenes, which the 1925 version struggled to create but never successfully managed. Most importantly, however, the additional love interests serve, ironically, to highlight Christine's focus on her career rather than her desires for marriage and a traditional family. In this *Phantom*, Christine's choice is not between the world of light and darkness, choices which in previous versions have always implied her dependence on one of the male characters. Instead, her choice is between marriage and the professional life of an opera singer. And it may come as quite a surprise to some, but in this 1943 film, Christine chooses her career over marriage and family.

Before turning to the plot, it is important to note that this *Phantom* is distinctive as a result of some of its technological innovations, just as the 1925 version was, notably the addition of color during several scenes, particularly the masked ball scene. The 1943 version, which uses the 1925 set, is distinctive for its interior design, particularly the dressing rooms (Castanza 195), the sound, and the art direction, which won this film its Academy Awards. Clearly, the horror film was growing up and gaining recognition.

This 1943 version, admittedly, was a horror film couched as a Hollywood musical or vice versa. It clearly capitalized on the incredible popularity of Nelson Eddy and the vocal prowess of Susanna Foster, a relative newcomer. Consequently, the sound system for the film was given priority. Sharon Rich, who wrote a tell-all biography, *Sweethearts*, regarding the tempestuous relationship between Nelson Eddy and Jeannette MacDonald, notes:

> ...the sound director, Bernard Brown ("Brownie") was intrigued by Nelson's voice. He felt it had never been accurately duplicated on film sound track, always being toned down or muffled. He had a special booth built for Nelson to record in. When Nelson heard the playbacks, he was astonished, "I sound like that?" Most people feel that Brownie did capture the power and the glitter of Nelson's voice; seeing *Phantom* in a theatre with a good sound system was like hearing him in concert [300].

Sound was now associated with film in a significant and professional way, not merely added on as in the 1929 sound reissue of *The Phantom of the Opera*. Ultimately, the sound in this film may be technologically advanced compared with that of other films, but its thematic use was fairly conventional. Like many musicals of the day, the plot would stop for a musical number or two, here with much more credibility as the characters were, in fact, opera singers who were spending time rehearsing and performing. That is, the film lacks some of the clumsy breaks in plot for song, but it finally presents the songs in a typical Hollywood-musical way. All plot stops while singing occurs. Gone are the somewhat erotic moments of the novel when Christine and Erik basically gain a level of intimacy that transcends physical bodies.

The film does not focus on many other special effects, particularly in the makeup department. Because of World War II and the number of wounded servicemen returning to the States, the studio decided to minimize the horrifying make-up that characterized Chaney's embodiment of the Phantom:

> The scar on Claude Rains was a big issue. Jack Pierce did the makeup. It was during the war, and a lot of boys were returning with these problems. They didn't want to offend anybody, or hurt anybody. So there was a great amount of talk on how they were going to handle the scar. Maybe [the audiences] expected something more grotesque or horrible. But I think actually that what they finally decided on, irrespective of the war, was classically the best [qtd. in Rich 300].

Foster may have been painting a much more complimentary picture of her co-star Rains here, since another report indicates that Rains was very touchy about the mask and makeup, fearing that any disfigurement would cost him roles as leading men (MacQueen 82). Such a conclusion may be true but very ironic, given the fact that Rains broke out of theatrical roles into film roles through his portrayal of the Invisible Man in 1933, directed by Universal's James Whale of *Frankenstein* fame. His early screen tests were riddled with performances more appropriate to a 300-seat London theater than the intimacy of the camera (Soister 28).

Whatever the case, the absence of many elements from the previous film and the original novel — the lack of spectacle, the gunpowder plot, the torture chambers, the Phantom's boudoir, the moody lighting, and the Chaney makeup —finally place our attention on the script, ironically a script that does not follow the Leroux novel very closely. Further, since film seemed to be making headways in terms of technological advancements such as sound and color, there was no need to defend the camera's power as in the 1925 version. As *The New York Times* critic Bosley Crowther observed, "You might almost think the picture was made just so he [Nelson Eddy] might sing." The loose adaptation also annoyed Crowther, who longed for the spectacle and the horror of the 1925 version. And though Crowther has a point, the focus on the storyline offers an unusual feminist variation on the Phantom theme.[14]

Like many scripts of the time, as well as the 1925 version, this film's was a hybrid. Universal Studio attempted to capitalize on both its successful Deanna Durbin musicals and its horror films. Durbin was approached to play the role of Christine, but she backed out because there was not enough music. Broderick Crawford and Charles Laughton were choices who were considered and for various reasons were unavailable (MacQueen 80). As we shall see, Nelson Eddy's appearance in the film adds a subplot to this film that the other two men could not.

The opening scene establishes a number of important elements in the film. First, Erique plays a violin, not the usual organ, and he is not playing very well. Second, the film fulfills stereotypes regarding opera with its choice of Von Flowtow's 1847 *Martha*, the only opera in the film, one noted for its accessibility, melody, and popularity (Batta 148). The excerpt is clearly what people who know nothing about opera think opera is: a good-fellow-well-met drinking song that includes tights, manly men, and a good number of "Tra-la-las." Eddy's performance is a bit overdone, but even the toughest audience member would have a difficult time dismissing this scene and the joy that Eddy communicates as he sings. Even the most hard-hearted critic would have to admit that he is a charming, capable, and charismatic entertainer.

In the meantime, Christine, who is in the chorus, looks admiringly at Anatole, but she also notices her other beau, Raoul, who waits for her in the wings. In this version, Raoul is manlier and more worldly than the other versions, including the original, which depict him as an innocent, having led an overprotected life. Here, however, Raoul is not only mature, he actually has a legitimate job. He is a detective with the Paris police department. Seeing her man in uniform, Christine forgoes the curtain call in order to greet her date. As they embrace, he encourages her to leave the stage and marry him, saying, "You've had your fling."

Later, when she is reprimanded by an opera administrator for leaving the stage, she receives a lecture on the importance of her work and
art. The director reminds her of her beautiful voice, her ambition, and
her responsibility to her music. He tells her that art demands her exclu-
sivity. The male music director in this 1943 film tells her that she may
have her flirtations, but she may not fall in love; her passion should be
reserved for her music, if she wants to succeed.

By placing these comments so early in the film, the script focuses
the audience's attention on the plight of a working woman and artist. It
is no easy path to the stage; sacrifices must be made. Of course, the film
does not indicate that Christine could have both, as the male characters
could, but the film is noteworthy in that it raises the issue at all. Further, the film articulates the tensions regarding work and family that
were implied in the novel. In the novel, for example, Christine's father,
as well as Erik, advise her to remain faithful to her music. If she follows
this advice, she will be rewarded with a strong, melodious voice, and by
implication, a successful singing career. Erik's admonition, of course, is
biased by his desire for her, but his love seems to afford her the opportunity for both singing and love. Unfortunately for Erik, she does not
love him in this way. Though she is tempted, it is difficult to presume
that she would leave the world of light and tradition for a musical career
that offered no audience and little sunlight. In the case of this film, however, the advice is untainted; it comes from a reliable authority and men-
tor who only thinks of Christine's career.

The tempestuous relationship between Nelson Eddy and his co-star
Jeannette MacDonald offers further insight into the feminine focus of this
Phantom. As Sharon Rich describes, the film is the first one that Nelson
Eddy did without the oppressive hand of Louis B. Mayer. Mayer made
Eddy's career and, through the film *Naughty Marietta* (1935), began the
screen and romantic relationship between Eddy and MacDonald. Eddy
wanted to marry MacDonald, but only on the condition that she leave
her screen career. Given that she was at the height of her popularity, and
that Eddy's own personality was mercurial at best, she declined these
offers. Behind the legend of America's "sweethearts," there was codepen-
dency and violence. Through a series of poor choices, the meddling of
Louis B. Mayer, and their own indecision, the couple married other people but continued their affair until their deaths, perhaps the only way
that MacDonald could retain her career and relationship with Eddy.

Such are the phantoms that underlie the 1943 film. At this point, however, the two were happily pursuing their careers and one another without Mayer, and that may account for the lighthearted treatment of romantic entanglements in the film. Nelson Eddy's noticeable brunet choice of hair color for this film may also be a comment on the Mayer relationship. Mayer was notorious for loathing blond leading men, and he frequently asked Eddy to dye his or wear a wig. Eddy never complied, except for this film, his first without Mayer. His fans responded negatively, so he never made another in a dark wig (Rich 300), but it is very easy to conclude that the wig in this film was his farewell gesture to Mayer.

To return to the film, Christine faces a clear choice between her two suitors, Raoul, the steady, responsible man, versus Anatole, the musical, creative, and unstable man. Her choice, particularly the fact that the story offers her one at all, unlike the 1925 version, once again provides the narrative with its energy and power. It also fuels the film's humor. In one scene, for example, both men appear at Christine's stage door to ask her out for a date. She solves the problem by inviting them both to dine with her and the other's rival. In a very comic scene, the men, neither of whom has been chosen singly, now fight over who will be the last to leave the room after her departure as all three go out to dinner together. There may be two men against one woman, but Christine is clearly in charge of her heart, romances, and decisions.

Her relationship with Erique is not so clearly defined. He wishes to make contact with her, and Christine barely even recognizes him even as the opera's first violinist. As we learn from his interaction with the conductor following the performance of *Martha*, Erique Claudin is a remarkable violinist, but he is aging. He plays a lovely "Nocturne in E Flat" based on "music by Chopin" (Castanza 192), but he can no longer sustain opera's grueling routine. He is unceremoniously sacked. We discover, moreover, that Erique has not been saving his money, as the conductor presumes, but rather has been anonymously paying for voice lessons for Christine. He has been Christine's Phantom by proxy.

In order to make more money and continue the lessons, Erique decides to sell his musical compositions. The publisher, of course, is "busy" with his mistress, creating etchings. This art form is a convenient choice, plot wise, since it requires trays of acid, and one is conspicuously placed on a work table when Erique confronts the publisher. The publisher tells Erique that his compositions are mediocre and that he will not use them. Erique was hoping to sell them in order to fund his own needs now that he has been fired. Just as Erique is about to leave, however, Franz Liszt, played by Fritz Leiber in a cameo, begins to play Erique's music, clearly impressed with Erique's talent as a musical composer. Hearing the music coming from the next room, Erique believes that the publisher is stealing his work. In a situation that will become more common throughout *Phantom* films, the individual artist, feeling betrayed by the musical institution or corporation, attacks. In this case, Erique kills the publisher, but immediately his mistress grabs the acid that has been conspicuously placed in the scene and flings it into Erique's face. He runs from the room in pain, struggling through the streets of Paris, fleeing the police. He enters the sewers underground to escape and in a very moving scene, we see him washing his face in the filthy waters under Paris, trying to stop the agony of the acid-induced burns.

In a classic scene shift, we return to the lush offices of the Paris Opera House administrators. The distinction between the "haves" and the "have nots" is clear here and throughout the rest of the film. Such a distinction is consistent with the Leroux novel, which contrasts the wealth and opulence of the opera world above with the dark poverty below. During this scene, we also learn that the master key to the Opera House has been stolen by, of course, the Phantom, who now has access to everything. As in the Leroux novel, the hard and fast distinctions between upper and lower classes are dissolved by Erique's efforts.

As a result of his unencumbered access, the Phantom plots the downfall of the diva and the triumph of his daughter Christine. The diva is drugged, cannot go onstage, and so is replaced by Christine. Christine appears on stage with Anatole, and, of course, they win over the audience with their duet and their extravagant eighteenth-century costuming. This scene is important regarding Christine's choice as well. It begins indicating that Christine will choose Anatole — they both sing brilliantly, and they both appear to be in love. It appears that the opposing choices, career and family, might be resolved through music, the great leveler, through this duet. A full frontal face shot of Christine, a rarity in film in general and in this film in particular, however, complicates the romantic duet. The camera lingers on Christine, who is clearly so happy to be doing what she loves, singing. No men are in the scene with her; she is alone, triumphant and fulfilled. Her face, in soft-focus, fills the frame with a beatific vision of music. Our conclusions about her feelings for Anatole are incorrect. The film shows us that she is not in love with Anatole, though she seems to be singing so. Instead, the camera shows us that she is in love with her vocation, not her leading man.

For most of us, the scene may be remarkable in that a woman is given such power in this 1943 film. For Edward Baron Turk, however, the scene is much more than a feminist statement; it represents a revolution in female representation, particularly the representation of the trained, female, soprano voice. By examining the works of Jeannette MacDonald, ironically Nelson Eddy's usual singing partner, Turk demonstrates how the trained female voice creates anxiety in male viewers who perceive a great deal of authority in this voice, a level of empowerment unique in patriarchal culture. Honoring and representing the female voice as *The Phantom* does, then, is yet another reason for the distinctive nature of this film.

Following the performance, the diva accuses Anatole and Christine of poisoning her before the performance. There is no evidence to support this conclusion, but in order to placate her, the opera administrators agree to have no reviews of that night's performance. As she leaves the room, she is attacked by the Phantom. Anatole runs to her rescue, but he is mistakenly presumed to be the attacker. This misunderstanding is quickly resolved, and the Phantom demands that Christine sing that night, once again. Like many opera managers before them and after, these managers disobey the Phantom. They use the diva, and disguise everyone in masks in the hopes of trapping the Phantom. During this production, police, including a young Hume Cronyn, stand guard. But as all good Phantom followers know, the masks never work, the chandelier must fall, and Christine must be abducted.

As Erique shows her his hideaway, it is clear that the once loving and reasonable violinist has gone insane. He describes the place as a haven, but it is a decrepit, debris-ridden cesspool. He says he has found resurrection, but the set looks like a tomb. What he says does not match reality. In this case, the spectacle serves to underscore the lies being perpetuated. While Christine attempts to assess the situation, Anatole and Raoul rush in to rescue her, and with one single gunshot, the entire hideaway crumbles. As the lovers escape, Erique is crushed. All that remains is a picturesque shot of his violin and his mask in the rubble, a symbol of a father's dream gone mad and destroyed. Erique's world was a fragile edifice of dreams and illusions.

In the next scene, again noticeable for its move from the crypt of the Phantom to the glorious dressing room in the Opera House, we find Christine, the new opera diva. She has triumphed. Anatole and Raoul enter, offering dinner engagements and bouquets. She finally makes her choice explicit. She leaves both men to meet her adoring fans, her true love. She does not have time for dinner with either or both of them; she must meet her fans. Comically, the two jilted and stunned suitors decide to have dinner together. Their next decision is how to leave the packed opera house. The film ends with Eddy signaling to the crowd, indicating that they are safe to leave anyway they choose because: "Who'd pay any attention to a baritone and a detective?" While comic, it is difficult not to see the conclusion as at least a nod in the direction of Rains's great ending with Humphrey Bogart in his earlier film, *Casablanca* (1942). In both cases, men let women pursue their lives, while they remain to nurse their wounds, *Casablanca* tragically, *Phantom* comically. This film, moreover, stands as one of the few in which a female character chooses career over conventional family life. Unlike the 1925 version, which represents Christine stereotypically, as a silent victim, this version affords Christine her voice in much the same way that the Leroux novel affords Christine her story. In the novel, however, she chooses a more conventional resolution to her desires. Here, the film does not merely give Christine permission to pursue her goals; the main female character makes and meets her goals on her own terms, without much concern for her male counterparts. Christine happily gains her primary desire: a life in music. This 1943 version clearly offers a unique interpretation of not only the Leroux story but female representation, particularly in traditional Hollywood films.

Taming of the Phantom: Hammer Films' Wholesome *Phantom of the Opera* (1962)

The 1962 version of *Phantom of the Opera* is the work of Hammer Films, a British film company whose name is "synonymous with horror" (Hunter 40). Begun in the thirties, most popular in the fifties, and defunct by 1980, Hammer Films' formula for fear was simple and effective:

> Up to the early '70s, Hammer had been preserved by a combination of factors: the credibility of their films, which resulted from the

unbending solemnity with which the characters undertook their
tasks, no matter how incredible; and the repetition of a successful
formula, modified only to take advantage of more lenient censorship
by upgrading the gore and nipple count. Only their later attempts
to update and diversify — such as bringing Dracula to the present,
the comedies or ill-matched international co-production ventures —
finally served to undermine their House of Horror [Hunter 40].

Hammer was notoriously appealing to teenage audiences; Jerrold Hogle
describes its *Phantom* as one of the many to reflect adolescent culture
(*Undergrounds* 173–204). It is no surprise, then, that its most recent resurrection — there were many — of Hammer Films in April 2008 would
be through a MySpace serialized film, *Beyond the Rave*, once again appealing to the younger generation in terms of topic and delivery method.

Hammer Films, however, did not begin as a horror studio, as Universal did, but its origins are just as apocryphal. According to legend and
Wayne Kinsey, a comedy team performing in Hammersmith were asked
what their stage names were, and the response by William Hinds was
"Hammer and Smith" (8). Hinds purchased a series of theaters, began
booking acts, and like the great Carl Laemmle, realized that there was
money to be made in films. Hammer Films Ltd. was born. This venture, however, did not produce full-length films, only a 60-minute comedy, *The Public Life of Henry the Ninth*.

Hinds then met Enrique Carreras, a Spanish immigrant, and the
two began working towards filmmaking. But Carreras, who probably
had commodities in his blood since his family had made their fortune
in cigarettes, could not commit until he had tried yet another invest-
ment adventure in toothpaste. When that "washed out," Carreras and
Hinds were reunited, and along with several others formed Exclusive
Films, which distributed, among other films, some of Laurence Olivier's
early works (Kinsey 8–10).

Like Carl Laemmle, Hinds's and Carreras's family members played
important roles in the company, with Michael Carreras serving as a Thal-
berg-type presence in the company. His jobs, though numerous and
omnipresent, did not have quite the same prestige and power as Thalberg. He was, for example, required to walk a secretary's dog (Kinsey 11).
His brother James worked in the company, only to be called into the
armed services, but when he returned in 1946, he decided to "relaunch
the company into film production.... Hammer was accordingly resurrected"

(Kinsey 11). The first film from this period was *Dr. Morelle*, a film based on a popular radio show (Kinsey 13).

In order to save money, the film company decided to find a location that would be best suited to filming, as no Hollywood existed in England at this time. And many of the books on Hammer are organized by their film studio locations, the first one being Dial Close, the second being Oakley Court, the third Gliston Park, and the fourth, Bray. The films during these early years were not horror films, and some of them were based on "sure things," popular radio series, which demonstrated the cultural shift from the aural to the visual, and stage plays such as *To Have and to Hold* (1951) and *The Last Page* (1952), again demonstrating the prevalence and reliance of film on older, more traditional art forms. In any case, the budgets were low, the work loads grueling, and the neighbors frequently unfriendly. Hammer, for example, had to move from Dial Close because "the locals complained about the noise of the generators and the arc lamps used for night filming" (Kinsey 16).

With the film *The Quatermass Xperiment* (released in America as *The Creeping Unknown,* 1957), Hammer turned a corner in terms of quality and distribution. The story is about the space race, with Dr. Quatermass examining the results of a rocket crash. He discovers "that the men's bodies were invaded by something alien" (Johnson and Del Vecchio 108). One of the survivors escapes to begin a murderous rampage. It is only through the intervention of Dr. Quatermass, and, no surprise here, a film production company, that the creature is stopped. The film was a huge success. Its sequel, moreover, sealed a very lucrative distribution deal with United Artists as well (Johnson and Del Vecchio 117–119).

It is, however, *The Curse of Frankenstein* (1957) that made Hammer Films, as well as performers Christopher Lee and Peter Cushing, household names: "When it went into general release in the U.K. on May 20, it broke records everywhere it played" (Johnson and Del Vecchio 124). For many, films from *Quatermass* to *Phantom* (1962) were Hammer's finest, their "golden age," since "key personnel left the company" after that *Phantom* as a result of financial constraints (Kinsey 6; 264). Later works tended to lose any artistic and moral standards, and there was even a moment in the 1969 *Frankenstein Must Be Destroyed* which included a rape scene. Subsequent films, such as the lesbian *Vampire Lovers* (1970), lost a lot of plot while gaining a great deal of cleavage.

Hammer Films, however, made important contributions to films and the horror genre. As Martin Scorsese writes, "In my early teens, I went with groups of friends to go see certain films. If we saw the logo of Hammer Films we knew it was going to be a very special picture ... a surprising experience, usually — and shocking" (qtd. in "Hammer Studios"). Its list of actors, in addition to Lee and Cushing, include Olivier, Oliver Reed, Ursula Andress, Joan Fontaine, and Raquel Welch, to name a few. Its archives, moreover, are filled with classic examples of the realities of an artistic repertory group on low budgets. During the filming of the sequel to *Quatermass,* for example, the location had one "'major problem.' While filming a windstorm powerful enough to overturn a Jeep, [leading man] Brian Donlevy's toupee blew off and according to [one observer] 'all the prop men tried to catch this thing which was flying around like a bat! It was complicated by members of the public watching from a nearby hill. They must have though we had gone mad'" (Johnson and Del Vecchio 118).

In the case of their *Phantom,* a version without sumptuous sets or notorious celebrities, the Phantom's mask was a challenge. As makeup artist Roy Ashton recalls, producer-writer Tony Hinds called in a master mask-maker to create some sketches as possible choices for the mask, and while beautiful, the renderings were not quite right. Ashton then thought about kabuki masks and created some drawings. Hinds, however, was indecisive:

> Three weeks later we were in the theatre where they had to photograph Herbert Lom with his mask on, and no decision had been taken yet. "Look," I said, "give me five minutes and I will make you one." I got an old piece of rag, tied it round his face, cut a hole in it, stuck a bit of mesh over one of the eyes, two bits of string around it, and tried it. "Great!" they cried out, "that's just what we want! Phantom of the Opera." I often laugh when I think back on that; only a piece of nothing, having had a professional artist there for six weeks, books, and God knows what! [qtd. in Kinsey 237].

Such are the delightful tales that haunt Hammer studios.

And like so many of the films made from *Phantom,* there is a story behind this film's inception, though Hammer's tight and hectic production schedules avoided many of the collaborative nightmares experienced in the 1925 film. This film began with Cary Grant's interest in making a horror film. According to Tony Hinds, he began working on the script right away, knowing that Grant's "agent would tell him he couldn't make it. And that's what happened" (Kinsey 233). Still, the opportunity led Hinds to continue work on the script, this time adding a henchman, a dwarf played by Ian Wilson, to do all of the Phantom's dirty work, just in case Grant was available and was concerned about his on-screen reputation.

As a result of the screen star's potential participation and Hammer's attempts to receive an "A," or general audience rating, the script for this *Phantom* is very tame. Given the financial difficulties Hammer faced at the time, they were desperate for a widely released film, one that would appeal to all ages all over. They edited the film heavily, shortening scenes and deleting others, in order to obtain what we now refer to as the "G" rating. One look at this film, and it is difficult to imagine anything "R-rated" occurring, but the early 1960s still had censors and censorious sensibilities. Here just one suggestion from the authorities as an example:

> On seeing this film again we felt that one further cut should be made in addition to those given.... At the opening of the film in the pre-credit sequence, there is a shock shot of the masked face with a gleaming eye. This, coming at the very beginning of the film, intensifies the shock element and we would like this removed. It becomes acceptable when partially covered by the titles.... [qtd. in Kinsey 244].

Such standards and their enforcement make it clear that any generally released film would be sanitized completely, and in the case of this *Phantom,* there is little doubt that the censors did their job well. The Phantom is a victim, and all his violence is caused by the loyal but misdirected dwarf. The romance between the two lovers is pure. In the end, the Phantom sacrifices his life for Christine, saves her from the dwarf, and affords her the opportunity to live "happily ever after." It is a feel-good *Phantom*, with little tension. It is so virtuous that it might be more appropriately called *The Sound of Phantom* or *The Phantom of the Music*.

With Cary Grant out of the picture, the studio chose Herbert Lom as the Phantom, also known as Professor Petrie. Heather Sears played Christine Charles, and Edward de Souza is Christine's love, who is not called by the French name, Raoul; instead, he is given the decidedly British name, Harry. Such changes not only help the film make the rating, but they also give the film a strong sense of British nationalism. The Opera House, for example, is in London, not Paris. The true villain of the story, moreover, is Lord D'Arcy, a French-named aristocrat, played by Michael Gough.

To highlight national loyalties further, and perhaps nodding vigorously to the censors, D'Arcy produces "his" version of, not *Faustus*, but *St. Joan*. Whether this choice highlights D'Arcy's evil or the studio's desperate need for the general rating is difficult to conclude. It certainly offers complicated representations of nationalisms. Joan, after all, led the French against the British, but she is such a popular character and her role as martyr to a greater cause so akin to the Phantom's that it is virtually impossible to untangle where national loyalties are supposed to lie. It may, perhaps, offer us a lesson in filmmaking: all is fair in production, particularly with the censors involved.

As in many other versions, Christine has the opportunity to sing as a result of an indisposed diva. After her triumph, D'Arcy invites her out to dinner and treats her badly. Now that the diva is out of commission, D'Arcy needs a new romance. Calling Christine a "delicious little thing," D'Arcy attempts to pounce, but Christine avoids becoming another course on the aristocrat's menu. One role the diva must play, apparently, is servicing this lord. As they are leaving the restaurant for the "private singing lessons" D'Arcy promises, the very distressed and uncomfortable Christine sees Harry, the attractive young new producer of the opera. As they converse casually, Harry invites Christine to dinner, which she readily accepts, although she has just dined with the lord. Given this public situation, D'Arcy accepts defeat, in this case, and he leaves the two to dine, in Christine's case, again.

It is over this second course that the love story begins. Following dinner, the two wind up at the Opera House, where they find evidence of the Phantom. As Christine retrieves something from her dressing room, she hears the sounds of the Phantom. Harry hears them as well, and as the couple leave, the rat catcher appears, but no confirmation of the Phantom's existence ensues.

The next morning, the couple meet at Christine's boarding house. Coincidentally, the housekeeper tells them the story of Professor Petrie, a former resident of the boarding house. Petrie was a music teacher who wanted to publish his music. Desperate for money, he makes a deal with the devilish D'Arcy. D'Arcy buys the music for a pittance, then has it published under his own name. Once again, the individual is overpowered by a powerful ruling or corporate class. Overcome by rage, the professor breaks into the publishing house and begins burning the musical score — his opera of *St. Joan* which D'Arcy has claimed as his own. Thousands of copies taunt the professor and confirm his suspicions of betrayal. A fire ensues, and everyone thinks that Petrie has been killed.

Harry and Christine begin investigating this mystery because they have their own suspicions — he is still alive, haunting the Opera House. As they return from their investigations, the couple ride in a carriage, complete with Miles Malleson, a very British character actor, as the driver. The two are clearly in love, have a big kiss, but then chastely separate for the evening. Unfortunately for Harry, the separation affords the dwarf the opportunity to abduct Christine. He takes her to the Phantom, who happens to be playing Bach's *Toccata and Fugue in D Minor*, a very popular and easily recognizable organ piece. Stunned and fearful, Christine is placed before the Phantom, whose first words are, "I am going to teach you to sing, Christine."

The Phantom is clearly obsessed, and forces Christine to sing despite exhaustion. He even slaps her in order to get her to sing more. Harry discovers that she is missing, and he begins to search for her by following the underground passages of the Opera House. Unlike the 1925 version, which presents the aquatic underworld of the Opera House as mysterious, mythic, and dreamily dark, the water here is some of the worst in film history. It is obvious that the valiant Harry is brave, for he must enter these slimy waters that make Grendel's home in *Beowulf* seem pristine and clear. In addition to what appears to be raw sewage floating in the water, Edward de Souza comments that the water was very cold: "They rather cynically left that for practically the last shot in the film in case I succumbed to the cold waters. It was made in the winter. They didn't want to have a dead actor to play in the rest of the film" (qtd. in Kinsey 239). Once again, the Hammer method continues: save the film, not necessarily the actor.

Fortunately for the film, Harry survives and launches into a battle with the dwarf. After Harry prevails, the Phantom tells the young couple the truth about himself and D'Arcy. As the housekeeper related, D'Arcy stole the professor's work, and the professor attempted to burn all the copies of the stolen librettos. He found himself on fire, disfigured, and the dwarf, who had been living under the streets of London, rescued and revived Petrie. He has since lived underground.

The professor then pleads with Harry to allow Christine to remain, to give him one week to turn her into a beautiful singer, not only for her sake, but for his own, for she will sing the lead part in the opera he composed, *St. Joan.* Through long, meaningful looks, Christine agrees. She does not need to speak. Her answer is a silent yes. In this film, she has no real connection with the Phantom. There is no passionate aural communication. Instead, she offers her voice as a charitable gesture to a wronged man. Further, her own true love, Harry, wants her to do so, so she agrees to perform, to go on stage, only for the sake of saving someone else, not making something of her own career. Even her passion for Harry seems decidedly sanitized. They are just a couple of good-hearted kids in a crazy mixed-up world, helping a disabled and distraught artist and father-figure.

Once Christine is ready, we see her singing her final song on stage. The dwarf, who has been watching the opera in the wings, jumps to the chandelier to escape the clutches of a stagehand who is trying to throw him out of the theater. The chandelier, of course, cannot hold the dwarf's weight, and the rope supporting the light fixture begins to fray, threatening to drop the chandelier, which is over the stage in this version, onto Christine's head. As the dwarf leaps to safety, the Phantom, unmasking, jumps from his box down onto the stage and shoves Christine into the clear. The chandelier falls, killing the Phantom. Harry and Christine live. In this way, the film offers a hopeful, wholesome conclusion: the bad have been punished (D'Arcy, having seen the Phantom's face earlier, has fled), and the good have been rewarded, if at great cost. Like many of the earlier versions, including the novel, this film still demonstrates that appearances may be deceiving. D'Arcy appears to be a member of society's elite, but through the search that Harry and Christine make, his true nature is revealed. Similarly, thanks to their curiosity and their persistence, the professor's good name is restored, and his art attributed to him. There is justice in the world, and fighting injustice among the upper and lower classes is possible for the British pure of heart like Christine and Harry.

Phabulous Phantom: Brian De Palma's Glam Rock Parody *Phantom of the Paradise* (1974)

Brian De Palma's *Phantom of the Paradise* (1974) is a cult-classic rock opera with close similarities to the mega-cult hit, *The Rocky Horror Pic-*

ture Show (1975). Though the movie version did not hit theaters until 1975, the London stage version of the antics of Frank-N-Furter and the gang was a huge hit, and there are several scenes that clearly mimic the stage classic. According to De Palma, however, he began writing the piece in 1969 in order to show the movie industry that the growing rock music culture was an important consideration, one that film executives were, surprisingly, ignoring at that time. His film introduces its audiences and Hollywood to the raucous world of rock opera. De Palma admits that he tried to capitalize on the incredible popularity of the Rolling Stones and the Who, "but, of course, you wouldn't even get them on the telephone" (qtd. in "The Making of *Phantom of the Paradise*"). Instead, the film starred Paul Williams, which might strike some as an unusual choice, but which, in the end, satisfied De Palma's vision for the film. He notes, "What is good about Paul Williams is that he's sophisticated enough as a composer to be able to write satiric music of a certain form ... he can write Alice Cooper-type music and he can write '50s Beach Boy-type stuff" (qtd. "The Making"). De Palma admitted that he did not follow the novel closely and reckons he may have watched the Lon Chaney version on several occasions as he worked on the film, but his goal was not an adaptation or homage to Gaston Leroux. He does admit that the film classic *The Cabinet of Dr. Caligari* (1919) influenced his decision to create a horror film: "I thought the rock world is so stylized and expressionistic to begin with, that it would be a perfect environment in which to tell old horror tales" (qtd. in Knapp 20–21). Rather than making a remake of *Phantom*: "I took the idea of a composer having his music ripped off, endeavoring to kill the people who are massacring his music and putting on the girl he loves to sing it the way he wants it to be sung. That was the basic concept" (qtd. in Knapp 14–17). Like the other versions, particularly the 1943 and the 1962 versions, moreover, De Palma uses the story to illustrate ambivalence — in this case, the ambivalence prevalent in the rock industry, the dark side of the "music of the night."

Jerrold Hogle argues that this film and the 1962 Hammer version reflect the growing youth culture, particularly young film viewers. He also connects these films to the later Lloyd Webber musical, arguing for a psychoanalytic continuity because Lloyd Webber must have been aware of these films, if not specifically, then the issues and sentiments which reflect this cultural period of youthful unrest (*Undergrounds* 183–188).

For Hogle, the films reflect adolescent ambivalence regarding authority and corporate power during the sixties and seventies which later influence the Lloyd Webber musical. The Phantom, for example, wants to rise in the corporate music world, but he is ultimately betrayed by the very processes that make the corporation possible (*Undergrounds* 188).

De Palma argues similarly, highlighting the dichotomy the film underscores:

> I am in the midst of a society that is very capitalist, and whose values I completely reject. But I, too, become a capitalist. The problem is that by even dealing with the devil, you become devilish to a certain extent. You need the machine. And once you use it, you are a tainted human being [qtd. in "Summary"].

De Palma articulates what is clear in the film: success in the music industry generally includes "selling out." To pursue a musical and creative goal demands concessions. De Palma's comments and his own difficulties creating the film reflect the growing American corporate culture that hinders rather than fosters artistic enterprise. He notes, for instance, that he had to negotiate with Universal Studios, which owns not only the book but also the three film versions: "They felt we were infringing on their story line — not so much the book, but some of their later versions ... so we had to settle with them for the rights in order to prevent the film from being held up for distribution" (qtd. in "The Making"). In addition, he had to make concessions to a comic strip called *Phantom,* an alternate title in the early stages of the film's conception, as well as Atlantic Records, since they have a subdivision called Swan Song Records. Swan's company is called Swan Song Enterprises, and though "it was never mentioned [in the dialogue], it was just that we had the words Swan Song on nearly everything around [Swan] and it all had to be optically removed" (qtd. in Knapp 17). Perhaps as a bitter comment, the name of Swan's company was changed to Death Records, a company out to destroy, not create, art. In today's climate, which lionizes multinational corporations and their operational methods, this *Phantom,* perhaps naively but refreshingly, illustrates a time when corporations and industry were not viewed as solutions to social problems, but rather the causes of those problems.

Before beginning the analysis of the film, it is also important to note that the film represents an important moment in film, stage, and rock history, through its rock opera genre. In a fascinating analysis of the rock musical, Elizabeth Wollman shows that the genre is inherently challenging. And while De Palma attributes its challenges to the movie industry in general, and that may in fact be the case, Wollman offers another perspective, demonstrating that rock and stage have been at odds since the inception of the rock musical *Hair*. She notes that unlike musical theater which clearly revels in its "artifice," rock music revels in its authenticity, its ability to express the "real," whether social, emotional, or personal (25–41). And with this distinction comes a certain snobbery, noted by De Palma, too: "It is a business without much sense of humor about what they are and what they do" (qtd. in Knapp 19). For Wollman, when it comes to rock opera, it is difficult to satisfy anyone: "A successful staged production offering a blend of rock and musical theatre aesthetics usually wins the favor of either the rock or the musical theatre realm, but rarely of both camps at once" (31). In keeping with the other *Phantom*s, this *Phantom* encourages viewers to sharpen their critical perceptions, in this case regarding the self-importance of the rock music industry, and its perhaps over-inflated view of itself, its effects on society and the art world.

The film begins with *Twilight Zone*'s creator, Rod Serling, offering a suitably creepy voice-over, articulating the great accomplishments of Swan and his mega-corporation, Swan Records. Immediately, the satire begins. According to the report, Swan, played by Paul Williams, won so many Gold Records for his work that he once tried to store his trophies in Fort Knox. His current discovery and success, a fifties-nostalgia band, called the Juicy Fruits, brings his record company and him great acclaim, but Swan remains dissatisfied. He longs for more, for something beyond wealth and fame, something meaningful. Even the corporate executive who fulfills the American dream is, ironically, unfulfilled. For Swan, he hopes to discover the ultimate music, what he refers to as the "music of the spheres." The choice of phrase is an interesting and classical one, one that bears analysis, particularly since it is placed in this modern film context.

Robert Reilly notes that research led Pythagoras to conclude that "music was the ordering principle of the world," as a result of the numerical relationship between whole numbers and musical notes: "Pythagoras wondered about the relationship of these ratios to the larger world [the Greek word for ratio is *logos*, which means *reason* or *word*]" (13). In a book outlining the entire history of the concept, Jamie James notes that "music of the spheres" was part of Pythagoras's concept of the order of the universe and music. There were three kinds of music: that of ordinary instruments; the music of each human organism; and the music of the cosmos or the music of the spheres (30). Reilly concludes that "this discovery was fraught with ethical significance. By participating in heavenly harmony, music could induce spiritual harmony in the soul" (13).

For later thinkers, composers, and writers, the relationship would also help the devout transcend the earthly plane and experience the divine. Dante Alighieri, for example, in the *Divine Comedy*, also indicates the music of the cosmos, and uses its beauty and harmony to epitomize paradise. As the narrator says, "The newness of the sound and the great light / Incited me to learn their cause" (*Paradiso* I, 82–83). Beatrice, his guide, explains, "All things, among themselves, possess an order; and this order is the form that makes the universe like God" (*Paradiso* I, 103–105). Johannes Kepler, too, links the cosmos to the spheres. Music, mathematics, and the divine are all interconnected in this concept of the "music of the spheres."

It is interesting, then, that such a reference appears in this popular film. One look at the Google search for the phrase, however, makes it clear that many have taken the verbiage and put it to uses far removed from the work of the philosophers, theologians, and scientists. It may mean a particular kind of wind chime or New Age music album. It becomes yet another marketing device, empty of its original meaning, particularly in a modern context. As John Adam, a popular American composer, notes, "[I] learned in college that tonality died somewhere around the time that Nietzsche's God died, and I believed it" (qtd. in Reilly). Given the modern context, references to the "music of the spheres" might appear anachronistic, out of place. For *Phantom* historians, however, the reference makes sense: like Faustus, one of the primary images in the original novel, Swan wants more. Dissatisfied with his success, he yearns for a greater understanding beyond human limitations. The parallels between Swan and Faustus do not end here. As we learn towards the end of the film, Swan has in fact made a deal with the devil in order to gain wealth, retain youth, and attain fame. Ironically, he desires the music of the spheres, the music of the heavens, and in order to obtain that dream, he makes a deal with the devil, and like Faustus, ultimately sells not only his soul but the possibility of fulfilling his dream, the moment he signs the contract.

Because Swan is devilish, evil, he cannot create something divine. He does, however, know it when he hears it in the work of Winslow Leach, a struggling but talented composer.[15] Leach, a youthful innocent, creates the "music of the spheres," and Swan offers to help the young composer make it big in the music industry. But like the selfish and evil Lord D'Arcy in the 1962 version, Swan steals Leach's music and presents it as his own.

After Swan takes Leach's music, ostensibly to review it, Leach attempts to see Swan to discuss his work. Of course, Swan has stolen the music and has no intentions of seeing the young composer, but while he is waiting, he meets his Christine, here called Phoenix, a young singer who hopes that Swan will make her a star in his next work. Unfortunately for Leach, Swan has him arrested on false charges of drug possession, and Leach lands in prison. Swan is now free to steal Leach's music and his girl. While in prison, Leach's teeth are pulled, and he is given steel ones. To make matter worse, while he is working on the assembly line, manufacturing tiddlywinks, he hears of Swan's newest project, a new musical creation to be performed at his Paradise concert hall. The musical clip he hears is, of course, his own. He discovers that Swan has robbed him. Enraged, Leach escapes, breaks into Swan's factory, and is terribly disfigured by an accident with a record album-making machine. Like many a Phantom before him, he runs to the river, and he is presumed dead.

In the next scene, we see Leach stealing a costume from the Paradise in order to hide his disfigurement. Through the accident and the new costume, he becomes the Phantom of the Paradise whose sole goal is to destroy Death Records and the musical venue. He begins by planting a bomb on the set of the Juicy Fruits stage. De Palma is noted for his use of split-screen technique, and he uses it to full advantage at this moment in the film. As the Juicy Fruits rehearse a bastardized version of one of his songs, Winslow Leach plants a bomb. Like the split between the upper and underworld in the other *Phantoms,* this split screen shows the oppression beneath the spectacle, as well as the violence beneath the entertainment industry. The technique also highlights the ironic world of Paradise. Leach, the Phantom, is actually a force for good, attempting to overthrow Swan's evil empire, but in this topsy-turvy world, he becomes the enemy, while Swan seems to offer salvation. He has gone to prison, but Swan is the thief; he is the terrorist, while Swan and the Fruits are the victims.

Swan realizes that the bomb was planted by Leach. He discovers Leach in Paradise, unmasks him, and then makes Leach an offer he cannot refuse. In addition to the physical disfigurement, the record-press accident has left Leach unable to sing or speak clearly. Discovering this weakness enables Swan to lure Leach into his world and his plans. Swam promises Leach the ability to talk and the opportunity to compose his own work. All of Swan's wealth, technology, and materials will be at Leach's disposal. With few other opportunities, Leach agrees to collaborate with his nemesis.

If the audience presumes that Swan has undergone any kind of change of heart by offering this opportunity to Leach, the film makes it clear that this relationship will only benefit Swan. He, after all, entices Leach to sign a voluminous contract, with insane clauses and legal jargon, to be signed in Leach's own blood. To highlight the irony further, the work that Leach begins is "the first rock version of *Faust* ... live, on the Death label." Such irony regarding creative artists and corporations is rare in postmodern America. The corporate is presumed and in many cases commended; here, however, we see the costs of doing business in satirical hyperbole.

To complicate matters further, Phoenix, Leach's past love interest, auditions for the starring role. Her voice is beautiful, and she is praised for her "natural," not glamorous beauty, as opposed to the other singers who wear too much makeup, show too much cleavage, and who are just too "glam." With Phoenix as his inspiration and with Swan providing plenty of drugs, Leach composes feverishly, nearly killing himself for the opera.

All of Leach's work, however, is undone by Swan, who decides that Phoenix is not right for the major part. Instead, a "heavier" glam rocker by the name of Beef is chosen for the title role, unbeknownst to Leach. Though full of satiric innuendo and comment, Swan's behavior is consistent with earlier presentations of the Faust myth. As in Christopher Marlowe's *Dr. Faustus*, the devil cannot create the divine, so it is entirely reasonable that Swan bastardizes Leach's beautiful work. He can only destroy, not create.

Leach discovers the shift and decides to take revenge. In a wonderful spoof of Alfred Hitchcock's shower scene in *Psycho* (1960), Leach attacks Beef in the shower, while Beef sings "Life at Last," one of the songs from the upcoming short. Rather than kill him, Leach takes a plunger and puts it over Beef's mouth, warning him that he must never sing his lyrics. Only Phoenix can sing the lyrics.[16]

Snorting massive amounts of cocaine, Beef makes a hasty retreat from Paradise, only to be redirected by Swan's ever-present henchman, Arnold Philbin. The show must go on, and Beef has also signed a contract with Swan, a contract in which there are no loopholes. The show, a cross between *The Cabinet of Dr. Caligari* (1919) and *Frankenstein* (1931), features a heavy-metal reincarnation of the fifties band, the Juicy Fruits, who harvest body parts from dummies planted in the audience. Against the Phantom's direct orders, Beef appears, "assembled" from these parts, and hams it up, butchering the lyrics and song. The Phantom, Leach in his disguise, resorts to violence, killing the glam-rock diva with a stage lightning bolt, De Palma's replacement for the chandelier. With Beef out of the way, Phoenix has her chance. As she takes the stage and begins to sing, she turns into an overnight sensation. Once again Swan destroys the beauty of art by promising Phoenix everything in exchange for her voice. She agrees, and but like Leach and Beef, she is no longer in control of her own destiny. She has allowed her ambition to enslave her to Swan.

The Phantom kidnaps her and warns her about the business, particularly Swan and the crowds. He warns her that the stage will take, not give, her identity. The crowd's desire for her music is insatiable; she will lose herself by giving the audience everything. Thinking him a madman, Phoenix escapes and returns to the arms of Swan, who gladly comforts and ultimately seduces the confused Phoenix. In a classic scene from this film, we see Swan on a round satin bed with Phoenix, also in satin. Fortunately, the satin remains throughout the suggestive, not explicit, scene. The Phantom, of course, watches from a skylight above, but little does he realize that he, too, is being watched by Swan via electronic surveillance. In a metaspectacular event, Swan enjoys watching Leach's tortured responses to watching him with Phoenix. The relationship between Swan and Phoenix is not about love or even lust; it is about revenge and hate, ironically, between Swan and Leach, not Phoenix. She is just the means by which Swan tries to destroy Leach.

Overcome with jealousy and grief, Leach stabs himself on the roof. The suicide brings Swan to his side to chastise him for his actions. He informs Leach that suicide is not part of the contract, which stipulates: "This contract terminates with Swan." Leach, then, attempts to kill

Swan, but Swan remains unharmed, explaining, "I'm under contract, too." There is no escape, and at this moment, this contract seems eerily eternal.

Given the publicity over Beef's death, Swan decides to try another publicity stunt — to marry Phoenix at the end of the *Faust*. Once again, however, Swan has alternate plans. He tells Phoenix that they will be married, but he plots to have her killed during the wedding scene. Again Swan's plan makes perfect sense in terms of evil, since evil cannot participate in a ceremony which honors love. Further, his behavior underscores the false promises of fame.

In the meantime, however, Leach uncovers the truth about Swan and the mysterious contract. Swan has made his own deal with the devil many years ago. Swan's deal keeps him young and prosperous in the recording industry, but his youth and vigor are, in fact, illusory, for as Leach discovers, he is not the only one wearing the mask. Like the title character in Oscar Wilde's *Picture of Dorian Gray,* Swan, too, has a mask, the boyish exterior covering his aged and rotting soul underneath. Swan and Leach, then, are perfect complements. Swan is appealing on the outside, but repellent on the inside, while Leach is repellent on the outside, but good and appealing on the inside. Leach finds the video taped contract files and burns them, and by this destruction, he removes Swan's power over Phoenix. He also discovers the murder plot, and just in the nick of time, Leach, as the Phantom, interrupts the onstage marriage and stabs Swan.

At this point, the complementarity between the two characters is fully realized, for by stabbing Swan, Leach has killed himself. Like a vampire and his vampiric offspring, the two are interconnected. Further, though the film has been critical of the oppressive relationship between the corporate and the creative, it must, in the end, recognize that the two are one. The creative cannot continue without the corporate, without the marketing, the advertising, the audience. They are inextricably linked. With the death of the two symbolic extremes, however, Phoenix remains, perhaps indicating another alternative for the relationship to continue. She, after all, embodies both, and though she has also sold herself for fame and success, she escapes her fate, thanks to the Phantom, the artist. In the end, she recognizes the Phantom and his sacrifice. Love and creativity have saved her from destruction, and this may be the way to negotiate the dialectic between the corporate and the creative, fame and inspiration.

The *Faust* overtones are clear, and in the end, Phoenix is saved, though her choice in the matter is not as active as in some versions. Since both of the men are dead, there is no Raoul with which to live a "happily ever after" life. Given the quirkiness of the film, its energy, and self-reflexive foolishness, it is easy to see the attraction to the entertainment industry despite some unsavory characters like Swan. On the one hand, the dark side of the entertainment industry is exposed as effectively as the underground canals of the Paris Opera House in the Leroux version, but in this film, there is so much fun through the parody that this film seems to suggest that in spite of it all, Phantoms, drugs, betrayals, meaningless sex, bad singers, stupid musicals, and cheesy costumes, it is still worth it, and there are still opportunities for performers like Phoenix who have perhaps managed to balance ambition and creation, the corporate and creative. In the end, she is silent, but it appears not for long. Her contract with Satan is up. She is now a free agent.

Decoys in the Danube: The TV Miniseries of *Phantom of the Opera* (1983)

Capitalizing on the successes of the miniseries, particularly their own *Count of Monte Cristo* in the mid-seventies, Norman Rosemont aimed the production company's sights on *Phantom* (*Undergrounds* Hogle 194). Set in Budapest rather than Paris, the 1983 television movie of *Phantom of the Opera* required name changes to accommodate the change in cities. Budapest is stunning, and some of the supporting roles are filled by Hungarian performers and musicians, giving the movie a real sense of place. The change also underscores the kind of competition that the Austro-Hungarian Empire created for the rest of the operatic world, a world that Leroux's Paris was so desperately trying to make a mark upon. The building that serves as the Budapest Opera House is substantial, and while it also has a number of underworld caverns, the underground is relatively dry compared to other variations of *The Phantom*. A passageway, for example, not an underground river, affords the Phantom the access necessary to terrorize the Opera House's inhabitants. As Jerold Hogle notes, moreover, the Opera House was actually a theater and the underworld was the tunnels of a brewery (*Undergrounds* 194), but the illusion of another world and another time is created very successfully, despite these departures.

For Hogle, the time period is a relatively safe one, one that comforts the viewers rather than challenging them to examine their lives, perspectives, and assumptions. In other words, it is pure television. Set just before World War I, the film attempts to "telescope the period ... into one safe, unthreatening time-frame before all of the twentieth century's major wars, hoping to achieve an escape for its audience that would bury their own anxieties behind those of a generalized 'other time' that seemed neither too close nor too far away" (*Undergrounds* 195). The period works, given the prowess of the Austro-Hungarian Empire prior to World War I, and, as we shall see, it also serves to lull viewers into a false sense of security, since like many *Phantoms* this one also challenges perceptions and long-held perspectives.

In addition to the impressive setting, the film also includes an impressive array of stars for the major roles. Jane Seymour, "queen of the mini-series," stars with Oscar-winning Maximilian Schell, as well as sixties star Michael York. The cast, along with the setting, brings "high culture," or the perception of "high culture," to a television audience. Schell was well-known for his work in the television production of *Judgment at Nuremberg* in 1959, a live production of the play. York, of course, was well-known for his work in Franco Zefferelli's *Romeo and Juliet* (1968). Born Joyce Penelope Wilhelmina Frankenberg, Jane Seymour had a number of successes behind her, including her role as a Bond girl in *Live and Let Die* (1973), and she continues to foster her "to the manner born" persona, offering interior decorating and makeup tips on various television shopping networks in the United States. Though all these cast members were no longer at the height of their popularity, their personas brought a certain high culture to this lowbrow medium.

The film opens with the Elena Korvin, played by Jane Seymour, practicing for the role of Marquerite in Gounod's *Faust*. Though talented, she has clearly not mastered the role. Nervous and self-conscious, she is a perfect mark for the Opera's lecherous owner, Baron Hunyadi. He propositions her, and she declines, despite his threats to ruin her and her career.

Like many *Phantoms* before, this version illustrates the corruption which lies behind the beauty of the music industry, the skull beneath the skin. Elena returns home to her husband, the conductor of the Opera's symphony, Sandor Korvin. Clearly in love with his wife, Sandor practices with and supports his vulnerable and talented wife. As she prepares her role, he hires a professional "plant" to start the applause as she sings. Unfortunately, the Baron also knows about this professional, and he buys him off with a larger sum to ruin Elena, the woman who has scorned his lecherous advances. As she sings her final piece in the opera, the professional stand and begins heckling her performance, screaming that she is the worst Marguerite he has ever heard. Other opera patrons join in and begin throwing paraphernalia on the stage. Ironically, of course, this has been her best performance ever. The reviews are even worse. Crushed and discouraged, Elena commits suicide by throwing herself into the Danube.

Devastated by the news of his wife's suicide, Sandor begins his revenge. First, he confronts the music critic, Kraus, played by Philip Stone, who may be best known for his masterful performance as Delbert Grady in Stanley Kubrick's version of Stephen King's *The Shining* (1980). Being the typical lackey he is, he says that the Baron forced him to write the bad reviews. In a scene that would make newspaper reporter Leroux proud, Sandor then forces Kraus to write a retraction, complete with a confession regarding the Baron's influence on the bad review, but the confrontation goes wrong. In a scene very similar to the Hammer *Phantom* of 1962, a fire starts in the office, and as Kraus and Sandor battle over a gun, Kraus is killed and Sandor is mutilated by a bottle of acid that happens to be in the newspaper critic's office. Sandor runs to the streets, collapses, and is rescued by a homeless man who takes him to the bowels of the Opera House. Once again, beneath the art, there is corruption and oppression.

In the underworld, Sandor recovers, creates a home, and finds suitable masks available in the Opera's costume department. What makes this film different regarding the masking of the Phantom is not so much how the Phantom became the Phantom, but rather, how his mask is represented. As has often been the case throughout the Phantom's history, deciding on the appropriate mask is sometimes an artistic challenge. Claude Rains's Phantom, for example, could not be "too disfigured," given the mutilations which occurred during World War II. Hammer Films' mask challenge was solved simply, but in all cases, for an actor to be masked, to have one of his most important features obfuscated, will always bring difficulties. Here, however, the Phantom's mask and even the Phantom himself are frequently depicted in black-and-white and shades of gray. The contrast is startling and significant, for when he appears in this way, he really looks corpse-like, someone buried alive, the walking dead. The mask does not distort Schell's appearance as extremely as other masks, but this gray pallor is certainly a notable contribution to the history of *Phantom* masks.

Several years pass, and the Opera House once again stages *Faust*. And like many other versions, a diva prevails on the stage. In this case, it is not necessarily her voice that is the problem, though it is clearly not great, but rather the fact that the diva cannot relinquish her diva status long enough to actually create a character. Though the film does not refer to method acting or Stanislavski, Michael York, who plays the "imported" British director, tries to bring realism to the opera stage. As he comments about the diva, Madame Bianchi, "If she sang Aida, we'd all ice skate down the Nile." She, of course, thinks he's an arrogant director, and to a certain extent, he is, so the rehearsals are in a stalemate.

Enter the "new girl," Maria Gianelli, Elena's "double," also played by Jane Seymour. In order to keep the diva in check, the director decides to audition other women for the role. Of course, Maria fills the role beautifully, and she is given a chance to sing. As she sings, the Phantom hears her and is reminded of his dead wife, Elena. She even looks like her, since she is played by the same actress in different hairstyles and colors, so he decides to help her develop her voice. This, he thinks, will be his best revenge.

Unlike many Christines, this Maria is ambitious and, by the way, American, which is ironic since the actress Seymour is English-born. On the way home after her brilliant audition, she meets the director, who, after a few moments, asks her, "Are you cold?" When she responds in the negative, he says, "That's surprising, because your naked ambition is showing." Unperturbed, she challenges the director's condescending tone, and reminds him that he has had a good life, full of all he needed or desired. Others, including the homeless on the streets, have not. He relents, and the two go out to dinner, where they begin their romance.

Here, again, the Christine role is updated. During dinner, she holds her own throughout the conversation, and when the discussion turns towards rumors regarding women in the opera house and their sexual encounters, Maria makes it clear that while she is no virgin, she would never sleep with anyone, including the Baron, just to get ahead in the Opera company. She says, "Lying on your back is not good for the voice." Though the exchange of Elena and Maria may suggest that women are interchangeable, or, as in the case of the diva and Maria, merely pawns in a male production, Maria's relationship with the director makes it clear that she is human, not an idealized victim. She knows what she wants out of life and romance. And as the film progresses, it becomes clear that such independent women have more to offer the men in their lives than sex; they, too, bring insights and perspectives that may complement and enhance a male perspective.

As Maria returns home, the Phantom waits for her. In a wonderful scene, Schell, in disguise, is positioned in front of an endless hall of mirrors. The scene underscores the Phantom's symbolic power regarding identity, an identity that, as far as his victims are concerned, is ever changing. The scene also signifies the power of art to change, represent, and alter. Once again, what we see may not be what we get. There are multiple perspectives.

At this point, Maria agrees to work with the Phantom, and he brings her to a studio where all her needs are taken care of and her lessons impeccable. Unlike other Phantoms, he even grants her a great deal of freedom: "The days are mine; the nights are yours." Unfortunately, he cannot uphold this bargain.

As Maria takes her lessons from the Phantom, she is also falling in love with the director. In another wonderful scene, the two kiss and the camera offers a close-up on Maria's jacket buttons. Several are being undone. The two awake in bed together, and they are clearly in love and happy, but the director admits that he is disturbed by this turn of events: "It's always such a bother caring for someone." He also asks Maria how she can afford the dresses, the voice lessons and other luxury items. Without believing her explanation of a platonic patron, he concludes that she is having an affair with the Baron. Maria will not betray her relationship with the Phantom and tries to defend herself. The two argue and separate.

During this separation, the Phantom attacks the director and warns him to stay away from Maria. The director presumes that the Baron has sent one of his thugs to keep him away from Maria. Not surprisingly, the diva returns to the role.

While attending the masked ball, then, Maria is besieged by problems — the Baron wants to seduce her and threatens her using the same tactics he did with Elena years before, and the Phantom torments Maria in the chaotic world of the masked ball. Maria attempts to escape, only to run to the Baron's carriage which is, ironically, being driven by the Phantom's accomplice. Both enter the Phantom's lair, and the Phantom kills the Baron for his treatment of his wife Elena. During a rehearsal, the Baron's body, not Joseph Buquet's, swings from the Opera rafters.

In the meantime, Maria and the Phantom get to know one another. Here, however, the Phantom's tactics are clearly condemned by the film. Sandor Korvin may have been a victim, but that fact does not justify his victimization of Maria. She stands firm, and does not waver in her determination to ignore his advances and escape from his prison. During an argument, she removes his mask, and this gesture seals her fate. Anyone who sees the Phantom unmasked cannot return to the world of light. "My fate is your fate," he cries out.

To ensure this end, the Phantom devises one of the more bizarre plots in Phantom history. He decides to deposit a decoy corpse in the Danube in order to stage Maria's suicide. Without getting too academic, the movie clearly illustrates the problems with gender in a culture which sees women interchangeably, not as individuals. The Baron uses the same tactics with all women. The Phantom cannot see the difference between Elena, his dead wife, and Maria, the new Opera star. He even thinks he can create another version of her in order to keep the living model under his control. Casting the same actress in the two roles also highlights this interchangeability and to a certain degree perpetuates it. But ultimately, the film does not endorse such a representation of women. Seymour's performance and character illustrates that strong women will not be typecast or remodeled under male hands.

The decoy plan, as well as Maria's imprisonment, is, of course, thwarted. The opera director, who happens to hear some cleaning women discussing the curse of the opera *Faust*, something like the curse of Shakespeare's *Macbeth*, discovers the history regarding Sandor and Elena Korvin. In addition to learning the truth about the Phantom, he also leans that the lower classes he treated condescendingly earlier have information to offer him, have something to contribute to his life. As he learns more, he realizes that Sandor is not dead, and that he is probably the Phantom of the Opera. Just as the Phantom deposits the decoy in the Danube, the director rescues Maria. Both turn to the authorities, who decide to lure the Phantom to the Opera, using the diva in the starring role of *Faust*, a diva whose voice he despises.

During the opera, Maria sits in the audience, another lure for the

Phantom. As the opera progresses, guards surround the audience and theater, while the Phantom begins to cut the chandelier from the Opera House's ceiling in order to kill the lead police investigator. What is not clear in this film is whether or not the Phantom at this point has a death wish, since he removes the chandelier in such a way that he would be sure to perish in the process as well. Whatever the case, through coincidence, Maria decides to switch places with the police officer, so that the Phantom is now readying himself to kill Maria. Once he notices this error, he tries to stop the chandelier's fall, but it is too late. Fortunately, Maria notices the chandelier, and alerts the crowd, and most are saved. The film concludes with the Phantom crushed under the weight of the chandelier, and Maria saved by the director.

In addition to matters regarding identity, in terms of the Phantom and Maria/Elena, the film also makes a clear distinction between various forms of love. The love between Sandor and Elena was pure, but it has been perverted and distorted through Sandor's desire for revenge. Throughout the film, his love kills, but at the very end, he literally makes a leap of faith, offering to sacrifice himself for the love and life of Maria. The relationship between Maria and the director, too, illustrates that love must be trustworthy and life-giving. It is only when the director realizes that his jealousy has blinded him to the truth of his beloved that he really begins to love. He, too, risks his life to save another for the sake of love. He, too, responds to the music of the night.

Nightmare at the Opera: Freddy Krueger Meets *The Phantom of the Opera* (1989)

Best known for his gruesome role as Freddy Krueger in the popular slasher films, *A Nightmare on Elm Street* (1984), Robert Englund makes his contribution to *The Phantom of the Opera* in his 1989 version. The Krueger concept is simple and lends itself to the *Phantom* narrative: Freddy, an escaped child-killer, is burned to death by an angry mob of concerned parents. He returns, complete with disfigured face and bad attitude, and he begins haunting the dreams of teenagers in the various film versions. He can, moreover, literally kill and does so in gruesome ways. In other words, he can cross over between the worlds of light and darkness. The valiant victims use various methods to overcome Krueger, but to this day, he still stalks among us. Originally directed by horror film great Wes Craven, *Nightmare* created numerous sequels and spin-offs. According to "The Nightmare on Elm Street Saga" Web site, New Line Cinema, the film company of the original and subsequent versions, is frequently referred to as the "house that Freddy Krueger built." Like Universal, New Line literally lines its pockets thanks to horror, specifically *Nightmare*. In this rendition, Englund also gains his power by blurring distinctions between reality and fantasy. His Erik crosses the boundaries of time and space as easily as the disfigured Freddy can, and though *The New York Times* critic Caryn James said the concept of this *Phantom* "results in all the terror and suspense of Charlie Brown in *Macbeth*," it is still worth discussing and seeing. It, too, offers a variation on the music of the night.

The film opens with a young singer, Christine, searching for a song that will be impressive enough to land her a leading part in a contemporary New York musical. She and her friend meet at the music library in New York City. There, they discover a composition by Erik Destler, who, as we will later discover, is the Phantom. As it turns out, the musical score the young women find is titled, *Don Juan Triumphant*, and it was, the documentation makes clear, written by an artist who was known as a great "composer by day and a serial killer by night." Christine uses the opening aria as her audition piece, and as she is singing it, she is hit on the head by a falling sandbag from the wings of the stage. Given the precedence established by other *Nightmare* films, it is no surprise that this event leaves her unconscious and hence susceptible to demon dream-stalkers. In her unconscious state, she returns to Leroux's nineteenth century, in this case, London, not Paris. According to one reviewer, the film's producer chose London for the dream sequences for very practical reasons: "Because we didn't want to have to incorporate French accents into the film" (qtd. in James). *Phantom* aficionados, however, will not be bothered by such a change, given prior relocations in 1962 Hammer film and the 1983 miniseries.

Christine suffers from neither the sandbag nor the time travel, and easily assimilates into nineteenth-century London. Oblivious to her New York past, this Christine continues her auditioning for the London opera, also hoping for a chance to sing and get her big break. We are soon shown the underside of the stage and London life, as is common in many of the *Phantom* versions. In this version, however, we do not see Erik with a mask, as is the case in the other film and television versions, but instead, we see Erik sewing human skin onto his face. His "mask" is nearly undetectable. It is a nineteenth-century version of plastic surgery. But like the serial killer in *The Silence of the Lambs* (1991), he must kill for fresh flesh; no rotting corpses will do. His looks very literally kill.

In this version, too, Joseph Buquet is not an innocent victim, but rather a drunken stagehand who blames the falling sandbag, in the nineteenth-century world, on the Phantom rather than taking responsibility for his mistake. Erik quickly remedies this situation by hanging Joseph upside down in the wings, quipping, "You're suspended." Then, while Buquet is still suspended, Erik guts him with a knife. In most versions, this moment would signal the end of Buquet, but we inhabit a late-twentieth-century horror film, so he will return.

With this errand out of the way, Erik visits Christine's room. She does not see him, but it is clear that the two have a long-standing relationship. The voice informs her that she will sing the leading role of Marguerite in *Faustus* that night.

Of course, there is a Carlotta, the diva who stands in the way of Christine's triumph, and Erik is only too willing to take care of her for his beloved Christine. Carlotta behaves typically, insulting all, throwing temper tantrums, and making unreasonable demands. While bathing, she refuses to sign her contract unless Christine is barred from singing. Frustrated, the manager of the opera leaves her to her bubbles. As she prepares to dress, she slips on some blood. She looks for the source, and in her closet is the skinned but barely alive Joseph Buquet, who asks for help, then immediately dies. Clearly the Phantom has entered the gore film culture.

With her rival dispatched, since Carlotta is too shaken to sing, Christine may now take the center stage. As she sings and the opera progresses, the Faustian deal is juxtaposed with the details of Erik's life. And like many Phantoms before him, notably the characters in the De Palma *Phantom of the Paradise* (1974), Erik makes a deal with the devil to ensure his music's immortality. The devil burns Erik's face as part of the contract, saying that people will love him for his music and nothing else. Clearly, this film is neither a classic nor filled with philosophical questions about the nature of fame, ambition, and art, but this depiction of the devil's dealings is an accurate representation of the Faustian theme in many versions of the classic tale: the devil's promises are not only empty but they are misleading.

When we return to the matter at hand, we see that Christine has triumphed in her starring role, and Erik is equally pleased. He cannot, however, express his love for Christine. Instead, he goes to a prostitute and kills her. In many horror films, sex and violence are paired, and here it serves as a deflection. Erik loves Christine and wants to be with her, but he cannot accept these feelings, so they are directed towards another love object, the whore, the opposite of the virgin, the prize in patriarchal culture. Erik's behavior reflects a dualistic view of women, those he sleeps with and subsequently kills, and those he loves, and perhaps allows to live. In this gore genre, the sexual tension builds, and it is only released in a spray of blood, again symbolizing a particularly male audience perspective. Destler, however, does not only kill women; he kills men as well, so the heterosexual projection and power are blurred here, as the sexual tension builds, and is then released through a man killing another man.

Perhaps by way of comment, Christine falls in love with Richard, a member of the opera company. This heterosexual and innocent love is contrasted to the perversions of Erik and the music of the night, which in this case is highlighted with screams.

After receiving an undeserved bad review, Christine goes to her father's grave for solace. Unbeknownst to her, her new love, Richard, follows. In the meantime, Erik has killed the music critic for the bad review, and he now waits for Christine in the graveyard. Upon seeing Christine with another man, Erik incapacitates his rival with an ear-piercing violin piece. Unaware of Richard's presence and subsequent unconscious state, Christine follows Erik, who tells her that her voice technique is good, but she does not understand the "meaning of music." Erik, of course, promises to teach her and directs her to his underground lair, what he calls the "soul of opera." Here, Erik confesses his love for her and explains to her how her love for music is, in fact, love for him. Swept away by the events and Erik's voice and promises, Christine allows herself to be wedded to the Phantom forever, a wedding symbolized by a small ring Erik gives to her during his profession of love. Like the audience, Christine is taken with this underworld, the world of music and darkness. Further, she does not unmask Erik, who, thanks to the human skin he has taken from his victims, looks fairly handsome. For her, Erik is as he seems. He is a handsome man, interested in her passion, music. It is only after Christine leaves that we see Erik unmasking himself, unveiling the complete hideousness beneath the mask. He is not what he seems.

Christine and Richard meet at the masked ball, clearly still in love. Christine has made a mistake, and Erik's romance is one-sided. During the ball, Erik creates another diversion — the diva's head is found in the soup. With chaos established, Erik abducts Christine again. In his underground lair, he makes himself clear: Christine can only belong to him; she is his obsession. In these scenes, the underworld is particularly effective. The film has one of the best representations of the hall of mirrors from the Leroux novel. We are disoriented. There is chaos. Identities are confused. We are lost in the funhouse. Nothing is as it seems. Erik tells Christine that love and music are the only immortal options available to them, and because she is his, he will have her for eternity. Richard attempts to rescue her with the help of the police, and the story ends with Erik being shot and the two lovers leaving the world of darkness to the world of light.

With the gunshots, the film returns us to the twentieth-century New York theater where Christine was originally auditioning. She awakens from her unconscious state, and it appears that the prior events set in London are just a dream. Like the final scene in *The Wizard of Oz,* we see that many of the characters from her dream were based on the people in her life. The producer of the show, Mr. Foster, for example, bears a striking resemblance to Erik, the Phantom, but he is so caring and handsome that it is easy to conclude that the similarities are coincidental, an accident of the unconscious. Christine merely cast Mr. Foster in the role of the Phantom because he was the last person she saw before she was struck.

Foster takes Christine under his wing and offers to escort her to a fashionable New York party to make up for her accident. While Christine waits, she notices that he has a copy of *Don Juan Triumphant.* In a quick cut to Erik, we see that he is still the Phantom, only his masks have become much more refined, apparently thanks to advancements in modern medical science. They are, for example, stored in special, high-tech boxes.

When he returns, he asks Christine to choose between watching something or listening to music, a choice between the visual and aural, between the world of light and the world of darkness. Christine chooses the physical, the spectral, and perhaps as a result, she is punished, for as they talk, he attacks her, and like a thoroughly modern twentieth-century female character, defends herself mightily. She realizes who he is, rips off his mask, stabs him, and apparently kills him. Without the help of the Persian or Raoul, Christine saves herself. Of course, the movie is not over.

As Christine enters the busy New York streets, she passes a musician playing the Phantom theme. Apparently the violinist is Erik/Freddy/Robert Englund incognito, waiting for another sequel. One was, in fact, planned, *The Phantom of New York*, but it did not materialize. Be that as it may, the Krueger version participates in the Phantom legacy in significant ways. The distinctions that we so codify and cling to are shown here to be very fragile and delicate. The division between fantasy and reality is blurred. Even time is flexible. Distinctions are blurred, and the Phantom, in particular, crosses centuries and continents. The image is particularly apt for the variations on *The Phantom* theme. Like Erik and Christine in this version, the retellings over the years illustrate an immortal tale, one that will not yield to changes in time, place, or culture. The Phantom, like Krueger, continues to return.

Red Phantom: Ronny Yu's Chinese *The Phantom Lover* (1995)

Set in China in 1936, Ronny Yu's *The Phantom Lover* (1995) offers a unique interpretation of the Leroux novel. Based on a rare film version of the *Phantom* filmed in the 1920s called *Songs of Midnight*, Yu's *Phantom Lover* is "a variation on *Phantom of the Opera,* inserting the primary elements from Gaston Leroux's creation into the framework of an archetypal Chinese romantic tragedy" ("*The Phantom Lover*"). Yu, who has made a number of action films, including Brandon Lee's first film, *Legacy of Rage* (1986), and coincidentally, *Freddy vs. Jason* in 2003, enjoys making his movies unique, even though they may be part of a longer series like the *Nightmare on Elm Street* and *Halloween* horror series. As he mentioned during one interview, he felt a responsibility to the horror film fans, but he also wanted to "sneak in my own little style and make it a little bit different" ("Culture Pulp"). Having received an MBA from Ohio University, Yu is also aware of the costs involved in moviemaking, particularly Hollywood, costs that make many studio executives fearful, which "handicaps them from thinking something different" ("Culture Pulp"). Like the other versions of *The Phantom* and Yu's own breakout film *The Bride with White Hair* (1993), in which one character is a Siamese twin, with one man and one woman playing the role, Yu's version of *Phantom* challenges traditional expectations regarding women, class, Chinese Communist art forms, and even obedience to parents in the face of true love. And like the Krueger version, this version also connects the past with the present through the love between the Phantom and his Christine.

The opening scene establishes not only one of the main romantic interests, but it also establishes the film's cinematographic and cultural differences as well. In this scene, a group of performers are on a journey. In this case, however, the young women ride a horse "bus," while the men ride separately. We learn that the Landy, a young actress, is in love with Wei Qing, another actor in the troupe, but they will have to wait for their wedding, since both are destitute performers. The troupe is on its way to a run-down theater they have just purchased in the hopes of generating interest in their company. As it turns out, the theater is not only haunted, but it was home to the great actor-director-singer Song Danping, played by Leslie Cheun, who is perhaps best noted for his role in the 1993 *Farewell My Concubine*.

Though we are far from the Paris Opera House in terms of culture and history, we are clearly on familiar territory regarding the *Phantom* narrative: a love interest, a tortured artist, and a haunted theater being taken over by new owners. In addition, and perhaps as a result of its setting, the political nature of the story, which has been alluded to but not fully developed in other versions, is much more pronounced here. That is, in addition to the love story, this version, like the original novel, highlights the political ramifications of resisting the status quo. In this version, loving someone unusual or behaving eccentrically or creatively results in real political consequences, not just social disapproval or marginalization. In this setting, Communist China, the consequences of alternative perspectives and dissent are heightened. They are also encouraged. True art, love, and artists need freedom of expression, not rigid adherence to convention. Artists and lovers must express themselves, no matter what the consequences from external forces. The alternative, not expressing themselves, is much worse and crueler than any punishment inflicted.

Intricately tied to this political agenda is the abusive treatment of women. While the 1943 version illustrated one woman's successful career, and other Christines demonstrate a certain amount of independence, *Phantom Lover* illustrates how little power Chinese women have. Audiences witness the devastating effects of abusive male behavior on women, themselves, their families, and ultimately, their communities. In this way, the Phantom character becomes a protector of women, a spirit of love which nurtures women through a culture of oppression and abuse.

Once the small troupe arrives at the theater, they realize the grave mistake that they have made. The theater, though originally beautiful and architecturally stunning, has been left to decay. Part of it has been destroyed by a fire ten years earlier in which the great artist Danping was killed, and the rest has succumbed to disrepair. While the others search for the caretaker and try to calm down after realizing their dream theater is in fact a nightmare, Wei Qing remains in the theater, visualizing what it once looked like, the beauty beneath the rubble. It is through his eyes that we begin to see that things are not what they seem. Unlike other Phantom versions, however, here we see the beauty beneath the rubble, not the skull beneath the skin or the abuses covered by the Paris Opera House.

Peter Pau's cinematography is stellar at this moment. Everything is beautiful and luminescent in the eyes of a creative artist. Even the scaffolding is beautiful. Instead of a chandelier, however, this version offers a dome with a huge walkway. This departure offers the film the chance to stage the lovers' meetings above and beyond the world of cares below, further emphasizing the transcendent nature of love and music. Wei, too, transcends the ordinary, for he perceives the spirit of the Opera House beyond the physical disrepair. He is a sensitive, artistic soul who has visions of the theater in its golden age. Flashes of the balcony, as well as the sounds of a woman crying and a man's voice, illustrate his ability to perceive reality well beyond the visual. Confused and frightened by the sounds and his experiences, Wei forgoes a night of drinking to meet with the theater's caretaker in order to discover the truth about his visions and the past. Again, he demonstrates his need to read beyond the superficial expressions and dig deeper to find the truth, or at least another layer of the truth.

The film now presents a lengthy flash back narrative chronicling the history of Danping and his love. The narrative begins with an explanation of the sounds Wei heard in the theater: according the legend, Danping sings to his beloved Yuyan every full moon. As in the original Leroux novel, sound takes precedence over the visual. Sound inaugurates the narrative and the film's visual retelling of the past. According to the caretaker, Danping came to the town and revolutionized theater: he brought in western plays and operas, elevated standards, and won over audiences. Yuyan, the daughter of town merchants, of course, falls in love with him, and the two begin a relationship. Of course, the trouble is, this is Communist China in the 1930s, and Yuyan has no business falling in love on her own, particularly with an artist, no matter how successful. She is bound to her family's decisions regarding her mate.

On one particular night, there is more at stake — Yuyan has an appointment at home. She does not know the details, only that she must appear at the required time. She is late because she has attended Danping's performance and met with him afterwards, without her parents' permission or knowledge. Their love is clear, but she must obey her parents. As Yuyan rushes home, we learn that the tea ceremony she will be presiding over is in honor of the arranged marriage her parents have made with Zhao Jum's family. Zhao Jum is not just a poor choice, he is a cruel, crude, selfish, and self-indulgent young man whose only positive feature is the fact that his father is a political official who can help provide Yuyan's family with steady business through questionable business deals.

Yuyan, of course, cannot agree to this marriage and runs to the arms of her lover. The two try to reason with her father, and Danping is certainly financially solvent enough to support the marriage, though not Yuyan's entire family. Yuyan's father remains unmoved. He has made his decision, and Yuyan must abide by that decision. The two lovers disobey her father, and they escape for a night of love on the walkway under the theater's dome. They are above and beyond the world at this point. Their love transcends earthly bounds.

Zhao Jum's father, who hears of the love between Yuyan and Danping, plots Danping's downfall by making his son the Minister of Culture. As Minister of Culture, then, Zhao Jum can do whatever he likes with the theater that Danping has so carefully built. Unfortunately for Yuyan, the wedding plans proceed, including a banquet at which Zhao is to propose publicly. Yuyan escapes to the theater to see her beloved in a beautiful rendition of, appropriately, his new operatic version of *Romeo and Juliet*. Given the play's focus on the true love that parallels that between Danping and Yuyan, the choice is much more appropriate than the conventional *Faust*.

A wonderful song is interrupted when Zhao Jum, his father, and his henchmen shut down the production, saying that it is immoral and corrupt. Danping plays the crowd beautifully, and no one wants to leave, even those who are generally fearful of Zhao. Truly, art is subversive, and no one in the theater misses this point. Unfortunately, this momentary victory appears to lead to the ultimate demise of Danping, for it fuels his enemies' determination to obliterate him from the romantic and community scene. To make matters worse, Zhao Jum sees Yuyan at the theater: she tricked him into believing she left the proposal ceremony as a result of illness.

Undaunted, Yuyan meets Danping for the final time. They promise eternal love, and Danping says he has a written a song for her which he will always sing to her on the night of the full moon. Inspired by their commitment of love, the two think that they can manage to persuade Yuyan's parents to approve of their love and stop the arranged marriage. As Yuyan leaves, however, she is abducted and locked away by her own family. Screaming for some kind of understanding and compassion, Yuyan tries to move her mother's heart, but to no avail, and it is one of the most difficult scenes in the film to watch. Her mother participates in her daughter's oppression and abuse. Her mother upholds the old ways, not her daughter's love.

In classic romantic style, Yuyan sneaks a letter to Danping, but the letter gets lost in the mountains of fan mail the young performer receives. Just when we think that Danping will open the letter which tells of Yuyan's imprisonment and impending forced marriage, Zhao Jum's men enter his dressing room, beat him, and set the theater on fire. Yuyan's maid, who helped deliver the letter and who supports the illicit love affair, is caught and beaten severely. Yuyan hears that Danping was killed in the fire, and the arranged marriage must occur.

Her wedding night with Zhao Jum is a rape, and when he discovers that she is no longer a virgin, he beats her, divorces her, and throws her out. In disgrace, her family disowns her and leaves the town, leaving Yuyan alone, with only occasional help from her maid. In the end, it is too much for Yuyan, and she goes mad. She continues to wander the streets of the town, and she returns to the theater at every full moon where she hears the song promised her by her long-dead love, Danping.

With the story behind them, the theatrical troupe begins working on their own performances in the town. Unlike Danping's artistry, this group's work is Communist propaganda that no one likes. They make little money, and they are about to abandon the town when the "Phantom" contacts Wei Qing with a play, his musical version of *Romeo and Juliet*. Unlike any other version, in this *Phantom*, it is a male character who is taught to sing more beautifully by the Phantom. And when Qing cannot sing particular notes, the Phantom, like Svengali to Trilby, sings them for him. During the first performance, the townspeople are shocked by the similarities between Qing and Danping. Beauty, art, and song transcend time, as in the television miniseries version starring Jane Seymour.

Of course, as we later learn, Danping is not dead, but is horribly disfigured from the fire. As a result, he has been unwilling to contact his love, Yuyan. Qing tries to bring the two lovers together, but Yuyan accidentally mistakes him for Danping, and Danping grows very jealous.

While much of the planning for the opera goes on, the opera's manager sets up a meeting with Zhao Jum, who is still the Minister of Culture, and whose treatment of women has ripened into even greater cruelty. When, for example, his female dinner companion tries to talk to the theater people, Zhao Jum tells her that women should not speak unless spoken to and forces her to eat 60 rolls as punishment. The unfortunate woman stuffs herself as the theater negotiations continue. Zhao Jum, of course, has his eyes on Landy, Qing's beloved, and offers to take her home in his private carriage. Against her better judgment but as a result of the prodding of the theater manager, who thinks that this harmless ride will result in greater support for their theater, she agrees.

As they are going through the streets, Zhao Jum sees the mad Yuyan, jumps out of the carriage, and begins to beat her and call her a whore. Coincidentally, Danping is on the scene, and he rescues her and publicly defends her. He also, of course, sees his Landy in Jum's carriage. He misunderstands, thinking that she is seeing someone else, and he becomes irate. Fortunately, she has time to explain the situation. But in this scene, it is clear that the film abhors Zhao Jum's treatment of women and applauds Qing's defense of Yuyan.

In the final scenes of the film, Zhao Jum once again attempts to kill what he cannot have, the true love between Qing and Landy. In a particularly dangerous moment, Danping reveals himself to save the two modern lovers and overcome the evil Zhao. In the process, however, the mad Yuyan is shot by Zhao, but she survives. While visiting her in the hospital, Danping removes his mask, a clear symbol of his vulnerability and willingness to trust. Yuyan has been restored to reason, but she has gone blind as a result of the shooting, so she does not see the disfigurement. In the end, the modern lovers are reunited, evil is punished, and Danping and Yuyan live together in happiness for several years before she dies, leaving Danping to continue his life with the young lovers and their families.

Through a romantic tale, the film uncovers numerous dichotomies and hypocrisies. The oppressive political machinery of Communist China is, in fact, motivated by petty personal concerns, not ideology. And though women may be mistreated, in this film they are ultimately rewarded. And perhaps more than any other version, unmasking, unveiling, reveals truth. Wei Quing unmasks the truth of the past; Yuyan unmasks the patriarchal oppression of Communist China, and Danping unmasks himself in order to open himself to love. In this way, Yu's *Phantom* is one of the more optimistic ones. There is truth to be found, and it can exist and succeed in a world determined by duplicity. Good can triumph over evil.

"When You Hear My Thoughts, You'll Know Where to Go": Dario Argento's Handsome *Phantom* (1998)

Italian director Dario Argento has gained a cult following with films such as *Suspiria* (1977) and *Tenebrae* (1982), which represent his "brand of supernatural, sadistic horrors," and the opening scenes of his version of the *Phantom* (1998) do not disappoint ("Blood Money"). As the film begins, a crying young woman accompanied by a man sets a baby in a basket. Like Moses, the baby and basket are set into a river. The basket flows downstream, dangerously near a waterfall. The basket and its cargo are fortuitously caught on a rock when a rat remarkably rescues both baby and basket. In a wonderfully campy scene, we see the infant's hand reaching towards the whiskers of a red-eyed rat. This scene completes the Phantom's childhood and tells us volumes about the baby's upbringing and new "family." Argento's *Phantom* is ultimately a rat-like creature himself; the darkness in which he lives reflects the darkness in his soul, finally. There is little to recommend him in the end. Ironically, this Phantom is one of the most handsome to date. There is no physical disfigurement, only emotional disability. The Phantom has degenerated into a monster in this latest film version.

Following the Phantom's childhood scene, the next takes place in the Paris Opera House, where a spectacular opera is in process. Like many *Phantom*s, there is a dark side to the beauty of the opera, and here, this dark side is represented by a group of workmen attempting to investigate a large cistern in the Opera's lower floors. As one of the workmen is lowered down to check out the masonry, he makes a discovery — there seems to be some sort of passageway. He sees a light. Suddenly, however, there is a bitter wind, and the man is hacked apart from the waist up. His friends try to rescue him, but they are trapped and captured as well. We leave the scene hearing only their screams and the terrible hacking sounds, a brilliant contrast to the world of art and high culture.

Clearly, the Phantom narrative has entered the slasher/shocker genre. And while even Argento's supporters do not think he was successful in interpreting the Leroux novel, it is an important permutation in the history of the *Phantom* genre: more than any other version, this film emphasizes the spectacle of the narrative, as clearly evidenced by the opening scenes, which have little or no dialogue. Ironically, however, the emphasis on the spectacle causes the film to fail, to pull itself apart. It is almost as if the Phantom narrative requires the tension between spectacle and sound, light and darkness, good and evil, in order to succeed, in order to be told. And when one of the two opposing terms is nonexistent or underrepresented, the narrative cannot continue. Ironically, without the "music of the night," the narrative cannot exist.

Given this emphasis on gore and spectacle it would seem logical that the Phantom would be one of the most disfigured. And the recent DVD liner for the film clearly raises those expectations by placing a masked man on the cover, with tears of blood coming out of one eye, and the other eye completely bloodshot. And while the image accurately reflects the film's overemphasis on spectacle and the look, it does not reflect the film's major character. As is true with many *Phantom*s, looks can be deceiving, and in this film, as mentioned earlier, the Phantom is an incredibly handsome man played by Julian Sand. Unlike the Freddy Krueger/Robert Englund version in which the Phantom attaches a handsome face to his disfigured one, here the Phantom is truly handsome, a departure from the Phantom legacy.

This Phantom's disfigurement is internal, not external. And while the film may not produce the tension between the spectacular and the aural, in the character of the Phantom, there is great tension. More than any other character in the film, he embodies the conflict between good and evil, beauty and ugliness. He is capable of great passion, but he is also capable of great cruelty. He may, for example, bite off the tongue of a victim, or caress Christine sweetly. He may be handsome, but he is so loyal to the rats that rescued him that he tells one victim: "I am not the Phantom, I am the rat man." In this way, his mask is figurative, but the duality persists.

Like the other Phantoms, he loves the young Christine, played by director Argento's daughter, Asia. (In addition to directing shock horror movies, Argento is noted for casting his beautiful daughter in his films. She has most recently been seen in the role of the Comtesse du Barry in Sopphia Coppola's *Marie Antoinette* [2006].) The Phantom first notices her on stage singing by herself after a performance by the opera company. He is so taken with her that he meets her in the hallway and accosts her. She is immediately drawn to him, and he appears to have a mystical control of her mind, one that she enjoys. Unlike Leroux's Erik and Christine who communicate through their music, this couple communicate telepathically, and there are many scenes in the film in which Christine "dials into" the Phantom frequency. In addition to being able to enter Christine's thoughts, this Phantom, like Svengali, also has the ability to force Christine to sing in ways that are uncomfortable for her. In this way, the music does not become a means for connection and relationship. Here the Phantom's musical power is a means for transcendent torture.

In addition to being drawn to the beauty and virtue of Christine, the Phantom is also sympathetic to the plight of the rats under the Opera House, who are hunted ferociously and unrelentingly by the Rat Catcher. The film takes great care to make the rats look sympathetic and less vermin-like, so when the Rat Catcher invents a machine that promises to kill thousands of rats at a time, we are genuinely disgusted with this invention. Later, the Rat Catcher becomes one of the most despicable characters in the film.

The Phantom's altruism does not stop with vermin. Like other

Eriks, he reaches out to the oppressed. In this case, he rescues an under-aged ballerina who is nearly sexually abused by one of the Opera House's patrons. Enticing her with chocolate, the man follows her into the underworld as she desperately tries to flee. The Phantom intervenes, albeit horrendously, by biting the man's ear off, killing him, and then giving the girl a long hug and sending her on her way to the safety of the ballerina dormitories. Clearly, then, Erik is confused and conflicted, an odd combination of compassion and brutality.

As is true of several other versions, Christine is also pursued by Raoul de Chagny, a virtuous man who, unlike the other film versions at least, also struggles with good and evil. Unlike the novel, this young Raoul is innocent, but not *that* innocent. In a somewhat gratuitous sex scene, Raoul's older brother takes him to a brothel to forget about Christine. Nudity, sex, and drugs abound. In the end, however, Raoul remains faithful to Christine, shouting out, "Get behind me, Satan." This struggle, however, educates him in the ways of the world and the human heart. Rather than jading him, this experience makes him more compassionate and a more realistic lover and character than some of the past Raouls. As he later tells Christine, no one is pure: "It's just part of being human, believe me."

Such an assurance is important to Christine, who also struggles with the choice between goodness and evil, rationality and passion. Like other Christines, she is confused about her choice between Raoul, a creature of the light, and the Phantom, a creature of art and darkness. Early in the film, she admits that she, who knows nothing of love, may, in fact, be in love with both of them. Such a violation of the heterosexual monogamous code by a woman is unusual.

When she first enters the Phantom's lair, she is completely taken with the Phantom and his power. She enjoys succumbing to his power, and they actually consummate their relationship, unlike any other *Phantom* pair. The next day, however, provides the awakening. Not only does she realize that her lover has an unnatural attachment to the rats that he caresses very seductively, but he wants to keep her a prisoner. Her lover requires that she remain in the world of darkness. He will not allow her to return to the world of light.

She escapes long enough to sing, after the chandelier falls and harms the diva, but when she returns to the Phantom's, she is clearly an interloper. She has betrayed him, and so he punishes her by raping her. The

Rat Catcher, who has been wounded by the Phantom but is still on the loose in the underworld, sees the couple but misreads the situation completely. He presumes that Christine is a willing participant, and he works to destroy her reputation and to avenge himself on the Phantom through his love. During the final scenes of film, after having once again escaped from the Phantom's lair, Christine sings on stage, only to have the Rat Catcher interrupt her performance to call her "the Phantom's whore." The Phantom storms onto the stage to rescue Christine from these accusations, only to proclaim that she is his: "We shall live alone in my world of darkness." Christine injures the Phantom, but oddly, simultaneously finds some compassion for her rapist. Raoul rescues her, but the conclusion is dissatisfying in a number of ways. The Phantom is killed by an angry mob, and while Christine returns to the world of light, she yearns for her abuser. Raoul indicates that he understands that she may not be pure, but he is willing to have her anyway. The Phantom's struggles have been erased by his own selfishness. Any sympathy that we held for him is destroyed, and he makes no final sacrifice to Christine's happiness. He has, in fact, become another beastly creature who haunts the slasher film genre, not a disfigured, tormented artist who yearns for love as much as we all yearn for love and connection. In effect, he has been objectified by the spectacle, transformed from character into object.

As the films of *The Phantom* have illustrated, the tension between spectacle and sound is essential to the narrative. And this tension is well-suited to the genre of film, which struggled itself with spectacle and sound. In this way, the technology of film and *The Phantom's* development have augmented one another, with one of the earliest films using the *Phantom* narrative to tell its own story and purpose. In the 1943 version, the film includes sound, and the music of the night, in this case, takes Christine to a world of her own, a world without her two suitors. The 1974 *Phantom* highlights the new world of rock music and the sounds it brings. In all, the relationship between the spectacular and the aural are highlighted, frequently showing us that the spectacle, even with the new technology of film, is not the be-all and end-all. There is still the music of the night, the music of the Phantom, a music that transcends the limits of the visual and calls us to examine the images presented to us daily a bit more deeply.

CHAPTER 3

Songs of Innocence and Experience: Stage Versions of *The Phantom of the Opera*

> When the stars threw down their spears
> And water'd heaven with their tears,
> Did he smile his work to see?
> Did he who made the Lamb make thee?
> — William Blake's "The Tyger"

The stage versions of *Phantom* are predominantly spectacular musicals, relying on either original music or opera scores to highlight the operatic setting of the narrative. Of course, the theatrical work which overshadows all versions is the Andrew Lloyd Webber musical, the longest-running show on Broadway, which continues to break records twenty years after its premiere in London. With the recent opening in Las Vegas, it may be the longest, most popular, most viewed musical in the history of musical theater (Freiss). Inevitably, Lloyd Webber's success led to other musical versions of the Leroux novel: because tickets were scarce and costly for many years, entrepreneurial directors, playwrights, and musicians created their own versions to satisfy the audience's craving for the "music of the night."

Lloyd Webber's version, however, was not created in a vacuum. Ken Hill's version began as early as 1976. This version is difficult to find, though the major changes to the script involve the musical score. In the 1976 version, Hill used modern lyrics by Ian Armit, as well as some references to Gounod's *Faust*. In its later incarnations, particularly those that Lloyd Webber and others saw, Hill replaced the modern music with opera arias, using different lyrics throughout the musical. The copies which are readily available are those that were produced in 1984 and the 1991 revival, but for all intents and purposes the musical existed in 1976 as it does today, and for that reason, it begins this chapter.

Much more interesting is the Arthur Kopit version, as well as the story behind its production, a production that predated the Lloyd Webber musical, and which also emphasized the romantic, not satiric, aspects of the story. As is clear from the discussion below, Kopit, in collaboration with composer Maury Yeston, created a musical version prior to the Lloyd Webber version. He even met with Lloyd Webber to discuss the possibilities of collaboration, but to no avail. In many ways, the story of the Kopit version reads like some of the earlier film versions of *The Phantom of the Opera*, with politics and production realities killing off, in this case, some great ideas, not any major writers or artists. The remaining stage musicals, John Kenley and Robert Thomas Noll's version (1988), Jack Sharkey's *The Pinchpenny Phantom of the Opera* (1988), Bruce Falstein's 1990 version, and Joseph Robinette's *Phantom of the Opera* (1992) are all minor works which bear discussion but which really owe their existence to the incredibly popular Lloyd Webber version. All, however, in their own way, ask audiences to see beneath the mask, to examine the skull beneath the skin and determine the truth that lies behind the facades which societies and people construct. All, in their unique ways, call us to listen to the "music of the night."

The Precursor Phantom: Ken Hill's *Phantom of the Opera* (1984)

In the apocryphal stories that seem to haunt the various versions of *Phantom of the Opera,* Ken Hill, like many before him, is said to have stumbled on an old copy of Gaston Leroux's novel in a "junk shop" in 1976. Like others before him, too, he was inspired by the story and in short order wrote a musical version and opened the piece at the Duke's Playhouse, Lancaster, on 26 July 1976. This version included a musical score by Ian Armit. Years later, however, Hill decided to revise the piece and include the music of Leroux's day, not the modern score of the 1976 version. To this end, he wrote new lyrics for the familiar operas. The revised version was subsequently produced by a joint venture between the Newcastle Playhouse and the Duke's Playhouse, Lancaster, and it is the version that was resurrected once again in 1991, and that is most readily available to readers.

It is also the version that Andrew Lloyd Webber saw with Cameron Mackintosh. Sarah Brightman was offered the role of Christine in the 1984 version, the same year she married Lloyd Webber, and though she turned it down, the show was popular enough to invite the interest of her husband. Hill and Lloyd Webber had worked together on a revival of *Joseph and the Amazing Technicolor Dreamcoat*. Initially, Lloyd Webber proposed collaboration with Hill, but that plan fell through, and Lloyd Webber soon announced his own musical version of *The Phantom of the Opera*. As Hill is reported to have said, "I'm not in the slightest bitter about it ... though he could have sent me a postcard about it, or something!" (Atkins).

Hill's nonchalance regarding the Lloyd Webber incident perhaps stems from his lifetime experience in show business, a career that spanned not only television, film, and stage, but writing, directing, and acting. Some other famous works that include supernatural themes include *The Invisible Man* (1993), *The Count of Monte Cristo* (1974), and *Dracula* (1974). As a protégé of Joan Littlewood, who ran the Theatre Workshop, he was "made associate director and resident writer from 1970 to 1974 and from 1974–1976 he took over as artistic director" ("Ken Hill"). His version of *The Phantom of the Opera* has received mixed reviews. As Tom Atkins notes, in 1988 it opened in San Francisco at Theatre in the Square and "grossed more than any off-Broadway show during that period." In 1991, it was nominated for Olivier Awards for Best New Musical and Best Director, and later it toured Japan, New Zealand, Australia, Germany, Korea and the United Kingdom (Atkins).

One of the play's most distinctive features is its humor and its representation of Christine, a representation that affords this female character the opportunity to tell her experiences with the Phantom, rather than showing them through the course of the play. While perhaps not the most dramatic decision, the decision to do so returns to the strategy of the novel, which affords Christine her own voice and perspective on the strange happenings under the opera house.

The musical begins conventionally enough with the new Opera owners learning about the reality of their situation: first, they know very little about opera; and second, there is a ghost haunting the opera house.

Characters attempt to disguise the truths of this situation by agreeing with everything the new owner says, but it is clear early on that they cannot escape the inevitable truth. Richard is the new owner who is better at "railways" than opera, and he is about to find out that the Opera is haunted (3). Through a slight change, Raoul is now the son of Richard in this version.

In this way, Hill eradicates the aristocratic class who, for all their faults, at least appreciated the arts. Now, however, there are only businessmen who run the arts like corporations. Debienne, who runs the company, for example, introduces Richard and his son to the company, and all of the Opera staff harmoniously pledge their allegiance to the new manager — in song. He responds favorably by mentioning his experience singing in "the Stock Exchange Choir" will indeed pay off (11).

Ironically, the first order of business is the fact that the diva cannot sing. There is also a ghost, and, most importantly, he demands 20,000 francs a month and box five. The "steadying hand" of the "Left Luggage Department" proclaims that the show must go on. They are to use the chorus girl, Christine, and they are to ignore the ghost's demands. The staff, of course, know that these proclamations do no good, but they bide their time.

In the meantime, Christine and Raoul reunite, despite Richard's admonitions to avoid chorus girls. Why the interdiction? As Raoul explains to Christine, "I think it's because Mother was one" (16). After this quick establishing scene, Carlotta and Christine battle in the usual *All About Eve* fashion, but Christine is set to perform the evening's performance. As the opera begins, Richard again illustrates his lack of music appreciation, commenting, "Managing the Opera House is one thing, but having to watch the wretched stuff...."(19) Unlike other versions, this inability to appreciate the music of the night, the alternatives offered to us through the Phantom and his art, is ridiculed but not entirely punished. Here, the innocent victims are punished, for as the opera begins, Mephistopheles arrives on a rope, only to be hanged before the entire audience. A note is pinned to him, and after a few jokes, it is clear that the ghost means business. He does exist. He is not a rumor.

And this technique is perhaps the downfall of this production. Just as the musical comes close to a serious conclusion, a joke intervenes and the illusion or the point is lost. Richard, for example, is followed by a

Radar O'Reilly–type assistant who finishes his every sentence and antic-ipates his every need. But such comedy dismantles the moments of seri-ousness. It is difficult to return so quickly to the world of the Phantom and Christine. After this incident, for example, Christine runs from the stage, and she meets the Phantom, who lulls her into submission, a kind of Svengali-like power exudes from the Phantom, and it should affect the audience, as well as Christine, but after the jarring jokes of the pre-vious scenes, it is difficult to surrender entirely to the Phantom's power. And it is here that Lloyd Webber succeeds. His *Phantom* is deadly seri-ous when it needs to be, so the romance and danger, the music of the night, the alternative to the world of the day is upheld. In one last exam-ple, Raoul comes to Christine's room, as he does in many other versions, searching for his love and hearing her with another. We have also seen Christine, who, under the Phantom's spell, agrees that she will know that her soul is his (24). Raoul enters the empty room, confused. Music continues to play mysteriously, but rather than allowing the haunting melody and situation to continue, Ken Hill's Raoul says, "Oh, for God's sake, will you stop playing that piano!" And it stops (25).

Hill, however, does represent Raoul's torment regarding Christine and her possible betrayal and has him sing a song expressing his anger and disappointment in this woman, a cross between the evil Eve and the beauteous Madonna. As the play progresses, it is reported that one of the Opera's horses has been stolen, and Richard believes that Christine may have something to do with the theft, as well as the letters he con-tinues to receive from the Opera Ghost.

Raoul defends her: "Father, much as Christine has broken my heart, I'm sure she'd never deceive the management" (37). He learns that she is probably at her father's grave, and all three, Raoul, Christine, and the Phantom, wind up there. When the Phantom sings, Raoul, as in the novel, is overcome by his power. That Phantom can overpower many, not just women.

The musical continues with the staging of the opera, and it is decided that Carlotta will mouth the music as Christine sings from the orchestra pit. Of course, the chandelier falls at this time, since the man-ager has ignored the Phantom's request, but here, the chandelier falls on the diva. Raoul and Christine meet on the rooftop of the Opera House, and there, Christine tells Raoul of her experiences with the Phantom on the other side of the mirror. She realizes that the Phantom loves her and that she cares for him, but not in the same way she cares for Raoul. She vows to be with Raoul after she sings Marguerite the next night, but of course, the Phantom has been listening, so their plans will be thwarted. Once again, this Phantom murders an innocent bystander as a means to express his anger with Christine and his situation as the unloved.

During the performance, the Phantom appears on stage and kidnaps Christine. The men attempt to find her, but it takes a good deal of time to find the underworld of the Paris Opera House. They rely on the help of the Persian, who says that he and the Phantom have been trained in the dark arts in Persia. He has been looking for him for some time, and he is eager to find his old companion.

Through a series of scenes, the men avoid the Punjab Lasso and endure the torments of the room of mirrors, and we learn that the Phantom is terribly disfigured and his life's work is "dealing death" (86). While they are suffering, the Phantom torments Christine, telling her that her beloved Raoul is already dead, so they will marry. At this moment, Christine tears off the mask, but it is too late. The Phantom has already earned her fear and anger, so the event is underwhelming. The Phantom, then, calls in a drunken priest and a chorus girl to officiate the marriage ceremony, and just before Christine must say "I do," the rescue team appears, Raoul, Richard, Madame Giry, and the Persian, among others. With the creatures from the light of day in the house of the prince of darkness, the truth is revealed. We learn that the Persian and the Phantom are actually brothers and that the Persian had traveled all this distance in order to confront the Phantom over the murder of their parents. As the Phantom explains, since they had seen his face, they could not live. And since now all have seen his face, he cannot live, and he concludes by stabbing himself while the rest of cast looks on.

The play clearly favors the world of the light and men, as opposed to the world of darkness and music. The Phantom is seen as a homicidal musician at best, loving Christine, but killing innocent bystanders for no reason. The world of light, however, is not entirely upheld because in it, there is no art, and little understanding of music, as evidenced by the character of Richard, who only years for money and commerce. In the end the play hints that without the world of darkness there could be no art, but it is only just a hint, and the rest of the play does not support the sympathetic conclusion articulated by Richard and Raoul:

RICHARD: Yes. Bit of good in him somewhere, I suppose.
RAOUL: There is in us all, Father, there is in us all.
THE PRIEST: Amen to that.
CHRISTINE: And he was once my Angel of Music. (107)

Through Christine's final word, it appears that Hill suggests that despite the Phantom's indiscriminate killing, he had the power to gain the attention of the captain of industry, and teach at least one person about the beauty of the music of the night.

Phantom Rivalries: Arthur Kopit's Forgotten *Phantom* on Stage (1991) and Screen (1990)

Inspired by Jean Cocteau's *Beauty and the Beast* (1946), as well as a desire to develop the relationship between Christine and Erik more fully (Dupont), Arthur Kopit and Maury Yeston created a musical *Phantom* several years prior to the Lloyd Webber version. The two had collaborated successfully before on *Nine* (1983), a musical version of the Frederico Fellini film *8½*. Yeston won a Tony for that score, and would later win another for his original songs for the Broadway version of *Titanic* (1997). Arthur Kopit had an established playwriting career with a number of successes to his credit, including *Oh Dad, Poor Dad, Mama's Hung You in the Closet and I'm Feeling So Sad* (1960), a satire of American life; *Wings* (1978), a moving drama about a stroke victim; and *End of the World* (1984), a play about a playwright writing a play about a nuclear holocaust. *Phantom*, then, looked like a winning proposition, and with the Cocteau inspiration, along with the musical accompaniment, it seemed there was a also a balance between spectacle and sound. According to Yeston, it was a dynamite proposition: "We were doing backers' auditions and they were throwing money at us" (qtd. in "The Kopit Yeston 'Phantom'"). What the two did not realize was that the Gaston Leroux novel was set to enter the public domain, thereby affording adaptators free rights to the novel, in Great Britain in 1985, which is when Lloyd Webber announced his *Phantom*. Given Lloyd Webber's lucrative past successes, "our project basically collapsed," admitted Kopit (qtd. in Hulbert).

Fortunately, however, the collapse was not fatal. Kopit's *Phantom* was produced. Interestingly, however, the show appeared first on screen, then on stage. And this unique method of development makes Kopit's work a perfect transition between the film and the theater chapters of this book. Unlike the traditional entertainment process whereby a stage production is picked up by Hollywood and then filmed, the Kopit-Yeston collaboration worked in reverse. Today, this process is clearly more dynamic, with examples of television films serving as the objects of Broadway musicals which are then transformed into film, or when a novel is first filmed, and then staged on Broadway, and then filmed again, as in the case of Disney's incredibly popular *Beauty and the Beast.* The process, then, by which Kopit's version appeared, reflected the content of his *Phantom*— things are not always as they seem; the stage has its secrets both in the novel and in the production of the Kopit version of the novel. Truth, art, and life are much more fluid than we perhaps believe.

As has become clear to most audiences, the reasons behind this fluidity are economic, not necessarily artistic or theoretical. Hollywood and Broadway are not challenging us all to think about the way that we live our lives by deciding to break with traditions by breaking the usual precedents regarding adaptations and genres. That is, Hollywood and Broadway are not self-consciously asking us to examine the art of interpretation when it is decided that a film should be a play first or a stage play should be filmed. There is no great philosophical underpinning here. Rather, film and stage producers are concerned with cost. The financial requirements of Broadway and Hollywood have risen to astronomical heights, so investors want "sure things," material that will sell. Revivals, adaptations, and imports serve as "good bets" in the costly entertainment world.

At the time of creation, however, Kopit and Yeston were discouraged and disheartened, and they decided to wait on producing their *Phantom.* After Kopit saw the Lloyd Webber version, however, he realized that his was distinct enough to deserve a production as well. As Yeston said during an interview, "Our story and characters are so different; they really are two completely different shows. I mean, we're not some exploitative production trying to bilk the public" (qtd. in Terry). Kopit made a deal with television for his version, but the producers of the miniseries did not care for Yeston's score, which Kopit thoroughly enjoyed because it was in the tradition of "*Oklahoma!* not *Jesus Christ Superstar,*" another Lloyd Webber hit (qtd. in Terry). Instead, the miniseries includes selections from real operas, as in the novel, which may have greater appeal to opera purists. What the miniseries may have lost with Yeston, they gained through visual production. This version is the only one filmed at the original Paris Opera House, and it is worth seeing for the details of this architectural wonder.

The stage version, which is very close to the miniseries, finally made its debut in 1991, receiving mixed reviews. Leah D. Frank of *The New York Times* concurred with the miniseries producers, noting the Yeston score "lacks the show-stopping hit numbers of the Lloyd Webber version, but the music is appealing." And Ed Siegel, in reviewing the televised version of the play, admits that "it may be the most intelligent Phantom we've seen, but it is far from the most passionate or mythic and far from the most satisfying." Siegel attributes this difference and deficiency to the script's sympathetic, even Freudian portrayal of Eric, noting that "Lloyd Webber grasped, or nearly grasped, what has eluded all the filmmakers — the Phantom is not a disfigured old man. He is not only a more romantic would-be lover than the Count, he is a sexier one." The problem, of course, with the reviewers' comments is that they are always comparing the Kopit version to the Lloyd Webber version, making Lloyd Webber the Mozart to Kopit's Salieri. But Siegel's observation regarding Eric has merit. Because Kopit focuses on the Phantom and his childhood, he does not have a great deal of time to focus on Christine's choice, thereby undercutting the tension of the choice between passion and convention, the dialectical energy that drives the narrative in the novel, on screen, and on stage. That is, Kopit exposes the psychological and historical influences upon the Phantom, unveiling the challenges Erik faced as a child. This unveiling is much more intellectual and less passionate or emotional. Erik behaves the way he does because he was abused as a child. His behavior is not the result of passion in a world of reason, a Dionysus in a land of Apollo. Instead, it is the usual domestic violence that we have become accustomed to in twentieth- and twenty-first-century America. There is no mystery. Many artists suffered as children.

Siegel's observation regarding the pace of the miniseries, and its lack of suspense, is in part the result of the miniseries format, a format that requires certain pauses in the action to make room for commercials. And these pauses do slow the play down considerably. On stage, the version is much more energetic and suspenseful. The Yeston lyrics, moreover, are satiric, a reflection of the original Leroux novel. Because the stage version was written first, its discussion precedes the television production.

The stage play opens with Christine entering Paris, selling music and singing. She is then "discovered" by the Count de Chandon, an heir to the champagne fortune. In the next scene, Joseph Buquet is ordered by the diva Carlotta to investigate the nether regions of the Opera House she and her husband "are inheriting" (11). This change from the two male Opera owners to the husband-wife team makes much more sense, since every other version implies that Carlotta's manipulations win her a place on the stage, which seems likely, since she sings so poorly. Even the most compliant manager would not risk losing his investments to please a diva or lover, while a henpecked and financially well-endowed husband would.

Like many Buquets before him, this Joseph Buquet violates the Phantom's underworld lair. In this stage play, we see the Phantom's lair is filled with a number of ragged acolytes, as well as an armoire filled with masks of "varying expressions" (11). While Buquet descends, the phantom completes a song, a fairly depressing work. His song is juxtaposed with Christine's, a more upbeat melody that she sings to the happy Parisians who have come to bid farewell to the old opera owners and welcome the new. The symbolism is clear: the Phantom sings of death and depression in his lonely underworld lair, while Christine sings of life, love, and happiness, surrounded by adoring audiences in the world of light above. He sings, "Paris is a tomb," while Christine and chorus sing "Paris is a melody" (12). Through Buquet's descent, the two worlds are no longer separate, and for this violation, he is punished. In addition, he sees the Phantom, and this spectacle costs Buquet his life. Again, the emphasis on the aural is clear. Here, in the Phantom's world, seeing is not believing. Seeing is not discovering the truth. Here, in this world of darkness, seeing is dying.

As the troupe waits, they sing, but in the background, we see Carlotta and her husband firing Gerald Carriere, an elderly man who has served as the director of the Opera House for years. Kopit adds this character to the usual cast and develops him throughout. In the television miniseries, the role will be played by Burt Lancaster, a substantial presence. Here, however, it is clear that the new owners do not value tradition, talent, or corporate loyalty. The old must be bad, the new always good. But as Carriere is dismissed, a note appears from the phantom saying that "Joseph Buquet broke the rules" (18). Ever the gentleman, Carriere explains the Phantom's demands and requirements to the new owners. And like the new owners before them, they are skeptical about these arrangements, confident that they will have no problems with this so-called Phantom.

After everyone leaves, Carriere calls to the phantom, asking if the note meant the death of Buquet. When the Phantom does not respond, Carriere calls the Phantom by his first name, Erik, and it is clear that the two have more than a passing relationship. This Erik and the opera director have a friendship. As the scene progresses, it becomes clear that the two have been working together for many years, perpetuating the myth of the Phantom of the Opera and bilking the Opera owners of some of their earnings. The two cannot decide on a reasonable course of action, but Erik knows that his life is changing. With Carriere no longer able to take care of the Opera House, Erik must decide his next course of action. Ironically, he calls for an "angel of music" to "restore a small glimmer of light to my gloom" (23). Here, the angel of music of the Leroux novel is, in fact, Christine, and this inversion demonstrates Erik's desperation.

In addition to firing loyal employees, Carlotta's "reign of terror" continues. Like an operatic Leona Helmsley, she is selfish and self-serving. When, for example, the Count de Chagny asks that his young friend Christine, having won everyone's heart in the opening scene, receive lessons from the great diva, Carlotta complies, presumably to keep the wealthy patron happy. Later, however, it is clear that she is more devious. Once the Count is out of sight, Carlotta relegates Christine to the role of laundress.

Carlotta explains that she is teaching Christine to sing by having Christine "watch" her sing. Once again, in this and other versions of *The Phantom*, seeing is never enough. It is useless when dealing with the "music of the night." To underscore this point, Christine sings as she completes the menial tasks Carlotta has given to her, and it is through her voice, not her looks, that the Phantom discovers her, and it is through his voice, not his appearance, that she agrees to work with him and learn more about this "music of the night." He sings to her, offering musical respite, world in which the two of them would be their own world (35–36). Cloaked in the darkness, the relationship begins.

Through clever staging, Kopit juxtaposes Christine's lessons with the pranks that Erik plays on Carlotta. He places bugs in her costume, so she must run from the stage, itching and screaming. A glass that she is to pick up during a scene is covered in glue, so it sticks to her hands, and worst of all, Joseph Buquet's corpse winds up in her closet. With Christine's music lessons nearly complete, and Carlotta on the verge of a nervous breakdown, the Phantom plans Christine's premiere, a public performance at the Bistro frequented by the Opera company, including the dreaded diva, Carlotta. Of course, Christine is a success. And it comes as no surprise that when the Count marvels at Christine's progress, Carlotta takes the credit for the ingénue's prowess and even offers her a place in the company — in front of the Count, naturally. During this scene, not only are Carlotta's machinations clear, but the feelings that Christine and the Count have for one another are also clear. Erik, hidden from the crowd, however, "sees" as much as the audience, and he becomes jealous.

Singing "A Diva's Work" (is never done), Carlotta prepares an herbal concoction designed to ruin Christine's voice for her first performance with the opera company. In a wonderfully devious scene, Carlotta persuades Christine to drink the potion and also tries to persuade Christine to reveal her voice teacher. In all honestly, Christine does not know, since she has never seen Erik without his mask. But the first half of Carlotta's plan is in place.

As though in a nineteenth-century version of *American Idol*, we see Christine falter on stage in front of the harshest judges, the Parisian Opera audience. It is her moment to triumph, but her voice, affected by the potion, cracks, and though the Count tries to rescue her, it is the Phantom who cuts the chandelier, brings down the curtain, and rescues Christine from this public humiliation (73). Thinking that she has been punished through some sort of musical karma for her dalliance with the Count, her first words to Erik are "Forgive me" (73), and she leaves herself to the mercy of her anonymous singing teacher.

The first act ends with the Phantom comforting Christine and taking her through the mirror in her dressing room to his underground lair. Of course, the mirror as prop in *Phantom* is common, highlighting the musical master's ability to defeat the spectacle, walk through the glass, and shatter the image. In other versions, we have seen the Phantom walk through the mirror alone, but, here, in Kopit's version, the two go through together. The mirror serves as almost an archway into the Phantom's world, the world of darkness, passion, and music. It is much more theatrical and dramatic, with the mirror serving as the gate between the world of light and the world of darkness. The moment also highlights the relationship between Christine and Erik. Theirs is a relationship based on music, not spectacle, true connection, not appearances. We have literally stepped beyond the looking glass; we now enter the realm of the music of the night.

The second act begins in the underworld, with Erik taking Christine on a boat to his rooms. This image, so hauntingly portrayed in the Chaney film, is one that neither Kopit nor Lloyd Webber could ignore. It is such a psychologically-charged image, harking back to the crossing of the River Styx, the world of the dead, the world of dreams and fantasies, the psyche itself. It is interesting to note that Erik, who frequently describes himself as ambivalently placed between the world of the living and the land of the dead, is Christine's chaperone to this underworld. Unlike other versions but similar to the original, Erik has adopted a number of what Kopit calls "acolytes," refugees from the Paris streets whom he feeds and cares for. In Kopit's version, Erik's world is populated by the homeless, not just vermin, and Erik is their savior. He cares for them, despite their appearances and social positions. And the money he has been receiving from the Opera owners has been funding some of these homeless creatures.

Once Christine is safely deposited in a bed in order to recover, Erik and Carriere talk. The inversion of darkness and light, chaos and order, passion and respectability are clearly articulated during Erik's conversations with Carriere, who urges Erik to return Christine. Erik's response highlights the ambivalent divisions between good and evil in this play's world and perhaps the world of the all the Phantom narratives. He says to Carriere: "The world up there is not fit for her! Up there is where hell is! I will not send an angel to hell!" (79). And in many ways, he is correct. The world of light and art is also filled with people like Carlotta. Erik is convinced that he is destined for Christine, not only to serve as her savior from the cruel world above but also to be saved by Christine: "I was born *so she could save me*!... From now on, she will be all I need" (81). He promises that he will die trying to protect her, even if it means her death as well.

It is a viewpoint that many understand — removing oneself from the world in order to protect the things or ones we love, but it is clear in this play that such retreat is never fruitful and frequently misdirected. Erik's obsession with Christine has Freudian undertones. We discover that his strong feelings for Christine stem from the fact that Christine reminds him of his mother, another great singer in the history of the Paris Opera House. Later Christine even finds a portrait of Erik's mother, attired in a wedding dress, which looks uncannily like her. Such details are far from coincidental, and may, in fact, hint at one of the reasons for the *Phantom*'s popularity over the years, genres, and cultures. The loss of self that Erik describes, the interrelatedness of savior and saved, mother and lover, is characteristic of infantile relationships with the mother. It is not difficult to see the undergrounds as a symbolic return to the womb, and with Christine's strong resemblance to his mother, the desire is explicit. Erik, then, embodies our own desires to return to a place of complete acceptance, care, interrelatedness, a world in which sounds prevail, the womb, with the mother's voice supreme. But as all *Phantoms* demonstrate, there can be no return.

Carriere, who lives in both the world of light and sight and the world of darkness and sound, realizes that the ideal that Erik yearns for is impossible. No one can avoid appearance and spectacle. Carriere advises Christine to escape because though she has seen Erik's eyes, which are full of kindness, she has not seen his face, which is a face of death. As Carriere says, "And to know him, you must also know his face" (84). Carriere's knowledge is given credibility when he makes an astounding confession to Christine. He admits that he is Erik's father, though Erik himself does not know.

In a flashback sequence, we learn about Erik's birth. Carriere had fallen in love with Belladova, the famous Parisian dancer turned singer, the singer who looks startlingly like Christine. The two had an affair, and Belladova wanted to marry, but Carriere could not because, unbeknownst to her, he was already married. Belladova leaves him and the opera, but eventually Carriere finds her, coincidentally, just as she is taking potions to induce an abortion. Carriere rescues both mother and unborn child, but when the baby is born, he is terribly disfigured. And while Carriere could barely look at the boy, Belladova loved her son: "She truly saw nothing ugly in this child at all. To her, he was beauty itself. And to him, ... so was she" (88). Given the various interpretations of Erik's mother, Kopit provides a refreshing one that shows this mother in a very positive way. Even the abortion attempt is presented as symbolic of her despair, rather than her wish to kill. It also illustrates the great consequences of Carriere's actions, consequences that he did not envision as he refused marriage to Belladova. She, of course, dies, and Carriere accepts his responsibilities and raises the boy in the underworld, protecting him for the cruelties of the upper world.

Carriere, however, like many of us, cannot face the consequences of his actions, and he literally masks Erik at a young age. Unlike Belladova, who could face her actions and the consequences thereof, Carriere cannot. This reluctance to accept the truth of the situation is perhaps what makes all the characters reluctant to observe the spectacle of Erik, a disfigured human creature, a constant reminder of our own spiritual disfigurements.

While Christine and Carriere are in the underworld, Erik takes his revenge upon Carlotta, initially telling her to leave the Opera, then finally electrocuting her, since she will not comply with his demands. His obsession and blood lust clearly escalating, he returns to his lair and shows Christine the "woods" he has created in his underworld, literally a staged forest complete with trees moving to an unseen wind. Thanks to the acolytes who live under the opera house, Erik creates his own paradise, complete with moving trees and gentle winds. Here, he is the creator of this paradise. To underscore this connection, during this scene Erik brings up the poet William Blake and confesses his interest in the nineteenth-century author of *Songs of Innocence*, best expressed through the poem "The Lamb," and *Songs of Experience*, best expressed through the poem "The Tyger." In many ways, these companion poems express Erik's personality exquisitely — how could he be both meek and terrifying, beautiful and ugly, loving and raging? How could God create both lamb and tiger, particularly in one man? These are questions that spurred Blake's creativity, and these are the questions that create Erik and fuel his creativity. They are also questions that create the tension in this *Phantom* narrative and help it succeed.

When he asks Christine to sing, she asks if she can see his face. She says, "Your mother saw your face and smiled. If love could let her gaze at you and smile ... why can't it do the same for me?" (98). She then sings a song professing her love and faithfulness. Of course, for those familiar with the Phantom story, the song ends in screams. When Erik removes the mask, Christine cannot face the consequences of her request or decision. As she escapes, the entire "forest" collapses, just as Erik's world collapses. It is a wonderful symbolic moment in the play. Erik has constructed a reality of beauty, peace, and art, a refuge from the world, his own private paradise, but such isolation can never last. It is illusory. No man is an island, and Erik is certainly not the omnipotent Creator. In response to the destruction of his illusions, Erik vows revenge.

After a period of reflection, Christine realizes her error regarding her reaction to Erik's disfigurement. She realizes that she treated him brutally, and she wants to make amends, but the Count, who has seen her terrorized, also wishes to protect her and encourages her to stay away from the underworld. Like Orpheus and Eurydice, Christine apparently has lost her one chance to make a compassionate gesture towards Erik. In the meantime, Carriere tells Erik that he is his father. Erik admits that he had his suspicions all along, wondering why it took Carriere all that time to confess his relationship. In this lull, a quiet moment after Erik's rage over Christine's departure, it appears that father and son have not only reconciled but Erik has come to some peace regarding his feelings for Christine. Such is not the case, in this musical or in the reality of human emotion. The play concludes with a spectacular finale.

Still desperate to make amends, Christine tries to make her way into the underworld. The police and the Count are simultaneously trying to capture Erik and prosecute him for the numerous murders he committed. The pace of the play accelerates, and Erik and the Count meet, with Christine looking on. The two men fight a duel, with Erik finally winning. As a result of Christine's intercession and Erik's love for Christine, however, Erik does not murder the Count. Instead, he hesitates. At this moment, the police succeed in wounding the Phantom. Erik knows the fate that will await him in jail, and he pleads with his father to kill him. He cannot face a life of imprisonment and ridicule. Almost as if to complete the abortion he interfered with years earlier, Carriere shoots his son, and in Erik's final moments Christine removes her music teacher's mask. She then kisses Erik, and he dies happily. She has been able to make amends for her earlier behavior, and Erik can die a "free man," not a prisoner of the Paris police. The Count escorts Christine off the stage to their future together, and Erik's corpse remains on stage, a symbol of love, passion, and misjudgments.

The version is much more sympathetic to Erik, and his anger, though extreme, is understandable, given Christine's betrayal. Further, given the childhood he has endured, as well as his life of pain and isolation, his behavior seems fully justified psychologically rather than presented as some aberration. He is not evil. He is all too human, and we, as audience members, cannot but help to feel for him. Such sympathy is present in many versions, but ultimately, in order for the Phantom to retain his power over us, he must represent something lurking within all of us, evil, passion, eroticism. Unlike us, however, he allows this "dark side," this unconventionality, this evil, to express itself first through his music and then through his love for Christine. Christine, like a moth to a flame, is drawn to this forbidden world as easily as we are, and she must struggle and suffer to make a decision. Though Kopit's version does not present her struggle as fully as other versions, Christine realizes her error, her participation in the world of the light, the world of appearances, ironically, the "dark" side of the Apollonian existence, and comes to reconsider it at the end of the play. In this way, she may be a tragic heroine who realizes, always too late, what she has done and what she has lost. Though she clearly loves the Count, she did not treat Erik respectfully and carefully. She overemphasized the spectacle, but in the end, she concludes her relationship with him by singing in his honor, honoring the music of the night.

Kopit's *Phantom:* The Television Version

The advantage to the miniseries version, in addition to the Paris Opera House setting, is the cast. In one of his last film roles, Burt Lancaster plays the father, Gerald Carriere. Charles Dance, a strong stage and film actor (*The Swimming Pool* [2003] and *Jewel and the Crown* [1984]), plays Erik. Ed Siegel admits that Dance "acts circles around not only [Michael] Crawford, but around the ghosts of Lon Chaney and Claude Rains as well (he sings, or, rather lip-syncs too, in the penultimate scene in the film)." Teri Polo (*West Wing* [2006] and *Meet the Fockers* [2004]) plays Christine Daae, and Ian Richardson, with numerous stage and screen credits, including Marat in *Marat/Sade* (1967), plays the new opera owner. His wife, Carlotta, is played brilliantly by French actress Andrea Ferreol. In addition, Kopit wrote the screenplay, which follows the stage version closely, and the miniseries is directed by Tony Richardson, noted for his film direction of the classic *Tom Jones* (1963). There is also an extensive production of *Faust* towards the end of the film. All make this a film worth watching. Conveniently, it is available in many formants, VHS and DVD. Of course, there are no commercials, but the commercial pauses are still apparent and a bit intrusive.

The film, like the Kopit play, illustrates the important relationship between Erik and his father, Gerard Carriere. It begins similarly, with the arrival of Christine and the new Opera House managers, and the firing of Carriere, which causes a great deal of trouble for the new Opera House owners. Some of the most entertaining scenes are those between the Opera House owner, Cholet (Richardson), and his wife Carlotta (Ferreol). Through these characters, the pretentiousness of opera lovers, the upper classes, and the nouveau riche clearly link this version to the original Leroux novel, as well as Kopit's own stage version. Carlotta is especially manipulative and cunning as she gains the trust of the innocent Christine, and one of the great highlights of the film is the singing "duel" between Carlotta and Christine in the Bistro, which does not occur in the stage version.

The film does not use the Maury Yeston score, affording the filmmakers the ability to utilize classic arias and operas for many of the musical numbers in the film. In the play, Carlotta sang a song praising Paris, the musical version's signature piece, then Christine gave her version of the piece, which was clearly superior. In the film version, the two are on stage together, with Christine, a veritable David to Carlotta's Goliath, but as the duet continues, Christine's power is clear, and she wins the hearts and trust of the operatic company, including Cholet, who proposes that Christine sing Marguerite in *Faust* the next night. Carlotta, who has been plagued by the Phantom's jests — the bugs, the glue, and the corpse of Buquet, as in the stage version — has vowed never to sing again, and her husband cunningly uses this argument to cast Christine in the title role. Of course, Carlotta ensures the demise of Christine's singing career the next day by giving her the herbal potion which makes Christine's voice falter.

Following her success, however, she spends the rest of the evening with the Count and they discover their childhood connection during a beautiful moonlit carriage ride. Erik, of course, is furious. The challenge with this role on stage is the mask. Emotional expression is a difficult here and in other stage versions of the novel, since Erik's signature feature, his face, is masked, thereby impeding an important means of expression on stage — the performer's face. Part of his success is ensured by Kopit's addition to the Phantom legacy, the use of multiple masks to express emotion. And throughout the film, Dance is seen with not only a white mask, but a devilish one, a black one, and a Pagliacci, crying-clown mask. These multiple masks also suggest Erik's narcissism, and director Richardson places Erik in front of the mirror frequently, trying on masks, admiring their effect. Such details highlight not only Erik's selfishness but also his search for himself, an identity which expresses who he is. He may be on the other side of the stage mirror in his underground lair, but in this version, he is searching as much as anyone in the world above for his identity and role.

The other reason the masks work so well is Dance's ability as an actor. He says, "Wearing a mask means you have to depend much more upon body language than eye language. Erik is a man steeped in theatricality — his whole wardrobe has come out of the Opera House costume department. I see him as a child, an innocent — I never think of him as being a murderous maniac. He's alone in a world he's created for himself, and into this world of music comes this girl with an exquisite voice" (qtd. in Dupont 48). Dance's perception of Erik is clearly communicated throughout the film, and we do feel sympathy for him, for the most part. What Dance's comment does not indicate, but what his performance clearly does, is that this isolated childishness has its dark side. As the explicit reference to William Blake in the stage version suggests, "songs of innocence and experience" intertwine in the character of Erik, particularly in this performance by Dance.

Once the chandelier falls and Christine is taken to Erik's underground realm, the film slows its pace considerably as a result of the embedded narrative regarding Erik's birth. In a filmic flashback, we return to Carriere's and Belladova's youth and affair. We learn that Erik is the love child of the singer and Carriere, and even though Burt Lancaster is a very sympathetic performer, it is still very difficult to understand why the young Carriere does not seek to console his pregnant mistress. In this film, it is particularly difficult, because during the flashback sequence, which does not include the sympathetic Lancaster, the young Carriere finds out that his lover is pregnant, tells her that he is already married, and nonchalantly continues fishing. It is a brief moment, but it is particularly cruel. Belladova attempts to drown herself in the river, and only then does Carriere realize the effects of his callousness.

Teri Polo also plays the part of Erik's mother, underscoring the Freudian images of the stage version, as well as making Erik's desire clearly highlighted in the film — his love for Christine is a desire for a mother who loved him unconditionally; he hopes to return to the womb.

As in the stage version, Carriere is incapable of such emotion and provides his young son with a mask. In a particularly moving scene, Erik looks into one of the underworld rivers and is frightened by what he thinks is a sea monster. Of course, he discovers, by the appearance of his father behind him, that the monster is none other than himself. Again, the gaze in the mirror is emphasized and critiqued. Spectacle is cruel, so Erik turns towards music, but in this version, even he must look into the mirror.

Mirroring Erik's childhood is Christine's youth. She, like Erik, is an orphan, but unlike Erik, she is beautiful and surrounded by beauty. Her father is a famous violinist who lives with the Count's family, as does Christine. Even here, however, there is darkness. As a result of the young Count's innocent but ardent interest in Christine, she and her father are expelled from the household — the Count, after all, cannot love someone from another class. Christine may appear beautiful, but her pedigree is incorrect, according to the Count's family. Even the beautiful cannot get what they want.

In this version, the Count himself has a bad reputation. As Erik warns Christine, the Count comes to the opera, not for the love of music, but to be seen, the cardinal sin of patrons of the opera in the Leroux novel. The Count overemphasizes spectacle, not the aural, so, of course, he is demonized. And when Carriere realizes that the Count and Christine love one another, Carriere warns the Count that he must not only risk his life to save Christine, but he must change his life, turning from appearances to realities, from spectacle to music.

Carriere's warning not only emphasizes the change that must occur in the Count, but it also shows the change that has occurred to Carriere over the years. He has made amends, realized his mistakes, and taken the responsibility required. He has been transformed as a result of his life with Erik, and the transformation has made him better. There is hope at the end of this *Phantom*. By experiencing the "music of the night," the world of darkness as well as the world of light, people may treat one another better. Love is possible.

In the end and as in the musical, Christine asks the Phantom to remove his mask, which he does, with horrendous consequences. She cannot stand the ugliness. She escapes from his lair, and as in the musical, feels deeply about her inability to withstand the ugliness that accompanies the Phantom's passion and artistry. Like Carriere, but much more quickly, she makes her tragic realization and accepts the consequences of her actions. Desperate to make amends to Erik, she admits to the Count that she loves Erik but in a way different from the way that she loves him. This admission of multiple forms of love is another hopeful sign in this version — love is not limited to romantic, heterosexual love. There are other options. This Christine articulates what has been implicit throughout many versions of the *Phantom*: there is more than one kind of love, more than one kind of music, a kind of music that expresses love and passion, light and darkness, and there is more than one kind of love, a love that blends innocence and experience, appearances and other realities. Christine is moved by the Phantom's passion, his darkness, and his creativity, an artistry that depends on the darkness, just as much as the Opera House depends on the dark foundations of its architecture. Beauty, passion, and ugliness are intertwined. The Count, who is repeatedly described as a man who does not appreciate music, may have treated women badly in the past, but he does not have the dark, obsessive, brooding and murderous temperament of the Phantom, and this lack may be the deficiency that explains why he cannot appreciate music and art. Music, art, and love demand an understanding of the darkness that makes the light possible, the silence that underscores the sound.

In the final scene, all these dialectics are brought to the forefront. Christine sings Marquerite in *Faust*, and the relationships between Faust and the Phantom are not lost. He has made a "deal with the devil" figuratively, a life with music but without human contact. The deal, however, has been compromised by the appearance of Christine in his life. He wants both passion and security, but like Christine's reluctance to face the dark side of passion, this desire is doomed. Not, of course, before a great duet between Christine and Erik. As Christine sings her Marguerite, the Phantom replaces the singer who was playing the role of Faust. The two are now on stage together. In these final moments, it is clear that Christine and he are connected in a way that the Count and Christine will never be, and Erik even says to the Count, "She sang to me, she is mine." And given the performances, as well as the reaction shots of the Count during this aria, it is difficult to disagree with these sentiments. There is something soulful, passionate, and unearthly about these moments, and they are as effectively connected through song as they would be through marriage.

In the end, however, the Phantom must learn that this love requires sacrifice. As he is about to kill the Count, Christine intercedes, saying, "If you love me, you will spare him." Like many Phantoms before him, he complies. Christine and the Count are united, and as Erik attempts to make his escape, the police wound him, a fate worse than death for Erik. Like the stage version, he asks his father to kill him. And like the stage version, Christine has her moment of truth with him, removing his mask, and kissing him goodbye. These moments, moreover, take place on the roof of the Paris Opera House, perhaps indicating the higher forms of love, compassion, and fidelity that are now forming as a result of the film's action. The Phantom is dispatched, the couple united, and the father forgiven. There is a return to the status quo in this version, like the others, but here there have been so many great changes in people's perspectives, Carriere's ability to love, Christine's ability to love, and the Count's ability to love, that it is difficult to see this world with anything but new eyes, with music underscoring the perceptions. Here music and spectacle become one, and though Christine cannot relinquish her role in the world of light, she has come to a greater understanding of the darkness that fosters this world.

Spectacular Phantom: Andrew Lloyd Webber's *Phantom* on Stage (1986) and Screen (2004)

Andrew Lloyd Webber's *Phantom of the Opera* (1986) is the longest-running musical on Broadway. Opening in 1988, it won seven Tony Awards, and its recent incarnation in Las Vegas, Nevada, ensures its position in the annals of theater history as one of the most popular and most-viewed musicals. Admittedly, recent years have brought poor sales and rumors of its demise, but the 2004 film version seems to have given new life to *Phantom* by introducing a "new audience to the show" and reminding "old ones how superior the musical is" (Zinoman). Of course, there are detractors, and it is easy to see the flaws in the musical. The plot is thin, and the entire musical is melodramatic. For Jerrold Hogle, the piece represents the "culture of adolescence" in its most derogatory sense: a young man with bad skin falls in love with a young woman who struggles to find her way between eroticism and convention (*Undergrounds* 173–176). One of the harshest critics, Robert Brustein, writes that it is "not a musical play so much as the theatrical equivalent of a corporate merger. We follow the plot with less interest than its box office reports" (33–34). Almost as if to prove Bentley correct, twelve years later, and as a result of the financial gains from *Phantom,* Lloyd Webber won a bidding war "to buy 10 theaters" in London's West End ("Lloyd Webber Buys"). And while some were concerned that the purchase would affect London theater negatively, appealing to popular rather than avant-garde tastes, Lloyd Webber is clearly good at theatre, knows how to market it, and reinvests in and reinvigorates the London theater scene.

Critics of the musical, however, are few and far between. Even the curmudgeonly *The New York Times* critic Frank Rich noted in his original review of the 1988 New York premiere of Lloyd Webber's *Phantom,* "It may be possible to have a terrible time at *The Phantom of the Opera,* but you'll have to work at it." Michael Crawford, playing the Phantom, earned most of the praise, as did director Hal Prince and the lighting and set designers. Rich had to admit that the musical expressed not the Leroux or Phantom phenomenon brilliantly, but the Andrew Lloyd Webber phenomenon: his "esthetic has never been more baldly stated than in this show, which favors the decorative trappings of art over the troublesome substance of culture and finds more eroticism in rococo opulence and conspicuous consumption than in love or sex." Given its immense popularity and the remarkable sales of *Phantom* paraphernalia, it is difficult to disagree with Rich regarding the conspicuous consumption. Hogle concurs, arguing, moreover, "the proliferation of *Phantom* T-shirts and other memorabilia bought by teenagers since 1986, all with the musical's logo of the phantom's white mask on them, attest to the appeal of this show for teenage sensibilities, alongside the attraction of adolescent elements to numerous playgoers of older generations" (*Undergrounds* 174). Hogle may be correct in attributing the musical's popularity to its adolescent appeal to audiences of all ages, but the musical itself seems no more adolescent than the great Rogers and Hammerstein works it hoped to emulate.

The romantic musical is simply built around love, obstacles to it, and its ultimate consummation. Our interest in the story, from its conception in the Leroux novel through its myriad incarnations, reflects the need, admittedly adolescent, to discover our identity and our soul mate. And while these quests seem sophomoric, they are also the hallmarks of the human condition.

Lloyd Webber's *Phantom,* in addition, serves as a signpost in the

history of theater and the entertainment industry in general. Its successful marketing campaign of its tickets, its recordings, and its memorabilia reflect the changes in entertainment industry. By a comparison of
the original *Phantom* to the Andrew Lloyd Webber version, the differences between marketing and art at the beginning and end of the twentieth century become clear. Initially, entertainment was advertised in and
of itself. Today, not only is the musical, movie, or drama advertised, but
it is marketed on almost limitless paraphernalia, from T-shirts to lunch
boxes. Market saturation is not the demise but rather the key to success
in a glutted consumer market. *The Phantom*'s marketing not only reflects
this concept beautifully but also embodies the steps necessary to attain
such saturation and success. First, tickets were very expensive and scare.
This scarcity provoked a "hunt" mentality. As Russell Baker wrote in a
very humorous piece on the then incredibly popular *Nicholas Nickleby:*
"I for one get very little pleasure seeing a show for which just anybody
can walk up to the box office and buy a ticket. Give me a show so sold
out that my friends will never be able to buy tickets, however, and I will
put up with anything." The same could be said of *The Phantom*. In
many ways, the Lloyd Webber phenomenon and musical not only reflect
the desires of his audiences, as the versions prior to his do, but his, perhaps more than other version, actually creates desire within his audience
members, desires that have resulted in a multi-million-dollar success. Of
course, if the show were not well-written and well-composed, it would
have gone nowhere. But the success was marketed, managed, and manipulated in order to capitalize on that success even further, perhaps even
undeservedly so. As we shall see in the discussion of the Las Vegas version, in the case of this *Phantom*, the art does not reflect cultural desire;
it feeds this desire.

Like many other versions of *Phantom*, Lloyd Webber's began through
a series of accidents, luck, and passion. As George Perry's *The Complete
Phantom of the Opera* notes, Lloyd Webber saw a version of the Ken Hill
musical, and he thought he could help with the music, which Hill had
struggled with as early as 1976. Lloyd Webber approached Jim Sharman,
who had directed *Jesus Christ Superstar* (1970), but he was not only busy
with other projects, but he was also unwilling to turn Erik the Phantom
into Frank-n-Furter, the transvestite from Transsexual Transylvania à la
the *Rocky Horror Picture Show*. According to Perry, Sharman told Lloyd
Webber, "You're missing a great romantic plot" (67). In an apocryphal

story, Perry continues, saying that as Lloyd Webber was mulling over Sharman's idea, he just happened to wander into a bookstore and found the original Leroux novel which he had not previously read.

The Lloyd Webber version is an important one, not only because of its popularity, but also because it brings the story and an original musical score together in a way that has never before been successful. Some versions resort to operatic scores, others to weak original compositions. Further, Lloyd Webber's abilities as a composer are noteworthy and popularizing. *The Phantom of the Opera* appeals to those who would normally abhor opera because Lloyd Webber's melodies are akin to popular songs, but for those opera aficionados, Lloyd Webber offers many nods in the direction of the great opera composers, particularly Puccini. In this way, Lloyd Webber appeals to an audience similar to Leroux's audience some one hundred years earlier — those interested in opera will be intrigued, those unfamiliar will be entertained, not overtaxed:

> The musical offers its increasingly broad-based audiences ... a sort of "ticket backstage" to the splendors of high-culture opera (at appropriately high ticket prices) without being so operatic as to alienate the many who aspire to the level socioeconomically but find real opera too slow and remote ... the musical's segments of "opera" are entirely new and fake ones devised by the composer of the score, this time without fully operatic features or direct echoes of well-known figures yet with attributions to such nonexistent but opera-sounding names as "Chalumeau" and "Albrizzio" [Hogle, *Undergrounds* 173].

Audiences may sit back and enjoy the "music of the night," without having to have the libretto or supertitles for *Faust* or *La Traviata*.

As John Snelson of the Royal Opera House demonstrates in great detail in his book on Andrew Lloyd Webber, *Phantom* represents an important turning point for Lloyd Webber, as well as the *Phantom*'s history. Lloyd Webber originally conceived of the work as a rock opera, and he even recorded a version of the title song with Sarah Brightman and Steve Harley, a rock singer.[17] As Michael Crawford points out, the title song retains some of its roots, "with its heavy rock beat ... [it] sounds almost an anomaly; it has a totally different feel to the other songs in the show" (270). This concept shifted considerably as Lloyd Webber began to talk to director Hal Prince; both concurred: "It's got to be romance" (qtd. in Snelson 38). And in another great story about its development, Lloyd Webber said that he played a version of the new, less rock-

influenced score for a friend who said, "You've taken one big step back-
wards towards the world of Rodgers and Hammerstein." Lloyd Webber
responded, saying, "I was delighted because I've always wanted to write
for a conventional orchestra and write real love songs and do my own
'Some Enchanted Evening.' I hope it's going to be about slightly old-
fashioned theatrical values because it's absolutely imperative the musical now goes back to the direction it was taking during the years of
Rodgers and Hammerstein and the best of the Americans" (qtd. in Snelson 38). Given these goals, the narrative winds up being fairly traditional
as well. As Snelson notes, Christine, in particular, faces "the old dilemma
of having your man or your career; the options in this nineteenth-century romance don't allow for a more modern solution ... romantic happy
endings conventionally require the restoration of the status quo" (92).

In addition to the traditional sound and narrative of the musical,
the publicity surrounding the work hark back to the showmanship of,
ironically, the filmmaker Carl Laemmle. With rehearsals in progress and
discussions about the musical reaching tabloid proportions, the musical
generated a great deal of interest beyond the story and cast. Reports on
the amount of dry ice continue to appear in the paper, as do reports on
box office sales, the number of ballet slippers, and other such details. Perhaps more than any other Phantom, there is a great deal of discussion
about the mask and the cosmetics necessary to create the disfigurement
underneath. In Perry's *Complete Phantom*, there are several pages devoted
to the makeup for Michael Crawford, Lloyd Webber's original Phantom.
There is even a sequence indicating the transformation of the handsome
Crawford to the disfigured Phantom (86–87). Crawford himself discusses the difficulties with the mask and the makeup. As he notes, one
of the biggest challenges to this production was the fact that the performance would not be filmed but live:

> My ears and nose had to be kept clear so I could hear the music and
> breathe freely, and my mouth had to be kept clear so that I could be
> completely understood when I sang. The idea of wearing a half-
> mask was [designer] Maria [Bjornson's] and it solved all our prob-
> lems, save one: the Phantom was a romantic figure and the exposed
> side of my face had to be appealing to the audience (272)

Crawford and others have indicated the hours it took to prepare the
mask, as well as the various materials used to create the final product
(273). In this way, the press surrounding the musical reproduced some

of the musical's main points — life behind the stage, life behind the opera. Ironically, the information, rather than clearing up mystery and suspense, only heightened the world's interest in the Phantom. In many ways the discussion of the spectacular elements of Lloyd Webber's *Phantom* actually brought in audiences to experience the aural, the "music of the night."

The story begins with the elderly Raoul searching for his past at an auction at the Paris Opera House. This quest serves as the frame for the story. Raoul's appearance, however, adds little to the story. It is not told from his perspective, and the remaining narrative is told from third-person objective. The audience, as in much traditional theater, observes through the fourth wall. The quest for "the truth" about the Phantom and Raoul's past is a dramatic device which gets the plot moving quickly and in a way the Kopit version did not. There are rumors of a ghost persisting even many years later. In this way, the play creates suspense, as well as suggesting the Phantom's immortality.

The opening musical sequence is perhaps one of the most famous of the musical. The organ blares in a pop overture reminiscent of Bach's *Toccata and Fugue in D Minor*, and we are whisked to turn-of-the-century France, as the chandelier is resurrected from the floor of the decaying Opera House to its golden age in the past. Once we return to the past, we meet the diva Carlotta, demanding as ever. The cast and crew prepare for a performance of *Hannibal*. Choosing *Hannibal* upholds audience stereotypes regarding opera —filled with spectacle, divas, men in tights, and lots of Italian accents. Christine's appearance, however, demonstrates that there is a beautiful, more natural side to opera. Her rendition of "Think of Me," which occurs immediately following Carlotta's extravagant interpretation, is clearly superior. It is, of course, ironic that the musical, one that is noted for its spectacle, advances the case of "natural music," not spectacular music.

For Snelson, the opera world of the musical is a backdrop for the more beautiful music of the piece. Originally, Lloyd Webber had planned to use parts of established operas to offset his writing, but that idea was abandoned, and in the end, the operatic moments in the musical are almost always comic. As Snelson proves effectively in his analysis of the score, "The point of the onstage opera in *Phantom* is that it is generic, playing to present-day, musical theatre audience's prejudices of opera, playing upon stereotypes. The onstage opera of *Phantom* is there for laughs" (108). It is no wonder, then, that Carlotta, singing in the style of high opera, almost burlesquing it, is overcome by Christine's musical simplicity, a triumph of musical theatre, a (perhaps) fun-loving snub to opera.

The usual rivalry erupts between Christine and Carlotta, and the new Opera owners are plagued by demands from the Phantom. Raoul also appears on the scene, this time without a reputation as a ladies' man as in the Kopit version. Christine and he remember one another immediately and rekindle their romance. While their love is clear, Christine is still loyal to her "Angel of Music," her teacher who holds her to high and strict standards. Initially, at least, Christine rebuffs Raoul's affections. Her duty is to her music, particularly the "Angel of Music" she presumes has been sent to her by her dead father, the famous violinist.

Given Lloyd Webber's composition and the poetic libretto of Charles Hart and Richard Stilgoe, the attraction Christine has for the Phantom is transferred to the audience — he is difficult to ignore or dismiss, given this music and these lyrics. The music that Erik and Christine share underscores their attraction, as well as the intimacy Leroux crafted in the novel. The song "Angel of Music," for example, illustrates the intimate connection, the oneness the two share. Erik tells Christine, as they look into the mirror, that there is no separation between them, between the reflector and the reflected. They are not separate; they are one another. They literally mirror one another's desires and identities. There is no other side to the mirror, according to Erik; they are one and the same. And in the very next scene, during the song "The Phantom of the Opera," their unity is further expressed in words and song. They are one and the same, inside "one another's mind." And it is through music that they overcome the limitations of spectacle. It is the "music of the night" that helps them overcome the obstacles of the day. The duets, as well as the Lloyd Webber score, highlight their supernatural interrelationship. It is a relationship, an interconnectedness that transcends the boundaries of space and time — they are united through voice, through breath, through song, not the physical realm. This distinction gives their relationship and this musical an otherworldly quality which is only manifested through the music of the night, not the light of day.

In this way, the musical relies on the songs to communicate the reasons behind Christine's fascination with Erik. It is no wonder: we are all fascinated by the music of the night this creature brings. The musical, consequently, does not offer the extended explanations from Christine as in the novel, but rather illustrates her passion through the music. For some this strategy might read as shorthand, but for those who actually listen to the lyrics and the melody, the rationale is plain. Ironically, the music helps us "see" the attraction. As *The New York Times* critic Mel Gussow observed, Lloyd Webber merged several myths to create his Phantom, including "that of Svengali ... and much more of a possible romantic alternative for Christine than in other versions." This resurrection also highlights the supernatural quality of the couple's relationship, a mysterious connection that defies the usual sort of romantic love.

Christine's passion and loyalty to Erik facilitate her triumphant debut on the opera stage. Her performance, in many ways, is a homage to her "angel," a prayer of thanksgiving. Of course, there is Raoul, her long-lost love. Erik, however, cannot abide this friendship, and his expectations about their connection are clearly unreasonable. To underscore his commitment, Erik asks Christine to follow him beyond the looking glass to his world of darkness, music, and passion. As in other versions, the mirror serves as an appropriate symbol for the competition between spectacle and music, the eye and the ear. Because she and the Phantom can walk through the glass, their relationship and their love of music is more powerful than spectacle. As they descend to Erik's lair, Lloyd Webber, ironically, offers one of the greatest spectacles in musical theater. Candelabras ascend from the depths of an underground lake as the two drift on along in the gondola to Erik's home. Here, in the darkness art, both visual and aural, is created. And it is here that Erik wishes Christine to stay in order to create an Eden of the underworld, to be his Eve to his Adam. Without her, he sings, he cannot create.

Erik's expectations, however, are unmasked as effectively as he is when Christine removes his disguise. Rather than opening himself to her gaze, to her vision, he abuses her, telling her she will never be free, now that she has seen his real face. The connection the two had is either ended or never was, as a result of Erik's anger and loss of control. As long as he was in charge of the relationship, the viewpoint, all is well. As soon as she takes control in some way, there is chaos.

Christine's reaction here is not as pronounced as in previous versions, particularly the early films. She is surprised, but she is still very tempted by this creature of the night. And this tension between her love of the night and its music, and her love of the day and its stability, moves the musical along, creating wondrous art. While attracted to Erik, she is a creature of the day, and even though she continues to triumph over Carlotta and win audience approval, she also realizes that she is in love with Raoul. Again, Lloyd Webber transforms one of the great scenes from the novel onto the stage, having Raoul and Christine discover and profess their love under the statue of the god Apollo and, unbeknownst to them, the watchful eye of the Phantom. Their theme "Say You Love Me" offers a world of light, not darkness. Again, the symbolism is clear: Apollo, the god of truth, light, and music, complete with by Erik, the disfigured creative genius and creature of the night. The act ends with the brilliant chandelier scene, representing the Phantom's formidable power, passion, anger, and apparent triumph over the world of day and light. He has literally struck out the lights of the Opera House, ironically using the lights to do so.

The second act begins spectacularly with the song and dance number "Masquerade." This musical piece emphasizes the duality of all human beings, not just the phantom. There is a dark side to us all, and suspicion is necessary. We may all wear masks, but for some, the masks are deadly. Christine and Raoul decide that their love places them in danger. The piece also pays homage to the Chaney film, and Erik's attire is clearly similar to Chaney's colorized Red Death costume in the film.

Christine decides to visit her father's grave, perhaps to gain insight into her romances. Erik, of course, is there, and as in the other scenes between the two of them, she is overcome by his music and power. Raoul appears on the scene and breaks the spell, and the men begin their battle, complete with spectacular fireballs. It is only as a result of Christine's cries to Raoul that the two men do not destroy one another completely. As Raoul and Christine run away, Erik curses the two of them, "So be it! Now let it be war upon you *both*!"

The company produces Erik's composition, *Don Juan Triumphant*, and it includes one of the most passionate songs in the repertoire, "Past the Point of No Return." Don Juan, played by the Phantom who has killed the singer cast as Don Juan, serenades Aminta (Christine), promising passions that negate separation and offer completion. And Aminta agrees, admitting that she has already imagined them satisfying their desires and becoming one flesh. As they sing, Christine, of course, realizes that Don Juan is the Phantom. And in a scene only found in the Lloyd Webber version, Christine unmasks Erik publicly. He is completely vulnerable, and the entire audience sees his deformity. In revenge, Erik abducts her at the conclusion of the song. In this way, Christine betrays Erik completely, exposing him to his enemies. But at the same time, she has lost all respect and admiration for Erik, who is behaving selfishly. As Raoul enters, the Phantom makes Christine choose between them, with Raoul's life in the balance if she chooses Raoul. Christine's anger subsides, and she looks upon Erik with compassion. Suddenly understanding his anger and hostility, as well as his selfishness, she kisses him tenderly, and Erik relents. Christine and Raoul escape together. Christine turns back quickly to return the ring Erik gave her earlier. As she and Raoul leave, we hear their theme, "Say You Love Me," as they move towards a world of light. The Phantom continues their song, and then disappears into his world of night, leaving his mask behind.

Clearly, Christine's music triumphs in the end, the music of the day, but a tension remains. The dark side, Erik, helped create Christine, giving her "natural voice" greater depth and power. But it appears that such passion and power must be tempered with moderation. If seen or experienced too fully, chaos, disharmony, and destruction result. Balance is necessary for beauty. But if we remember the opening of the musical, Raoul, the ultimate representative of the world of light, day, and order, continues his search for the Phantom, a remembrance of things past, a remembrance of his love for Christine and her love for the Phantom. There is no peace once you have experienced the "music of the night."

The 2004 Film Version of the Lloyd Webber Musical

After many years of waiting, wondering, and gossip galore, including rumors of the dashing Antonio Banderas playing Erik, the film of Andrew Lloyd Webber's musical *Phantom* arrived in 2004, nearly twenty years after its London stage premiere. According to interviews with both Lloyd Webber and director Joel Schumacher, the two had discussed a film version in the late 1980s (8–9; 48–49), but Lloyd Webber thought that the "film would damage the proliferation of the stage show." In addition, notes Lloyd Webber, there was still some uncertainty regarding audiences' interest in a musicals, but then "*Chicago* came along and proved that there was an interest" (8). For Schumacher, the transference from stage to screen was one of the most important reasons he decided to do the film:

> ...there were two main things that appealed to me about *Phantom:*
> firstly, it's a beautiful and profoundly tragic love story and secondly
> there are millions of people in the world who can't afford to go to
> legitimate theatre, either because the tickets are too expensive or
> because it is too expensive a production to play where they live, and
> those things combined gave me a huge amount of motivation [48].

And despite Lloyd Webber's belief that the film expanded the stage
play's "emotional center" (9), the film did not deliver, and it opened to
consistently poor reviews. It is easy to assume that Lloyd Webber pur-
posefully created a weak film in order to keep up the interest in the stage
play in New York, as well as the scheduled reincarnation in Las Vegas in
June 2006. That is, given the Lloyd Webber team's ability to manage
and manipulate marketing, perhaps the film was a kind of planned obso-
lescence similar to those used in the creation of computer technology
and electronic entertainment. The most damning review, by A.O. Scott
of *The New York Times,* takes Lloyd Webber's music to task for popularizing the eighteenth- and nineteenth-century operatic tradition: "His
attempt to force a marriage between that tradition and the modern musical theatre represents a victory of pseudo-populist grandiosity over
taste — an act of cultural butchery akin to turning an aviary of graceful
swans and brilliant peacocks into an order of Chicken McNuggets." Kirk
Honeycutt notes that the lack of creativity with the adaptation resulted
in a film that would appeal to an older audience: "A Baz Luhrmann
might have found a way to make the film version hip and relevant to
younger audiences. But Lloyd Webber clearly maintained a tight grip on
his baby as producer and screenplay collaborator with director Joel Schumacher, so little rethinking of the stage show went into the filmization."
It is interesting to note that this interpretation of the film, made twenty
years after the stage version, contradicts an earlier critic's view that the
Lloyd Webber musical appealed to adolescents (Hogle, *Undergrounds*
173). Perhaps *The Phantom* has grown old.

Other critics found fault elsewhere. First, it is important to men-
tion the fact that while Emmy Rossum, who plays Christine, is a clas-
sically trained vocalist, the Phantom, played by Gerard Butler, is not,
so expectations of another Michael Crawford, the singer who immortal-
ized the Phantom role on stage, would not be met. Other critics com-
plain about set design and direction. Film critic Roger Ebert faults the
underworld sets, which he says look more like they are in a "really neat

cave," not the underworld lair of the pseudo-prince of darkness. He adds that the Phantom is too handsome, and "the mask is more a fashion accessory ... a kinky babe magnet." Peter Bradshaw's commentary makes Ebert's look praiseworthy: "Weirdly, though, this new movie version of the stage musical ... is a reminder of just how compelling this tale could still be as a Gothic chiller, if the composer, with his legendary counter-intuitive talent, did not insist on smothering it in the rich vanilla sauce of good taste." And while the review is certainly extreme, Bradshaw does have a point. The tensions between good and evil, between virtue and sin, have been surgically removed from this film version. Specifically, Christine's struggle between the erotic and the conventional is absent. Ironically, and despite many successful adaptations, including Lloyd Webber's own stage musical, Christine returns to the role of victim that characterized the 1925 film. Given the cultural changes over the eighty years between 1925 and 2004, it is surprising and perhaps discouraging to see Christine once again cast as a passive victim, trembling at the hands of a dastardly villain. It is clearly several giant steps back for feminism, but it is also a step back for the *Phantom* story and the Lloyd Webber musical.

Not surprisingly, such representations of femininity abound in the modern, popular cinema. And it is remarkable how fully feminist and fit heroines on stage or in print become stereotyped victims during the process of adapting the novel, short story, or drama into film. Very few strong women exist on film, and when they do, they are frequently seen driving over the edge of a cliff, as is the case with *Thelma and Louise* (1991). Much has been written about such representation, but it is very easy to see the process when the Lloyd Webber stage and film version are compared. In many respects, this film even follows the structure of an American film Western, with the underworld lair serving as the Wild West from which the outlaw Phantom emerges, and over which the young hero must gain control in order to "get his girl."

With only a few exceptions, the film follows the musical very closely. It opens with Raoul bidding on the musical monkey and the great chandelier returning to its original position in the ceiling during the brilliant overture. Christine is beautiful and talented, and she succeeds at her debut at the Opera House. Like the other versions, the relationship between the Phantom and Christine is interrupted by the appearance of Raoul. Unlike the musical version, however, the film implies an almost incestuous desire on the part of Erik for Christine. Here, Lloyd Webber does not trust his music and libretto and explains why Christine and Erik are so close. They have been raised together by Madame Giry, and Erik, though older, has had an almost pedophilic attraction to Christine throughout his life. Raoul, too, has known Christine since childhood, but their love is pure, not tainted by dark, forbidden passion, as Erik's is.

After Christine's triumph at the opera, Raoul takes her out, and they travel around Paris together all night. Christine, of course, has abandoned her teacher, but the film forgives her this indiscretion by focusing on her innocence. It is not her fault if she wants to see an old childhood friend; it is Erik's for presuming that she would not succumb to the rewards of a glorious musical triumph. By presenting Christine in this way, the film transforms her from a passionate woman torn between her love for the mysterious, passionate Erik and the conventional Raoul to a victim lured into the darkness by a treacherous man, basically a child lured into a car on the promise of candy.

This simplification of Christine's character is clear during the song "Past the Point of No Return," a wonderfully seductive piece. Unlike the stage play, which presents this scene as a moment of truth for both Erik and Christine, a moment when Christine admits to herself and everyone else that she is attracted to the dark side embodied by the Phantom, in the film version, Christine becomes a nineteenth-century Ophelia, manipulated by the Opera owners and Raoul. As she sings the song, she does not keep her eyes on Erik; instead, she frequently looks at Raoul reassuringly. He, of course, is surprised by the seductive and sultry tones his seemingly innocent girlfriend expresses, but her gaze reassures him — he is the only one she sees. It is also important to note here that this moment undercuts the power of the voice and dramatically places the full power of the scene on the eye, on sight, the most important sense in film viewing. Again, as in the 1925 version, which is more about the film industry's ability to penetrate almost every area of human experience and existence using the camera than it is about the *Phantom* narrative, this film foregrounds its visual prowess, displacing aural power. Music may seduce, may transcend time and space, but a look can do so as well. There are no limits to the eye and its offspring, the camera. Christine, moreover, is completely in control of her feelings; she will not be swept away or even be tempted to be swept away by the Eros of music, sound, and breath. She is, in the end, a "good girl" who merely feigns understanding the "music of the night" in order to capture her sexual predator.

The film concludes like the musical, with Christine offering to marry Erik in order to save Raoul and with the Phantom then realizing what true love is about, and releasing her to her "happily ever after" life with Raoul. The film returns to the opening scene, with Raoul and Madame Giry once again exchanging knowing glances and affirming the power of the spectacular. They say nothing, they sing nothing, but they "see" all. Erik's world, the world of the music of the night, is now fully co-opted by the world of spectacle. Raoul then returns to Christine's grave with the musical monkey, only to find red roses, presumably left there by the Phantom. And while it is a moving image, it is an image that seals the Phantom's fate. He will be heard from no more.

That *Phantom* in Vegas

Capitalizing on the recent trend of Broadway musicals moving to Las Vegas, with some even bypassing Broadway altogether, Lloyd Webber's *Phantom* opened in Las Vegas in 2006. With its original running time of two and a half to three hours, "it's easy to see why the property stayed away from Vegas for so long ... no self-respecting casino wants its customers to be otherwise occupied for that long" (Quzounian E03). So the new version was cut to ninety minutes, with much of the material taken from the back story, as noted by Phil Gallo of *Variety*. Further, the original director Hal Prince "has lit a fire under his thesps, making sure they skedaddle quickly between numbers and keep the pace bordering on the frenetic." (Gallo 4). The shortened time also affords the Venetian, the casino hosting this extravaganza, the opportunity to offer more showings, thereby increasing profits in many ways — lots of attendance, lots of time to gamble. *Phantom* has clearly taken consumerism to a new level.

All reviewers, moreover, note that the production focuses on the spectacle, creating "a chandelier that dwarfs every lighting fixture ever assembled for this war horse" (Gallo 4). The spectacle is emphasized, and even the songs are hurried along with only "All I Ask of You" sung slowly and luxuriously, providing what Gallo notes as a "respite in the mayhem."

But this is Vegas, after all, and in many ways, this *Phantom* is perfect for this adult version of Disney World, where people who do not go to New York experience the city through a hotel called New York, New York, or who experience Venice through the Venetian. It is safe, sanitized, and easy. In many ways, this version does for *Phantom* what *Phantom* did for opera — make it palatable for novices who wanted to experience an art form as painlessly as possible. The advantage is that more people will see *Phantom* than perhaps any other musical in history. And perhaps, even though they are rushed through the music of the night, they might consider listening for it once they leave the spectacle of a city like Las Vegas and a production like *The (Ninety-Minute) Phantom*.

Phantom of the Midwest: John Kenley and Robert Thomas Noll's *Phantom of the Opera* (1988)

For many American Midwesterners, the name John Kenley is synonymous with theater. Beginning in the early sixties, Kenley was responsible for bringing Broadway talent to the heartland, first through Kenley Players in Gambier, Ohio, and later through the Carousel Theatre in Akron, Ohio. Elaine Stritch, in her recent one-woman show, remembers working with Kenley and Gloria Swanson during a production of *The Women*. From all reports, Kenley was a showman and eccentric. According to one rumor, he was said to have been asked if he was a hermaphrodite. He responded, "I'm not even a registered voter."[18] No matter; he was an entrepreneur, a showman on a much smaller scale than Lloyd Webber, but a showman nonetheless. He was driven to bring the stars of television to the heartland stage and to keep the audience wanting more. As one former Kenley player noted, he would encourage performers to take vitamin shots, not just for the double performances but to keep them energetic for the long autograph-signing sessions following productions. *Phantom,* then, seems like a perfect choice: through his rendering, Midwesterners could experience the "music of the night" without the expense and travel difficulties of going to New York and only trying to find tickets to the Lloyd Webber version.

As with many variations of the Leroux story, some elements remain consistent throughout the Kenley version — the chandelier scene, the love between Raoul and Christine, as well as the demanding diva. The

Opera House is also under new management, and the Phantom makes his usual demands on the new owners, who initially do not adhere to his rules but then realize his power, as always, too late.

One of the most notable additions or expansions in this piece is in the role of the Persian, who functions as a kind of narrator, opening the play with a few words about the Phantom:

> He was not, as was long believed, a creature of imagination. He was not, as was long believed, a product of superstition. No. He was flesh and he was blood. He lived in this House of Music and Dance. He was a man obsessed. He was a creature feared. He was a magician of the night. He was the infamous ... Phantom of the Opera! And he is with us tonight! [9].

Once the play begins, the Persian's role is much more active than in the novel. He serves as a liaison between Erik and Christine, and he even warns Raoul to stay away from Christine when this young suitor appears on the scene, thereby clearly establishing his loyalty to the Phantom and his singer, Christine. But as is often the case, true love overcomes such obstacles, and in this version, it is clear that Raoul and Christine are in love and destined for one another. Once the Persian realizes the seriousness of the relationship, he helps the young lover rescue Christine from the clutches of his friend and foe, the Phantom.

Like many other variations, Christine is also faced with a difficult decision: to marry Raoul or to remain married to the Opera. Like the novel and other versions, the two have known each other over the years, and Raoul admits that he has been writing to Christine over the years in the hopes of establishing at least an epistolary relationship. Strangely, the letters never arrive. Of course, Erik has intercepted these missives. Such a detail, then, not only indicates the depth of Raoul's feelings for Christine, but the depths to which the Phantom will lower himself to get his desired love object. In this way, too, much of the mysteriousness regarding the couple's past and their current reunion is clarified. Raoul loved Christine from afar, and his epistolary wooing was intercepted by his rival.

Christine, however, has yet another love. Like the 1943 version, this version emphasizes Christine's dedication to her art. She confesses, "I'm already married, Raoul.... To my music—to the opera" (14). Her commitment to art, of course, leaves her vulnerable to the machinations of the Phantom. Again, she is innocent and blind to Erik's dark side.

Ironically, this later version, over forty years after the 1943 film, is actually less feminist than the previous version. Here, Christine's passion for success on the stage leads her to potential destruction, but in the 1943 version, her dealings with the Phantom help her succeed, and though she risks everything, she ultimately triumphs on stage. Akin to the morality plays which fostered *Faust* and its variations, in this play, when Christine unmasks the Phantom, she also uncovers her own error — she has been led down the path to sin and destruction by her own desire for success. Her ambition has blinded her to the realities of her teacher and the realities of success on the stage. Here it is she, not Erik, who is likened to Faust. She has made a deal with the devil, and she now realizes the error of her ways. In this way, the play upholds the novel's admonition to examine superficialities, but here it is at the cost of female representation. She is weak, and she is misdirected. It is only through her association with Raoul that she redeems herself and fixes her mistakes.

In the end, like many other Phantoms, Erik realizes that he cannot accept this blind or forced sort of love from Christine. When she kisses him, as many of the Christines have done in the past, he realizes that she closes her eyes. She is doing it out of love for another man, not for him.

In a reversal of some of the spectacular imagery in previous *Phantoms*, Erik tells Christine he has dreamed that she would look at him, kiss him with eyes wide open (49). Here, Erik does not want Christine to be a mere object of his affection; he would like a reciprocal gaze. But, in the end, like all the other Phantoms, he wants to control this gaze, to direct the eye as well as the ear. Kenley's version emphasizes the Phantom's desire over that of Christine or Raoul. The Phantom wants love, a perfect kind of unconditional love, but he cannot attain such transcendent passion. The Persian attempts to comfort him, but the Phantom dismisses him. Christine finally kisses him with her eyes open, but she immediately returns to Raoul — this was a passing gesture, not a true expression of perfect love. At this point, the Phantom shrieks in pain. There is an explosion, and he is gone.

In this version, Erik is guilty of the misjudgment. He misreads and misapprehends the ability of humans to love. Like us, he imagines a perfect love, which overlooks flaws. Like us, he imagines that he can control this illusive love. With Christine chastised for her ambition, she is now perfect, and her reward is the perfect Raoul. For us and the Phantom, we only have our dreams, and for many Midwesterners at this time, one of these dreams was seeing a production of Lloyd Webber's *The Phantom of the Opera,* a dream that was also unfulfilled for many, many years.

A Phunny Phantom: *The Pinchpenny Phantom of the Opera* (1988)

Also copyrighted in 1988, Jack Sharkey's *The Pinchpenny Phantom of the Opera* clearly takes advantage of the "Phantom frenzy" surrounding the Lloyd Webber musical with hilarious results. Simply, this musical may be described as Gaston Leroux meets The Reduced Shakespeare Company. The musical is not accelerated, but its cast, costumes, and props are truncated, and the entire show is performed by two men and two women, one of whom plays a total of seven divas. It is a refreshing relief from the usual reverential Phantoms, but ultimately it is a third-rate comedy in need of editing and some better jokes.

The story begins with Gaston, the theatre director, trying to calm the condescending and nervous diva, while Bubby, the versatile and ubiquitous male character, prepares his operatic role for the evening. The musical blurs the distinction between fact and fiction from the start of the play. And in this way, it is consistent with previous *Phantoms* regarding nature of appearances. The main character, here called Pristine, is forced to share her dressing room with the male singer, Bubby, indicating not only the tight budget of the fictional story, but also the tight budget the creators of this musical are working with. Gaston, who loves Pristine even though she mispronounces his name and most others as well, cannot give the young woman a part because they need a diva to bring in the crowds. The Phantom, also known as Airwick, then appears, and proposes to make her the Diva of the Opera. Why? As he notes, "Why not?" Then comes an aria about Pristine's future, punctuated by a very dramatic exit of the Phantom: "*The Phantom always Exits this same way: Right cloak-swathed forearm goes horizontally across lower part of his face, he leans slightly backward from the direction he plans to depart in, then suddenly leans into the direction and swoops off, running in very short steps on his tippy-toes, cloak swirling behind him: this is not a sensible way to depart, but it looks nicely mysterious*" (14). The rest of the play includes a number of very interesting methods of murdering operatic divas because unlike other adaptations, this version does not promote Christine imme-diately. There are divas galore to go through and, consequently, mur-der — a veritable cast of a thousand divas, played by one character, of course, but who must be killed off in numerous ways. One diva is frozen while she performs the dance of the seven veils in the opera, *Salami*. Another is killed by poisoned fleas. The list goes on, and this repetition slows down the pace of the musical considerably.

Throughout the murder sequences, various comments are made about Pristine's inadequacies as a singer, and hence the reluctance to promote her. But in the end, she and the Phantom descend into his lair, where he unveils his newest opera, *La Triviata*, an opera that he com-posed on a child's toy piano. The lair is a dank sewer full of rats, noth-ing like the lovely underworlds of previous novel, stage, or screen versions. As the Phantom says, "It *is* kind of moldy, but at least it's a short commute to work!" (59). And when the unmasking occurs, the Phantom turns out to be none other than Gaston, the man whom Pris-tine loves anyway. Pristine, like most of the audience, is befuddled. The Phantom, in song, admits what most of us know about love — it ain't easy. There are days that our beloved is wonderful, and days that our beloved is not (60). With Pristine telling Gaston to take her as she is, the love story is interrupted by an opera.

And after a ridiculous version of the *La Traviata*, again another moment which slows down the musical, the couple agree to marry. The opera is a success, and all live happily ever after, even Bubby, the Opera's jack of all trades. He assumes he will only be a lowly chorus boy for the rest of his life. Suddenly, a mysterious figure appears — the Phantomette. Bubby's happiness and perhaps a sequel loom in the future, but thank-fully, no sequel has appeared.

Like all comedies, this funny Phantom gets much of its energy and momentum from ridiculing and subverting all the usual conventions. The young ingénue cannot, in fact, sing. The Phantom is actually the love interest, not a threat to it, and there is even a female version of the Phantom. Further, by emphasizing the low-budget nature of the play, the authors imply that illusion is expensive but they manage to create, if not art, then at least entertainment, even under financial constraints. The effect is fun and humorous, and the Phantom's lair becomes more canivalesque than a dark underworld subverting the light of day. It is a place to romp and play, and then return to the daylight. If only the pace of the musical were as tight as this analysis, the play would make its financially strapped creators some money, if not a sequel.

Flexible Phantom: Bruce Falstein's *Phantom of the Opera* (1990)

Once again capitalizing on the popularity of the Andrew Lloyd Webber musical, the Hirschfield Theatre in Miami Beach commissioned a version of the Gaston Leroux novel, using Bruce Falstein for the adaptation, and Paul Schierhorn (1986's *The News*) and Samuel Barber (music for the 1986 film *Platoon*) for the music and lyrics. The play opened in Miami in 1990, but made its way to New York as a videotaped version which was "staged" at the 57th Street Playhouse for a limited, two-week engagement.

As Stephen Holden of *The New York Times* notes, "Surprise: it is not half bad." It is also not too long, running about 90 minutes, but the video version, which is still available through libraries and eBay, has the same problems that Holden noted in his review: "The colors are drab and washed out; the pictorial resolution only fair, and the sound so thin that it borders on atrocious." The plot, however, is worthy of analysis, since Falstein offers a few important changes to the version that help underscore some of the themes that have appeared through the many variations.

The play begins like Hamlet's "Mousetrap," with a dumb show depicting Christine, her father, and Raoul when they were younger. A voice-over establishes the relationships, which clarifies the later interactions. After this prologue, the opening scene depicts Christine practicing her singing and the Phantom beginning to give her instruction. The setting, by Ken Kurtz, is clever. A mirror is at the center of the stage, and as Christine and Erik's relationship develops, Erik becomes clearly visible to Christine and the audience. As the two sing and establish the teacher-student relationship, the lyrics highlight the sense of oneness the music offer both characters. Through their passion for song, they will become one, and the Phantom will find the "angel of music" within Christine and bring it to life. During a brief interlude, Madame Giry arrives, and helps Christine interpret the events — the voice is the "spirit of music" her father promised to send her after he died. Thus encouraged,

Christine and the Phantom finish their song, with the Phantom saying, he will be "whatever you want me to be."

This admission is an interesting one, and it may account for the popularity of *The Phantom* in all its variations. Erik, the misunderstood, passionate, dark artist, becomes a "lure" or "icon" of audience desires. He may, for example, appeal to those who wish to see themselves as mis-understood artists, loners, individuals in an all-too-structured world. To others, he may represent escape from the mundane, perhaps a descent into the forbidden realms of desire, art, and music. But whatever the case, this version makes explicit at least one explanation for the Phan-tom's enduring appeal — he is a cipher, a mystery, an enigma which we may fill with our own fantasies, longings, desires, and explanations. He is, in effect, the very act of interpretation. We may figure, analyze, and enjoy, perhaps forever, the journey of an explanation of the Phantom.

To return to this version: as usual, here the opera house is under new ownership, but rather than having two bumbling owners under the spell of the diva Carlotta, Falstein's Firmin and Moncharmin are not only bumbling, but they are also at odds with one another. In a very funny scene, the Phantom uses their animosity against them, making each think the other has stolen important materials from the him. Further, it is clear that the business relationship puts art in jeopardy — concerned only about ticket sales and marketing, the two corporate types neglect the reason for the opera in the first place: music. Falstein's version high-lights the irony by having the death of music through money described in a song.

Christine's stage debut is very deftly and simply staged. With only a light on her, she sings, while Raoul recognizes her from his box on stage right. He stands, sings along with her, separate but also in the light. On the other side of the stage stands the Phantom, disguised, in the shad-ows, in his beloved Box 5. He, too, sings with Christine. In this way, not only is Christine's dilemma clear, but it also demonstrates how this love triangle is aided by music, an art form that transcends the physi-cal. Christine is musically connected to both men.

After her triumph, which is so much better than any other per-formance she has ever rendered, she follows the Phantom to his lair, where he sings and seduces her, hoping that she will not be like "all the others." During the song, he seems to undergo a transformation, almost indicating his dual nature, at once tender and destructive. He wants

Christine only for himself, and he effectively describes a life without anyone but his beloved, making it appear feasible to Christine and his audience. The play, however, demonstrates that such a desire is ultimately selfish, and though Erik tempts Christine, she must return to the world. She cannot forsake the world for him. In an interesting variation, she chastises Erik for living alone, leaving the world, and wearing a disguise, basically not facing the world, but running from it and its challenges.

She, however, does not entirely live up to these courageous words, for when she unmasks Erik, she responds like every other Christine, shrinking from the reality of his deformed face. This Christine, however, more than many others, recovers quickly. She moves towards the devastated Erik and takes his hand. Through this simple gesture, we see Christine's compassion, as well as her struggle regarding her feelings for Erik.

Christine returns to the world of light, and her lover Raoul, however. The compassion cannot overcome her feelings for Raoul. The two meet at the masked ball, and again, the lovers escape to the rooftops. Here Raoul confesses his love for her, but makes it very clear that he will share Christine with her passion, her musical career. Unlike many other Raouls, Falstein's version recognizes Christine's gift and the need to share this gift to the world. In many ways, this generosity of spirit is what differentiates love from lust. Love, in this case, makes us better, more generous and open.

Christine's feelings for both men at this time and through the rest of the play are not clearly articulated. She, of course, is very pleased that Raoul understands her need to be free and to express her art, but she also confesses her attraction to Erik and the beauty and passion he offers. There is always something more she hopes to attain, but by the end of her confession, it is clear that she has chosen Raoul for no clear reason.

At this moment, Erik appears and kidnaps Christine, returning to his lair. The Daroga, who here presents a great deal of comic relief, placing Raoul in danger rather than himself, leads Raoul to the Phantom's underground world, where the two lovers argue over the object of their affection. The Phantom gives Christine the choice — the mundane, as exemplified in his rival Raoul, and the passionate, the place where true beauty exists, exemplified in Erik and his new opera, *Don Juan Triumphant.* Christine says that she cannot leave the earth to create music; she must feel the sun and rain.

Unlike most other Phantoms, this Erik takes the news well. He, too, has been transformed by love, this time without the need of torturing his rival. As he dreams, his reverie is interrupted by the appearance of the Daroga, the Persian police officer who has apparently been chasing Erik for some time and for some unknown reason. Similar to the relationship between Rick and Captain Renault in *Casablanca* (1942), these two men come to some understanding, one that helps the betrayed Erik establish a reason for living. The Daroga agrees to continue to pursue Erik, and Erik agrees to continue that game because it "would be no fun at all."

Once again on top of the Paris Opera House, Raoul and Christine confess their love for one another. Ironically, however, Christine admits that she only wants to sing for Raoul. She resolves to leave the Opera and establish a domestic life with Raoul. In this way, the play reinforces the idea that love changes people and makes them more generous and compassionate. Raoul allows Christine her independence and freedom, and she chooses to remain with him. Erik initially thinks that capturing Christine will bring her to him, but as is often the case in the various versions of *Phantom*, his attempts to control her only push her further away.

Erik's motives, however, are not entirely condemned by the play. In the final scene, one of the ballerinas practices on a bare and dimly lit stage. Erik approaches her and encourages her to follow her soul, the same words he used when he first met Christine. The young woman listens, and performs much better. Erik is clearly over his previous love. He is on the move again, searching for a new Christine. The young woman asks, "Who are you?" He answers in the same way that he does when he meets Christine for the first time: "I am whatever you want me to be."

Earlier in the play, Erik referred to himself as beyond mortal, somehow inhuman in a spiritual sense. He makes this claim during a rather self-important speech to Christine. During this speech, he argues to her and Raoul, that, of course, Christine would choose him, since he offers pure beauty and passion. Who could resist? When Christine chooses Raoul, the play seems to undercut Erik's claim as the rantings of a handsome, talented, but egomaniacal artist. Here, the play asks us to reconsider. Perhaps Erik is the "spirit of music," the muse or force which moves throughout the arts encouraging perfection and the many sacrifices necessary for art to be art. As he tells his new protégé, through difficulty, she will attain mastery.

In this way, Erik is literally whatever you want him to be, since he now symbolizes not just a particular artist or the artist in general, but the art itself, the force that breathes life into the music, dance, and performances we see and will see. Erik, here, is no mere mortal; he is the spirit of art that tempts us all, honors a few, and must eventually leave even the most talented. He is the music of the night.

The Invisible Phantom: Joseph Robinette and Robert Chauls's *Phantom of the Opera* (1992)

Perhaps also inspired by the popularity of the Lloyd Webber musical, Joseph Robinette and Robert Chauls's *Phantom of the Opera* offers a musical adaptation that follows the Gaston Leroux novel much more closely than the Lloyd Webber version. Rather than concentrating on the technical effects of the Phantom's lair, these collaborators spend their time on the script, expanding it in unique ways. Their emphasis is on the class distinctions that were prevalent in the novel, but not as pronounced in other versions. In the end, however, the specter of the Lloyd Webber musical haunts this version. It is very difficult to respond to this version without comparing it to the Lloyd Webber extravaganza.

The play begins with the usual appointment of the new Opera managers, their opening night festivities, the performance by Christine, and the obligatory rivalry between Carlotta and Christine, as well as a number of unusual misunderstandings. Unlike other versions, Christine and Raoul do not share a childhood, so there is considerable effort and time placed on establishing the love interest between this couple. Raoul, moreover, mistakenly assumes that the Persian is the Phantom, so there is some time spent developing that difference.

The usual difficulties arise with the opera box, the Phantom's salary, and the Christine-Carlotta rivalry. This version presents an unusual twist in the salary negotiations. In previous versions, the Phantom's salary has gone towards his music and, presumably, the poor people who live in the underworld with him, the lost souls who have been marginalized from the upper world. Here, however, it is clear that the Phantom's salary has put a strain on the livelihoods of the arts, so the new opera owners offer

the artists raises when they stop paying off Erik. To complicate this econ-
omy further, we later learn that the Phantom has adopted Madame Giry
and her daughter, generously helping them survive the often brutal world
of opera. The economic pie in the artistic world is clearly limited. When
the owners punish Giry for her affiliation with the Phantom, which they
think is just a means of taking money from the opera, they force her to
take on the duties of Yvette, a lowly cleaning lady. Yvette, in turn, is
given greater status, dressed in fine clothes, and invited to the opera.
When the chandelier falls, it is Yvette who is killed, not a pretentious
first-time opera patron, as in the novel. In this version, perhaps as a
result of monetary limitations, the chandelier's collapse occurs offstage
and is reported to us rather than staged. Be that as it may, the Phantom's
actions and the owners' responses are clearly connected, perhaps illustrating that we are all, indeed, connected. There are consequences to
treating people badly, for both the owners and the Phantom. And dressing up a cleaning lady in fine clothes will not make her an artist, and
dressing down an artist will not make her a cleaning lady.

The remaining action of the musical focuses on the relationship
between Christine and Raoul. Erik's ambivalence and Christine's struggle between the two men is gone. We hear that Christine reminds Erik
of an early love, the Shah's daughter, which further highlights the interchangeability of women in this version. They are one and the same in
this world, Giry, Yvette, Christine, and the Persian princess. In the final
scene of the musical, Christine is forced to make the usual choice: marry
Erik or Raoul. And like the novel, her decision to marry Raoul will result
in the destruction of the Opera House. Raoul gives a surprisingly selfish
speech urging her to choose him: "The Opera House can be rebuilt.
Mortar and stone are expendable. Ideals and principles are not. Say 'no,'
Christine. If we cannot be together in this life, we shall surely be joined
in the next" (111). On the one hand, the sentiments are noble. Stand for
your truths and your love. But on the other, the entire fate of the musical arts of Paris will be sacrificed on the altar of a domestic romance.
The musical only raises this issue, but clearly sides with romance. All of
civilization should be cast aside for the true love that occurs between these
young people. Romance is all.

In an uncharacteristic *deus ex machina* moment, Christine says "No"
to the Phantom, "Yes" to Raoul, and throws a conveniently placed bottle of chlorophorm in Erik's face, which blinds him but somehow does

not render him unconscious. Raoul and the Persian have a chance to save themselves, the Opera House, their ideals, and their ideologies, but they do not manage to save Christine, who is once again abducted by Erik. Conveniently, however, the men are armed, give a quick chase, and in two bullets' time, they solve the problem by killing off the Phantom, who dies saying the name of his beloved. Christine and Raoul sing a song about their eternal and immortal love, and the musical ends with the Phantom at the center of the tableau, "The lights fade slowly, leaving Erik in the spotlight" (115). Ironically, it is an Erik we never had the opportunity to meet. We do not understand his obsession with the princess nor his transference of his affections to Christine. We do not understand his musical passion and power, so in many ways, this version presents a truly phantom Phantom.

CHAPTER 4

Variations on the Theme: Novels and Miscellaneous Versions of *The Phantom of the Opera*

> For all the women who thought Christine should have stayed
> with the Phantom...
> — Colette Gale's Dedication to *An Erotic Novel*
> *of "The Phantom of the Opera"*

The Phantom of the Opera's persistence is nowhere more pronounced than in the novel industry that has sprung up around the Phantom's tale. Perhaps inspired by Leroux, perhaps inspired by the Lloyd Webber version, whatever the case, there are a good many offerings when it comes to Phantom variations in novels. One look at Amazon.com, however, reveals that many of these novels are self-published works, representing one of the newer trends in entertainment and publication. Thanks to computer technology, particularly desktop affordability, publication costs have decreased, enabling many to publish works on their own at their own expense. Though vanity presses have been around for many years, the Internet now offers many self-published authors a good deal of marketing assistance from sites such as Amazon, which collects a small fee for books sold through its website.

Clearly interest in the *Phantom* is not subsiding, and the sheer volume of self-published works illustrates the resiliency of the *Phantom* tale and the passion with which its readers and viewers respond to the narrative. It is also important to note that Erik's seduction moves beyond the pages of novels, beyond the films, and well beyond the Leroux original.

Most of the self-published works choose to continue the story, perhaps in the hope of reliving the Leroux narrative in their own way. That is, Erik is no longer a character in a novel or film, written or adapted by someone else; in the hands of these authors, he becomes one with them, creating a sort of literary romance between author and character. Debra P. Whitehead's *Into the Light: A Phantom of the Opera Story* (2006) takes up where the story leaves off, with Erik wandering into the night, the police in pursuit, Russians to come, a murder to commit, and a higher purpose to find. Shirley Yoshinaka's *Deception: A Phantom of the Opera Novel* (2006) and Jodi Leisure Minton's *Darkness Brings the Dawn: Erik's Story* (2006) also offer a follow-up to the events of the novel and films. And while most receive supportive online reviews, Minton's work is universally condemned for sloppy editing, spelling, and storytelling, perhaps a casualty to her passion for the Phantom.

The reviews are also worth a look, and many of them offer straightforward advice in a chatty, homey tone. One reviewer, "Kittypro" from Texas, for example, noted that one *Phantom* sequel not only contained a misspelling in the title, but admitted:

> ...the main thing that bothers me about this book is the way the characters TALK to each other. For instance, wouldn't it be more likely someone would say, "He bled to death" rather than "He exsanguinated"? This book is full of florid vocabulary like this, and I'm sorry, but even in the 19th century, I doubt people spoke to each other with such pompous, contrived language.

Dawn A. Skinner from Michigan writes of another version, "Bad, bad, bad, bad." While others applaud novel plots twists and new authors, also mentioning that "free shipping" accompanied a particular version. According to Amazon's list, there are over a dozen such novels, and though I will not discuss any of the self-published versions, the phenomenon of self-publication and *The Phantom* is a noteworthy one. As both novels and their online critics illustrate, the Phantom story continues to appeal to audiences. It piques imagination, curiosity, and creativity. And given the recent reports from the National Endowment for the Arts' grim statistics on reading fiction for pleasure, it is refreshing to see such an interest in a particular narrative from both professionals and amateurs. In some strange way, the Phantom's unrequited love, unfinished symphony, and unclear conclusion generate rather than negate creative responses. Leroux's story continues to birth others, some fully-formed, some deformed.

With the publication of the more conventionally published novels, Susan Kay's *Phantom*, Frederick Forsyth's *Phantom of Manhattan*, R.L. Stine's *Phantom of the Auditorium*, and Colette Gale's erotic version, *The Phantom of the Opera* gains great literary ground and respectability. With these novels, *Phantom* joins a long line of literary classics with companion pieces. Jean Rhys, for example, wrote *Wide Sargasso Sea* (1966), her imaginative retelling of Charlotte Brontë's novel *Jane Eyre* (1847), from the perspective of the madwoman in the attic, a fairly minor character in the Brontë novel who becomes a feminist cause in Rhys's hands. Others include John C. Gardner's retelling of the poem *Beowulf* from the perspective of the monster in *Grendel* (1971), and Robert Louis Stevenson's *Dr. Jekyll and Mr. Hyde* (1866) and *Mary Reilly* (1990), a reworking of the story from the maid's perspective by Valerie Martin. Perhaps the most famous adaptation/revision of this kind is Tom Stoppard's *Rosencrantz and Guildenstern are Dead* (1967), a reworking of Shakespeare's *Hamlet* from the perspective of Hamlet's school friends and in the tradition of absurdist playwright Samuel Beckett's *Waiting for Godot* (1952). And though not every *Phantom* version has attained such success, they are worth reading in order to appreciate more fully the narrative that continues to delight audiences into the twenty-first century.

Given the novel form, moreover, these works can offer extensive retellings, sequels, or reinventions of the Phantom that could not be done on stage or on screen.

The story's return to novel form, after many years outside of the genre, suggests a resurrection of the Phantom myth, a rebirth and a return to its familiar generic literary expectations which at once comfort and confront audience expectations. Susan Kay's novel *Phantom* (1991) offers lengthy details on Erik's past and his time in Persia in order to humanize and help us understand his motivations and his struggles. In Frederick Forsyth's *Phantom of Manhattan* (1999), a sequel to the Leroux story, we learn that Erik did not die at the end of the story, but instead made his way to New York City, where he is currently running a successful entertainment empire. Erik, with his demons and his demonizing, is humanized, rationalized, and analyzed.

With this shift in focus and perspective, Christine's relationship with Erik also changes, and, perhaps coming as a shock to *Phantom* purists, she actually consummates her relationship with Erik in some of these versions. In Collette Gale's erotic version, there is more than consummation. There is lots and lots of sex, and if it were ever to be made into a movie, it would receive an NC-17 rating.

As a result of these retellings, we begin to feel for the "masked man" perhaps more deeply than in other versions, perhaps as a result of the return to its original generic form. Erik is no longer "other," an outsider, a mystery or cipher; he is one of us, struggling against the prejudices of his age and the longings of his heart and soul. In addition to masking his deformity, he wears the mask to hide his desires from himself, as well as hiding his desires from the world. In this novel form once again, Erik becomes a symbol for the rebel, a renegade who fights for the rights of the eccentric and the disfigured in a world that increasingly values physical perfection and intellectual and political conformity. He challenges us to look beneath the mask. He continues to embody the "music of the night" as opposed to the spectacle of day, but in these longer novelistic versions, which are also influenced by their film and stage versions, we see Erik perhaps more deeply than ever before. These novels, after all, are not only influenced by Leroux but the adaptations, so there is a great generative power among versions, creating and recreating the Phantom beyond the original conception embodied in the Leroux novel.

The Donald Barthelme short story, however, returns the Phantom to his role of symbol, mysterious cipher. The Phantom in his story barely appears, and we are treated to a description of what it would be like to be the Phantom's friend. Barthelme humorously concludes that it cannot be easy, but as this study has shown, it may be difficult, but getting to know the Phantom is definitely worth the effort, and it will continue to be for many readers and audiences in the future. Because the Phantom challenges us to see our worlds differently, to listen to the music of the night, and to participate in art, in many ways, as audience and as authors.

The Romantic Phantom: Susan Kay's *Phantom* (1991)

Susan Kay's *Phantom* (1991) was inspired by the Andrew Lloyd Webber musical, as well as other variations. Interestingly, the novel went out of print for awhile, and it was rereleased in 2005 by a self-publishing company, thereby affording Kay the dubious distinction of having a book printed by a traditional publisher and then the increasingly popular self-publishing industry, thereby existing in both realms of *Phantom* novel existence. The phenomenon also indicates the persistent popularity of romances based on the *Phantom* theme. As the current publishing house Llumina's website indicates, "In its original printings in the early 1990s, *Phantom* sold over 80,000 copies in hardcover and over 600,000 in paperback versions.... The original publishers were Transworld (in the UK), Random House, and Bantam/Doubleday/Dell. The novel won the prestigious British Romantic Novel of Year in 1991." With this new publishing trend, a popular book can literally never go out of print.

Using the luxury of time and space provided by the novel form, Kay provides an exhaustive interpretation of the Leroux story, filling in the gaps she perceives in Leroux and the musical version. As Hogle notes, "This novel depends on enough familiarity with *The Phantom of the Opera* tradition, at least by way of the musical" (*Undergrounds* 215). As a structural nod in the direction of the *Phantom's* operatic origins, Kay structures her novel musically. There is, for example, the opening chapter which is told from Erik's mother's perspective. In effect, it is her solo, her aria. The next section is again told in first-person, this time from Erik's perspective. The third section is told from the perspective of an Italian architect, Giovanni, who meets Erik in Rome. The fourth section is told by Nadir, a friend from Erik's Eastern travels, commonly known as "the Persian" in other versions. The fifth section is told by Erik at a later date, after his departure from the Orient. The sixth section is titled, "Counterpoint: Erik and Christine 1881," a section in which both characters have the opportunity to speak. This is, in effect, a verbal "duet" between Erik and Christine, with the narratives intertwined. Each character, each narrative, however, retains independence, and the compilation results in a compelling story, just as such strategies result in beautiful music. The final section is told from Raoul's perspective. In the end, the novel, like many of the other versions and the Leroux novel itself, is about the choice between passion and convention, as well as the love and sacrifice involved in both. It is also a romance novel, complete with exotic places, erotic moments, and all-too convenient coincidences that conspire to highlight the enduring power of romantic love. And like so many versions before it, Kay's novel challenges us to see beyond the superficialities of life — in this case, very literally, to see beyond the Lloyd Webber narrative, and to value the "music of the night" which underscores our world of light and sight. More than any other narrative thus far, Kay's offers, for example, more detail regarding the psychological motivations and reasons behind some of the characters' behaviors.

In the opening section, "Madeline," it is clear that Erik was a much-wanted child, and the pregnancy was the result of a happy union between Madeline and her husband. Unlike the other versions which portray Erik's mother as delinquent or distressed by the pregnancy, Madeline is overjoyed by the event. She is also a "good pregnant mother," not prone to abortifacients, drugs, or alcohol. Unfortunately, fate, the prime mover of romance novels, intervenes, and her beloved husband is killed prior to the birth of the child. When Erik is born, he is, of course, disfigured. Her description of the baby immediately following birth moves us to pity. Moreover, the scene is characterized by silence, an ironic choice, given Erik's later passion for sound and music:

> I did not scream; none of us screamed. Not even when we saw it make a feeble movement and we realized that it wasn't dead. The sight of the thing that lay upon the sheet was so unbelievable that it denied all power of movement to the vocal chords. We only stared, the three of us, as though we expected our combined dumbstruck horror to melt this harrowing abomination back into the realm of nightmare where it surely belonged [4].

Madeline is so shocked and so repulsed by her son, she suggests letting him die of neglect. The priest in her town advises her to love the child "as God does" (7). But she cannot, and though she sees her own cruelty, she cannot bring herself to love the creature, even going so far as to allow him to sleep with the family dog, who loves him more than any in the household.

In addition to treating him like an animal, she isolates Erik. As he grows older, she keeps him from the outside world for his protection and her reputation. She realizes, however, that this strategy ultimately leaves her imprisoned as well: "I felt as though I had been sealed up in a tomb to serve the corpse of a child-pharaoh in its afterlife" (28). Townspeople who do catch a glimpse of Erik make the family's life miserable, throwing rocks through their windows and writing threatening notes.

For awhile, however, Erik appreciates the domestic fortress, and his genius thrives in the isolation. The son of an artist and a creative mother, Erik also demonstrates an unusual ability for architecture. Most importantly, he begins to sing, not only beautifully but seductively. His mother believes that any woman who hears his voice will not "die in a state of grace" (30). And though she cannot love Erik like a son, his voice and its strange power entrap her in some oddly sexual way. This paradox, Erik's physical deformity combined with his erotic power over women through sound, explains the many Christines in the past — who can resist the transcendent nature of music? But Madeline herself is a paradox, for though she is attracted to the music Erik makes, she is sometimes cruel, highlighting his deformity, not his musical powers. When, for example, she finally shows him his face when he is five years old, she realizes that she has "scarred him for life" (41).

Her confidante and helper, the local priest, believes the young boy is educable and worthy. He begins training Erik's voice for God and his mind for architecture with the help of another tutor. The domestic pressures, however, increase when Madeline begins a romance with a new doctor in the village. Erik, of course, is jealous, and he attempts to thwart the relationship. Behaving as many children do, Erik torments the doctor, and the doctor, rather than responding as a mature adult, torments him in return. In the end, the doctor proposes that Madeline commit Erik to an asylum for his own good, as well as the good of the community and their love. On the one hand, the doctor helps Madeline remove herself from the power that Erik has over her, a sort of aural incest, but on the other, the doctor's desires are unclear, as are Madeline's. There is, for example, some suggestion that the young doctor may be using the beautiful young widow for personal gain. In the meantime, Erik overhears the plans to have him put away, so he runs away from home, feeling unloved and unwanted. And unbeknownst to him, at least until much later in the novel, his mother does not marry the doctor. Instead, she lives her life cloistered in their little home, perhaps awaiting Erik's return and the opportunity to make amends.

Like Joseph Merrick in Bernard Pomerance's play *The Elephant Man* (1979), Erik is captured by a disreputable man, Javert, who puts him on display as part of his gypsy caravan. Erik is treated like an animal and part of the "freak show," until it becomes apparent that he can sing, as well as repel people with his monstrous features. He negotiates a deal with his captor that wins him more freedom and some luxuries. Also during this time, Erik learns herbal and healing arts from an old woman in the caravan, as well as magical skills. Through these negotiations, as well as his mistreatment, Erik also learns about power, how to use it, how to wield it over others, how to manipulate it, and how life is lived without it.

In the end, there is one more lesson in power that Erik learns from this time with the gypsy caravan — sexual power. As Erik matures and becomes more popular, Javert becomes more threatened. After a night of drinking, Javert attempts to rape Erik. Erik, however, has also been trained in the art of knife use by his other gypsy friends, friends that appear to like him for who he is. Luckily for Erik, unluckily for Javert, Erik uses this knife training to fend off Javert's advances. Upon killing his captor and potential rapist, Erik escapes from the gypsy caravan with his virtue intact.

The next chapter in Erik's life brings greater creativity and culture. He is discovered by a reputable mason in Rome whose own life was marred by the lack of a male heir to carry on his family trade. With many daughters and a disappointing number of apprentices, Giovanni welcomes Erik to his home when he discovers the young man's architectural and intellectual abilities. Erik's prior training in architecture and masonry made him the perfect pupil for Giovanni, the narrator of this chapter. All would have worked out well between the two men, if it were not for Giovanni's beautiful, ethereal daughter, Luciana, his last born. She and Erik become infatuated with one another, though Erik tries to resist. On a fateful night, on a rooftop in Rome, Luciana demands that he remove his mask. When he does, she cries out in horror only to fall to her death as a result of a crumbling balustrade. Again, Erik must flee for his life.

The next section brings Erik to Persia, told from the perspective of an admirable character named Nadir. Nadir's relationship with Erik is complicated by the Shah and the political demands and intrigues of a corrupt court. The Shah has heard of a great magician, Erik, and sends Nadir to bring him to the court. Nadir leaves his ailing son to persuade Erik to come to Persia. Erik comes to the court and establishes himself as an important confidante to the Shah and his manipulative and cruel mother. The Shah's mother makes Erzsebet Bathory, the "bloody countess," look like Florence Nightingale. Manipulated by the mother through drugs, sex, and power, Erik agrees to use his creative abilities for evil, rather than good. He constructs methods of torture for the Shah's mother to use on innocent young women in the court. Rewarded with money and hashish, Erik becomes an irrational, violent drug addict. At this point in the novel, Erik is at his worst. As Nadir observes, Erik even kills for pleasure using the mirror room and the Punjab lasso:

Before he came to Persia and fell under her malevolent influence, I do not believe that Erik had ever killed purely for pleasure. But with her drugs and her insatiable demand for novelty she awakened his sleeping hatred of men, releasing a demon of savage ingenuity which he could no longer control [251–252].

The only joy in his life is a palace he is constructing and his friendship with Nadir's ailing son, Reza. Using the herbal remedies he learned from the gypsies, Erik manages to prolong the boy's life, but ultimately, he can only provide the boy with a peaceful death, one that is free of pain and suffering. Much to the father's dismay, he is forced to agree and allows Erik to kill his own son in a humane manner. With the death of Nadir's son, the chapter winds up quickly, with political powers shifting after the death of the Shah. Erik falls out of favor and leaves quickly and in disgrace.

The next section follows the previous one chronologically, but the story is now told from Erik's perspective. Haunted by the deaths of Luciana and Reza, Erik accepts his destiny, to be alone. He also discovers that his mother has died, and he realizes that his reason for leaving in the first place was founded on false pretenses. His mother never married, as he presumed. She remained faithful to her son.

While visiting his childhood home, he learns that there is a competition to design and construct a new Opera House in Paris. This opportunity is too good to miss; it unites his two loves, music and architecture. He meets with the architect, Charles Garnier, the real architect of the Paris Opera House, and proposes his ideas. In the end, Kay suggests that Erik creates the Paris Opera House through Garnier. He is, in effect, the "ghost architect."

Through the numerous trials and tribulations of construction and war, Erik survives, manages to complete the Opera House, and then takes on his role as the Opera Ghost, never to live above ground again. His friend Nadir reappears. And he discovers Christine, the young singer who had a "perfect instrument" but "lacked the inner will to play it" (382). He is determined to be her angel of music, and as the chapter ends, "wherever this shadowed path might lead, we were both irrevocably committed to follow to it to the end" (388).

The next chapter, "Counterpoint," includes perspectives from both Christine and Erik. It follows the Leroux version very closely: the diva, Christine's triumph, the time in the underworld, and the complicated love triangle. And once again, as a result of Christine's desire and curiosity about Erik, his intellect, and his passion, the narrative is much more successful and suspenseful. In this version, Christine's interest in music is secondary to her interest in Erik and his musical and passionate prowess. Unlike other versions, with the exception of Dario Argento's *Phantom* (1998), this Christine consummates her relationship with Erik as a result of his moving musical composition, *Don Juan Triumphant*. She regrets the fall, and she wishes that she would have never met Erik and lived a "simple, cheerful normal love" with Raoul.

Confused and shocked by her own passion, Christine returns to Raoul, which infuriates Erik. He rages, and as in many other versions, threatens to kill Raoul if Christine remains with him. And Christine, like many others, calms him with a kiss, making him realize that he does, in fact, love her, and this love enables him to sacrifice his desires for hers. He disappears, leaving Christine and Raoul with their new life.

In the final chapter, we meet Raoul with his sixteen-year-old son, Charles. They are attending the opera. Charles is especially gifted musically, and the proud heir to the DeChagny clan. We learn, however, that the child is not Raoul's — he is Erik's. Unable to have children of his own as a result of a dueling injury, Raoul raised Erik's son with Christine as his own. Perhaps moved by his love of Christine, as well as Erik's music and mystery, Raoul loves this child: "This brilliant, loving boy, who calls me father in his innocence, has taught me so many things I might never have grasped about love. I see the world through his eyes now, I glimpse my appointed place in the grand order of things. Like a weary sparrow I can look with fond pride on the giant I have raised as my own" (528). He even raises the child after Christine's early death. In this way, the novel absolves Christine of her indiscretion. The love between Erik and Christine creates a new love and new life, not dissension and disability. It has taught Erik to love less selfishly. It has taught Raoul to love differently. And perhaps it may inspire some to live, love, and look differently.

Admittedly Kay relies on coincidences, untold past events, and the heavy hand of fate, but she offers us an interesting perspective and some explanation for many of the details of Erik's life left open or unexplained in the Leroux novel. And while certainly the mystery behind the Phantom is what gives it its life, Kay's job as a romance writer is to wrap matters up for us, to answer our questions. Here the satisfaction of the

Phantom is not his symbolic nature, but the explanations for his behavior. It is as if Kay were functioning as the Phantom's psychologist, bringing the true nature of events and repressed information to the surface. Here then, the surface is what Kay creates, and by association, we see that there was an underworld that needed to be explored. In this way, though Kay answers many questions about the Phantom, the fact that she answers them indicates that the questions existed in the first place. And to bring matters to their natural romantic conclusion, Kay also offers us something the Leroux novel and many of the other more symbolic and figurative versions could not — a happy ending, perhaps not for Erik, but for the many people in his life.

Taking a Bite Out of the Big Apple: Frederick Forsyth's *The Phantom of Manhattan* (1999)

Best known for his documentary thriller *Day of the Jackal* (1971), which some compare to Truman Capote's *In Cold Blood* (1966), Frederick Forsyth both deviates from and builds upon his traditional "nonfiction novel" form in his *The Phantom of Manhattan* (1999). Set in Manhattan during 1906, this version is a very readable and exciting sequel to the Leroux novel, illustrating Erik's life after his departure from Christine and Raoul in the underground caverns of the Paris Opera House. Forsyth credits his conversations with Andrew Lloyd Webber with inspiring his work. As Terry Byrne notes, Lloyd Webber and Forsyth worked together on the film version of *The Odessa File* (1974), for which Lloyd Webber wrote the music: "It's easy to imagine the cocktail party where the two men started talking about what fun it would be to put together a *Phantom* sequel." It is also safe to conclude that Forsyth, too, hoped to capitalize on the Lloyd Webber musical's popularity. And though it may be coincidental, the novel itself is also organized similarly to Susan Kay's *Phantom*, with each chapter offering the observations by various characters including Erik himself in order to provide "first hand" narratives which taken together tell the complete, and given the verisimilitude of the characters, the "real" story of Erik's survival.

Ultimately, the book contains many of the same themes as the Leroux and Lloyd Webber works, and those who enjoy the Lloyd Webber musical will be pleased to see the Lloyd Webber "Masquerade" and the toy monkey-music box included in this version. The usual themes of greed, love, sacrifice, and the tensions between passion and convention, what we see and what is true, are apparent as well, but this version provides us with a look at Erik as a parent, an interesting perspective on the *Phantom* narrative. Not only do we get an idea of Erik behind the mask, but we see him interacting with his offspring as well.

The book begins with rather off-putting and condescending analysis of the Leroux novel by Forsyth in the preface. Forsyth criticizes Leroux:

> The basic idea is there and it is brilliant but the way poor Gaston tells it is a mess. He begins with an introduction, above his own name, claiming that every line and word is true. Now that is a very dangerous thing to do. To claim quite clearly that a work of fiction is absolutely true and therefore a historical record is to offer oneself as a hostage to fortune on every single claim made that can be checked must be absolutely true [xx].

The criticism is understandable coming from Forsyth, who is a researcher and creator of what he and his critics call "faction," a "blend of truth and invention" (xx). Ironically, however, his style is closer to the investigative reporting that Leroux not only did himself as a journalist but also the style he imitates in his fictional tale. This parallel may prompt Forsyth to criticize Leroux so harshly; they both work in the same business of reportage.

The criticism, however, overlooks the fictional narrative stance of the Leroux novel. The narrator pretends to be a journalist, but in fact is not one, though the author is. Again, this rather tangled relationship between the narrator and author is complicated further when the reader presumes that the narrator and the author are one and the same. Further, Forsyth overlooks the literary convention popular during the nineteenth century, particularly in gothic horror stories such as Bram Stoker's *Dracula* (1897), which uses numerous diaries, journal entries, and newspaper clippings to give his unbelievable tale some credibility. Henry James's *Turn of the Screw* (1898), too, uses this method, arguing that the story of the governess and the young children in her care is a true one — the narrator, after all, is reading from her journal. Such conventions are common and effective in literature, and there are few who demand rigorous documentation of these fictional facts.

Forsyth's need to point out the weaknesses of the original novel, moreover, neglects to highlight the universality of the story, as well as its continued appeal. There is something about this story which prompts readers and writers to review it and perhaps even rewrite it. Forsyth need not "set the record straight" and attempt to write a better book than Leroux, which is debatable finally, but instead, merely indicate his interest in the story from his perspective or from the perspective of a sequel. Ultimately, Forsyth credits Andrew Lloyd Webber with the narrative's continued success. Without the musical, he argues, the narrative would have died. Perhaps that is true, but if the narrative were not as compelling, not even Andrew Lloyd Webber could have resurrected the Leroux novel.

With the unfortunate preface aside, the story begins, and it is a compelling read. We begin at the deathbed of Madame Giry, who wishes to make not only a confession but to have a document delivered to Erik Mulheim, the subject of her confession. According to Giry, she served as Erik's mother for most of his life. As she tells her confessor, a young French priest, she found the unfortunate and disfigured boy performing in a freak show in France. She rescued the boy, and she raised him as her own. She also tells the cleric about the love between Erik and Christine, as well as Erik's noble decision to release Christine to Raoul. Since that time Christine and Raoul have married, and Erik, pursued for several murders at the Opera House, escaped France and is now living in New York City. At death's door, Giry realizes that she must communicate a secret, a secret that she has kept for many years, before she dies. She writes these details in a mysterious letter which she asks the young priest to deliver to this equally mysterious Erik Mulheim.

While the young priest, Armand Dufour, makes his way to New York, we learn, through several intervening chapters, that Giry helped Erik escape, and he landed in New York and began a career in the carnival world of Coney Island, a place where a mask would not bring suspicion. It is one of the perfect sites for Erik to hide, and it also marks a return to his childhood experiences in the freak show.

Throughout the years, he eventually comes to design amusement parks, and he makes a great deal of money doing so. At this point in his life, he has a Howard Hughes-like persona, successful but eccentric and isolated. One of his henchman, Darius, is not only unreliable, but as we find out through his discussions, he is literally in league with the devil. In this way, Forsyth resurrects the Faustian themes of *Phantom*, which have been buried under the voluminous psychoanalytical analyses in other versions that have humanized and domesticated Erik. We may realize through this version that the story may work more effectively if he is not "like everyone else," if he is in some ways different from us.

In this case, however, Erik is the potential victim, not the perpetrator of evil. This deal that Darius has made requires that he keep Erik under his spell, while pretending to serve. With no heir to the entertainment fortune accrued by Erik, both Erik and Darius decide that Darius will inherit the wealth upon Erik's death. All of these plans and assumptions, of course, are soon to be challenged by the mysterious letter from Madame Giry.

Armand Dufour, the priest who was unlucky enough to be on call when Madame Giry made her confession, finally makes his way to New York, a city he hates (30). After several false starts, he finally meets a very enterprising reporter who helps him find the mysterious Erik Mulheim. The reporter, of course, hopes for a story, but after the letter is delivered, the story is squelched because Erik has "his people" call the reporter's "people" in order to silence any observations about the eccentric millionaire.

Initially, the contents of the letter seem as mysterious unveiled as they were veiled, but it soon becomes clear that Raoul is not the father of Christine's child. As in the Susan Kay version, the child that Christine has is Erik's, and Giry's sin was not telling Erik earlier. Erik, however, holds no grudges against one of the only women who ever loved and cared for him. Instead, he is convinced that he will not only meet Christine again, but that he will attain a certain level of immortality and power through this child he sired years ago. He says, for example:

> But even if I am repulsed yet again [by Christine], everything has changed. I can look down from this high eyrie onto the heads of that human race I so loathe, but now I can say: You can spit on me, defile me; jeer at me, revile me; but nothing you can do will hurt me now. Through the filth and through the rain, through the tears and through the pain, my life's not been in vain; *I have a son* [95].

Given Erik's obsession with composing *Don Juan Triumphant* in the Leroux and the Lloyd Webber versions, a composition that would bring him immortality and fame in the world of opera, it is no surprise that he envisions his offspring as yet another opportunity for immortality.

Using an inspired setting, the hall of mirrors at Coney Island,

Forsyth stages the Erik-Christine reunion. Appearances, as we have seen repeatedly throughout the *Phantom* stories, are not what they seem. And what better place to stage this theme but a hall of mirrors? Christine just so happens to be in New York, singing in an opera. Erik proposes reconciliation, but Christine, who is still in love with Raoul, refuses Erik's advances. Then Erik asks for his son, Pierre, and Christine is not only shocked by the fact that he knows the truth about their son, but she is also concerned that Erik is an inappropriate father. She stalls, telling Erik that he may have the boy when he is eighteen, five more years. Erik, of course, agrees during his discussion with Christine, but he immediately begins to develop a scheme to abduct his son right away. He will not wait patiently during the remaining years.

In the meantime, God makes an appearance in the novel, as the devil did in an earlier scene in which we discover Darius's true nature — a man who has made a deal with the devil at the expense of another human being, Erik. God, of course, does not embody the message of greed and selfishness. Instead, during this interlude God shows incredible understanding for human frailty, as well as reminding Pierre's tutor and priest that Erik is a man who "hates himself" and loves another man's wife (130). So any reconciliation between the boy and his father should be entered into cautiously.

The book's climax is related some forty years later by the news reporter whose story was squelched by Erik's public relations people. He now teaches journalism at Columbia University. During a lecture, he discusses one of the most important moments in his journalistic career — the meeting between Erik and Pierre. Going against the advice of both her priest and her husband Raoul, Christine agrees to meet Erik with her son at New York's Battery Park so that the two might meet one another. When the husband and priest realize that Christine is away, the journalist steps in and admits that he has been shadowing the reclusive Erik, so he, in fact, knows where the three are meeting. Within moments, all are assembled at Battery Park.

Darius, in the meantime, has realized that Pierre's existence thwarts his inheritance plans and, consequently, his own deal with the devil. He attempts to shoot Pierre, but Christine intercepts the bullet, saving her son, but is mortally wounded in the process. Erik, who shoots with the accuracy of a marksman, kills Darius immediately.

During her final moments, Christine, like Giry, admits that Erik is

Pierre's father, and offers Pierre the chance to choose between the two men. In this way, Forsyth offers a masculine revision of the usual *Phantom* story. It is not Christine who must choose, but her young son. In another revisionist moment, the young boy, not Christine, removes the Phantom's mask. And whether Forsyth intends it or not, there is a bit of gender difference underscored here. Rather than screaming in horror, as every Christine for the last nearly 100 years has done, this young man feels compassion immediately. Of course, the reasons behind this difference are numerous. On the one hand, Pierre may be responding sympathetically to Erik as his father, not a stranger who has abducted him or is about to abduct him. On the other, he could be seeing himself, his own facial features or emotional makeup, in the distorted face of his father. There may be more interpretations of this moment, but it is noteworthy in its emphasis on gender difference. Pierre, moreover, decides to stay with Erik, not Raoul, arguing that Erik needs him more than Raoul does. Pierre thanks his stepfather for his love and support in the past. Raoul, clearly moved by the loss, decides to return to "take the only woman I ever loved back to lie in the soil of France" (171).

In the end, the father-son relationship between Erik and Pierre is quite successful. They both run the entertainment corporation, and, perhaps as a result of the absence of Darius's influence, use their enormous wealth for philanthropic purposes, particularly building hospitals for the disfigured as well as homeless children. As the reporter tells us, during the Second World War, the family changed their name from Mulheim to "another, still widely known and respected in America to this day" (176). Admittedly, our sympathies are with Erik and his son, but it is difficult not to feel for Raoul as well, a cuckolded man who had raised Pierre faithfully for many years. The novel also supports the cultural assumption regarding a natural emotional affinity between biological parents and children, since Pierre so willingly relinquishes the man he has known as father for his entire life for a man he has just met but who is actually his biological father. With Christine out of the way, moreover, the novel not only erases the mother's wishes, but replaces the mother with the male philanthropists who serve as figurative mothers to the community, nurturing the needs of New York. Furthermore, the novel eases the tensions between the conventional and the unconventional, between the good and the bad, the passionate and the domestic, because in this new American world, the two are intertwined. God and

Satan live side by side. The entertainment industry provides Erik a way to express his passions in a very lucrative and socially acceptable way, not hidden in the underground of the opera house. In this way, the novel may ultimately demonstrate the effects of capitalism on the *Phantom* narrative. The subversive ideas are tamed. Even God is proven wrong. Love conquers all. Satan does not succeed. But money continues to flow.

A Chapter Book Phantom: R.L. Stine's *Phantom of the Auditorium* (1994)

R.L. Stine is best known for his *Goosebumps* series for young readers, and his version of *Phantom* represents the growing number of books dedicated to retelling the Leroux novel to younger audiences. His version, published in 1994 under the title *The Phantom of the Auditorium*, is part *Phantom*, part *Hunchback of Notre Dame*, part *Macbeth*, part *The Shining*. It also reflects a children's literature genre known as a "chapter book." Narratives are broken down into discrete chapters, so that children may read a chapter at a time. Stine, however, uses the genre to its greatest advantage, so that every chapter ends with a "cliffhanger." For adult readers, who can probably manage to read this book in one brief sitting, the effect is rather manic. Every chapter builds suspense and every chapter concludes with a surprising revelation, shock, or nail-biting open-ended conclusion. Stine continues to move the story forward, but the effect is one akin to sailing — readers ride the tumultuous narrative waves as they make progress toward the story's final port.

The story itself is an adaptation rather than a retelling of the Leroux novel. Stine borrows heavily from the Leroux work, but he amends certain characters and plot twists to make the story his own. The narrative begins conventionally enough. Students rehearse a play, and they hear rumors of the Phantom. In Stine's version, however, the Phantom multiplies like two mirrors reflecting upon one another: the students perform a play called *Phantom*, which releases the Phantom, which creates Stine's retelling of the Leroux novel. Similar to the frame narratives of such classics as *The Canterbury Tales* or *Wuthering Heights*, Stine's story has narratives to spare, and the effect is to give the impression that his story is the "real" one, while the play version is just a "story."

The play the children perform is a "very scary" one about:

... a man named Carlo who owns a very old theatre where plays and concerts are performed. Carlo thinks the theatre is haunted.

It turns out that there really is a phantom living in the basement. His face is scarred. He looks like a monster. So he wears a mask. But Carlo's daughter Esmeralda falls in love with the Phantom. She plans to run away with him. But her handsome boyfriend, Eric, finds out.

Eric is in love with Esmeralda. He tracks down the Phantom in his secret home in a dark passage far beneath the theatre. They fight. And Eric kills the Phantom.

This breaks Esmeralda's heart. She runs away, never to be seen again. And the Phantom survives as a ghost. He will haunt the theatre forever [22].

Clearly, the Stine version borrows heavily from Victor Hugo's *Hunchback of Notre Dame*, but it is also interesting to note that he forgoes the happy, heterosexual ending, allowing the young woman to remain independent.

The "real" Phantom, the one who is released through the performance of this tale, is more frightening and powerful. Like Shakespeare's *Macbeth*, this play is cursed. As the teacher informs the students, the last time the play was performed, many years ago when the school was originally built, a young boy who was playing the part of the Phantom in the play was never seen again, though a "frightening scream," "like an animal howl," was the last anyone heard of the boy (15). Clearly, there is more at stake than a couple of shivers.

In the end, the two main characters of the "real" story, Zeke and Brooke, explore the basement of the school auditorium, which has many levels never before discovered. Like the underground of the *Phantom of the Opera*, this version has its share of spooky crevices. During their investigations, they meet Emile, the night janitor. Of course, they soon discover that the school does not have a night janitor.

To add to the story's eerie quality and strangeness, a new boy, very interested in drama, arrives at their school. His name is Brian Colson. Brooke befriends him and encourages him to participate in the play. He does and soon joins in the search for the "real" Phantom of the auditorium. Of course, along the way, while exploring, Zeke and Brooke are wrongly accused of vandalism, poor conduct, and breaking and entering. And though the real Phantom, the goal of their journeys and quests, is not found, teacher and parents reasonably excuse the two young people's indiscretion and allow them to participate in the play.

On opening night, Brooke, who plays opposite the Phantom, real-izes that the Phantom is the "real" Phantom, and when she tries to unmask him, he disappears. The play is a huge success, but both Zeke and Brooke know that the Phantom participated. Unable to find their new friend Brian, they realize that someone has tampered with Brooke's locker. Inside is a yearbook from the 1920s, the time the school was orig-inally built. In a moment similar to the conclusion of Stanley Kubrick's version of Stephen King's *The Shining*, in which the crazed Jack Nichol-son appears in a photograph from the hotel's early era, here, too, a photo of their new friend Brian Colson is found in the yearbook. As it turns out, he is the boy who was killed during the original *Phantom* produc-tion.

The story is clearly well-plotted, and it, too, upholds many of the traditional themes illustrated in the more adult versions of *The Phantom of the Opera*. The young people, for instance, find out first-hand that things are not what they seem, and their detective work will help them uncover the truth. Given the age of readership, however, this are no love interests or affairs. The two young people are just friends who want to find out the truth about the play and rumors surrounding the play. It is also reassuring that the parents and teacher, despite their knee-jerk reac-tion to the teens' misbehavior, ultimately allow them to participate in the play. In this way, art's importance is also retained.

A Steamy Phantom: Colette Gale's *Unmasqued: An Erotic Novel of "The Phantom of the Opera"* (2007)

Colette Gale's *Unmasqued: An Erotic Novel of "The Phantom of the Opera"* (2007) is much more adult in content than the R.L. Stine ver-sion, or any version, for that matter. As a matter of fact, moving from the Stine version to the Gale version is a bit like leaving a Disney film to go to a pornographic bookstore. Though a number of the self-pub-lished *Phantoms* indicate that they are romances, and one can assume there is a fair amount of bodice-ripping in any modern romance, no other traditionally published novel has interpreted or retold the *Phan-tom* narrative erotically until Gale's. And it would be a mistake to dis-miss Gale's version as mere Harlequin trash. According to Gale's brief biography, she has written historical fiction in the past, but this novel is her first foray into erotic romance fiction under this pseudonym. According to her website, she confesses that she was always disappointed with the ending of the Leroux narrative, with Christine leaving with Raoul, so she decided to fix this problem by retelling the tale from her perspective, one in which Christine remains with Erik ("Colette Gale"). And as her dedication indicates, she is convinced that there are many women who would agree: "For all the women who thought Christine should have stayed with the Phantom." In addition to this important change in the text, Gale also withholds nothing from the reader regarding the sexual practices, preferences, and partners of many of the characters in the Leroux story. In a word, Erik is not the only character exposed in this novel.

Gale begins her retelling in much the same way that Leroux began his novel, with a claim to verisimilitude. She says that she has gleaned this "true" version of the Phantom narrative through Christine's diaries and other historical documents. In other words, the previous stories have gotten it wrong, and she is out to set the record straight. In addition, she argues that the myth of the monstrous Phantom was created by both Leroux and the Parisian officials to protect the reputations of the Chagny brothers and their royal clan.

Sex, politics, art, and a cover-up? It's beginning to sound like the Kennedy assassination, but it is all part and parcel of the historical romance novel phenomenon. Historical romance novels, like those of Bertice Small, who often writes of the court of King Henry VIII and who praises Gale's book as "erotically wicked" and "spellbinding," follows a very conventional pattern: plot or historical background interspersed at rhythmic intervals with sex. It is, in a way, an imitation of the rhythms of sexual intercourse. Gale's novel, for example, establishes Christine's triumphant singing debut, her new assignment as Juliet in Gounod's opera, the new Opera owners, and the rumors of the Opera Ghost. As she thinks about her debt to the Angel of Music, prepares to perform, and expresses her desire to meet the Phantom in person, he visits her, commanding her to sing for him on this night. Though she does not see him, she feels his body. While wearing his mask, he presses her against her mirror which does not, ironically, enable her to see the man, but instead prohibits identification. She does, however, conclude, "He was a man, perhaps more," and he promises that he will "reward" her for her performance with his "devotion." Of course, Christine sings beautifully, and she is "rewarded" through sexual pleasurings which Gale details. Again, during this encounter, Christine cannot see the Phantom, her "Angel of Music," but his presence definitely enflames her passions through some mutually satisfying sado-masochistic bondage.

Here, then, Gale literalizes the transcendent passions of many of the previous versions. Rather than become soulfully entwined in their music, these modern lovers not only share their love of music, but their love of mutually satisfying sado-maschochistic love play.

Since they did not consummate their love "completely," i.e., through sexual intercourse, Christine's interest is piqued but not satisfied. Enter Raoul. As in the original novel and many subsequent versions, he appears at the opera and sees Christine's triumphant debut. Since they have known each other as children, this meeting offers them a chance to rekindle their relationship. Mistakenly, of course, Christine, whose sexual desires have not been satisfied but only awakened by her meeting with the Phantom, at this moment thinks that Raoul may be a better choice. Unlike the Leroux novel and many of the subsequent versions, female desire here is clearly supported and presented sympathetically. Gale also allows Christine to make her mistakes in choosing love interests.

Many of the women on this stage have power, not just over their careers, but over men. Madame Giry is their teacher: "The theatre was a profession, Madame told them, that allowed a woman quite a bit of control over her life, including her choice of lover or protector — if she was young and pretty, or at least if she was talented both onstage and in the boudoir" (21). Further, she "urged the girls to make their own decisions and taught them how to utilize their feminine power to the best of their ability. And how to be certain they were not gotten with child, what to do if they should" (47). In this version, then, women, as well as men are encouraged to enjoy sex and sexual relations responsibly and frankly. Women, as well as men, have desires and deserve to have those desires fulfilled.

So, when the Phantom leaves Christine unsatisfied following their second meeting, Christine justifies her response to Raoul, thinking, "It was Erik's fault for leaving her wanting more.... Any guilt she may have felt for her response to Raoul's feverish kisses so soon after her intimacy with Erik was quickly dismissed" (32). But, what she realizes through her experiences with both men is that "Raoul did not burn her" (48). It is only Erik who touches her soul, her voice, and her life, and from this

moment on, she remains interested in Erik alone. Her comparison shopping has benefited her.

In preparation for her performance as Marguerite in *Faust*, Erik visits her once again, and this time, they sing together, consummating their
love in breath and music: "She closed her eyes and sang, felt Erik's presence and the gift of beautiful music he awakened within her. She knew
then, in the deepest part of her core, that she could never be without
him" (65–66).

In keeping with the erotic novel genre, even after this level of intimacy, the couple still do not consummate their love sexually, just to keep
us all waiting for "the moment." Again, Erik fondles Christine, admittedly very seductively, not just in front of the mirror, but on it, using it
as a bed upon which he ties the very willing Christine. The image of the
mirror-as-bed is an interesting one because once again, the two lovers are
mingling to such an extent it violates traditional representation, particularly visual representation. In the Leroux novel and other adaptations,
characters walk through the mirror, indicating that the separation has
been broken, perhaps even suggesting sexual intercourse, with the hymen
being broken, as the two enter the deep, wet undergrounds of the Opera
House. Here, the mirror is part of the lovers' play; they express their love
together on the mirror, perhaps taking this image to its logical conclusion,
a conclusion that Gale makes literal in her rendering of the narrative. The
couple do not merely walk through the mirror, they express themselves
on it. They are becoming one; their identities are indistinguishable. At
the same time, it is ironic that the mirror plays such an important role
in their love play, since Christine cannot see Erik's face. Perhaps, in keeping with the *Phantom* narratives in the past, this narrative highlights the
importance of spectacle only to dismiss it once and for all. The couple
do not need to see each other to know that they love one another. But
unlike other versions in which the lovers connect ethereally, these two
connect very physically, ironically without spectacle. As Christine sings
after meeting with Erik, she realizes that she is singing only for him. Gale,
then, makes the mirror image clear: "And she felt as though she and her
angel sang together, somewhere, alone. And joined together as one."

Raoul, of course, interrupts this romance with his own professions
of love, and at this point in the novel, he appears to be a minor nuisance
who would be attractive if it were not for the Phantom, a larger-than-
life creature with whom no man could compete. Raoul, however, is a

man and attempts to seduce Christine, all the while assuming that she will be his wife. Raoul's assumption, though common among men, is clearly presented as presumptuous in this novel. His status and his condescending manner are presented here critically. And while Christine has feelings for him, he does not have the same effect upon her that the Phantom does. She has found her true love and will remain true.

As in many romances, however, the course of true love is frequently challenging. When Christine steps through the mirror and enters Erik's realm, following the chandelier incident, Erik chastises her for allowing another man to touch her. Christine attempts to explain, while Erik tortures her by making her desire him even more, this time using a harp to titillate her until she begs him for sex. Christine also sees his mask for the first time, and the two finally become lovers, completely: "She had never felt so settled and happy since her father had died. Her Angel of Music had turned out to be more than a muse, more than a tutor. He was her love" (143).

This is an erotic romance, so the story does not end here. As the plot continues, the Chagny brothers and their dynasty become more menacing and ultimately violent. Moreover, and as is the case in many of these romances, a secret is revealed. As it turns out, Phillipe, Raoul, and Erik are all brothers, with Erik being the deformed, forgotten brother who, until he falls in love with Christine, has been living contentedly under the Opera House. While determined to have Christine for himself, Raoul is no real threat to the lovers. Rather, Phillipe is the menacing, homicidal presence. He even blames Erik or the "Opera Ghost" for the women he has killed though his deviant sexual behavior, behavior which makes the Marquis de Sade's pale in comparison. Erik kills no one in this version, not even Joseph Buquet, who dies accidentally.

The novel, however, does not tame Erik. Rather his passions run to Christine and music, not violence and death. Even the opera he composes is "beautiful," according to Christine, not the discordant musical monstrosity of previous versions. But like the Eriks before him, he, too, longs for a "normal" life with Christine. And when she removes his mask on their seventh day as lovers, she is shocked and responds as all Christines: "What she saw was horrible—*horrible*—and she screamed as his eyes flew open and he launched himself off the chaise" (157). But unlike other Christines, she realizes immediately that she has "done the unforgivable" (157).

Shocked, overwhelmed, and guilt-ridden, Christine returns to her world, meets Raoul, and succumbs to his seduction, with Erik, of course, watching. While he wails in pain, betrayed by the woman he loves in so many different ways, Christine thinks that marrying Raoul may be the most sensible thing to do: "It was easier, much easier to agree to marry Raoul. To become the Vicomtesse of Chagny. To live a normal life with a man who loved her, and who had nothing to hide. And who did not wear a mask every day" (179).

Of course, the misreading is obvious. For those familiar with the *Phantom* original and variations, everyone wears masks, and though the Leroux novel and many other variations end with a happily-ever-after conclusion for Christine and Raoul, there is little doubt that the world of light and domesticity is easy. There is, after all, always the remembrance of the Phantom, his love, and his sacrifice which makes the sweet conclusion for many versions a bit less satisfying. Here, however, Gale exposes the façades of the ruling class with vigor. Everyone wears a mask, but in the case of the Chagny family, there is more to hide than physical deformity. There is cruelty. In this version the cruelest character is the eldest brother, Phillipe. And what Erik and Christine do not realize is that by separating from one another, they make themselves all the more vulnerable to Phillipe, the novel's true monster.

In addition to preying on the gentry and lower classes to fulfill his and his wife's deviant desires, Phillipe preys on Carlotta, who, up until her relationship with him, is the fun-loving dominatrix of the opera company, frequently finding young, well-endowed men who will do anything for and to her. The rivalry is still present, but Carlotta is not the mean-spirited diva of prior versions. As a matter of fact, after her encounters with the Phillipe, the novel directs our sympathies towards her. Thinking that Phillipe is like other men, who enjoy the sado-masochistic love play that she enjoys, she agrees to meet with him. But Phillipe does not merely perform cruelty, he embodies and embraces it. In addition to other sexual crimes, Phillipe chokes Carlotta so hard that she can never sing again.

Through the course of several encounters and scenes, Phillipe manages to imprison Erik and send Raoul on a wild goose chase so that he may take Christine to his chamber of sexual horrors, a chamber that we have already seen a formidable presence such as Carlotta enter and leave with great pain and horror.

It is Christine that Phillipe wants. She, of course, surpasses all other delights he may have had in the past, and he wants her for his own. At some point, Christine manages to reconnect with Erik, and the two affirm their love for one another, disfigurement or not. Of course, at this moment of reconciliation, Phillipe separates the two and begins his devilish plans to ravish Christine.

Surprisingly, Carlotta comes to the rescue in this version. Having been ravished and abused herself by Phillipe, she escapes from her prison, discovers Erik, as well as Madame Giry, who also tried to help Erik and Christine escape, and the two of them work to free Erik so that he might rescue Christine before Phillipe abuses her. Through juxtaposed scenes, the tension in the novel builds, Christine is rescued, but just as Erik is about to kill Phillipe, she pleads with Erik to let him go, to not become "like him." Of course, this hesitation costs Christine her freedom, because as Phillipe is about to kill Erik, Raoul enters, incapacitates Phillipe, and kidnaps Christine. Carlotta and Madame Giry also enter, and Erik leaves Phillipe in Carlotta's hands.

Through this revision, not only does Erik remain pure — he kills no one, not even his lifelong tormentor — but it also creates an important bond among the female characters. Carlotta and Giry, for example, work together to help Christine and Erik. In the end, Carlotta does what Erik could not, and there is a great deal of satisfaction in her revenge. When Raoul takes Christine, and Erik leaves to rescue her, Giry and Carlotta have Phillipe all to themselves, and he dies a tormented tormentor. As we learn in the epilogue, moreover, Giry, who loves sex, and Carlotta, who loves sex, decide to open a brothel together, and it becomes one of the most famous in Paris and the world. The female bonding, while admittedly unconventional, is refreshing. Women may enjoy sex. Women may enjoy the friendship of other women. And women may honor the love of others. They are not competitive monsters, out for selfish interests. The death of Phillipe, moreover, saves many women from his murderous lust, so Giry and Carlotta are, in fact, helping future female generations.[19]

Returning to Erik, he, of course, pursues Raoul and Christine, but appears to fail. Christine is locked in the room of an inescapable inn, and she collapses from exhaustion, only be awoken by a man in her bed. After a lengthy sex scene, during which the identity of the man in her bed remains unknown, Gale cleverly has Christine ask, "Raoul?" Careless readers might conclude that the man in the bed is Raoul, but careful readers are rewarded: "He's confined to his carriage" (333). Christine is not questioning her lover; she is asking about her captor. Love has triumphed, and like the 1943 version, so does Christine's career. Erik does not demand obeisance. That was for Phillipe, the oppressive sadist. Instead, their love creates. Erik and Christine move to New York, and then to Hollywood. There they meet Lon Chaney, who would star in the movie *The Phantom of the Opera*. Again, Gale mingles old and new, traditional genres and modern technologies.

While certainly an adult version of the familiar tale, the narrative offers a great deal of refreshing revision, particularly from a feminist viewpoint. Female desire is addressed and frequently satiated, and both career and romance exist. They are not mutually exclusive as they are in many versions of *The Phantom*. The lessons from previous *Phantoms* might also be applied to Gale's version — things are not always what they seem. Romances may have some substance.

Phantom of the Short Story: Donald Barthelme's "The Phantom of the Opera's Friend" (1981)

Donald Barthelme's "The Phantom of the Opera's Friend," found in the collection *Sixty Stories* (1981), tells us about the Phantom from a friend's perspective. Of course, given the Phantom's personality, he is not a very close friend. As he admits, he has "never visited" the Phantom's lair, "across the dark lake" (138). He is, however, close enough to observe that while the Phantom is prone to moments of merriment, "it is not often that the accents of joy issue from beneath that mask" (139). And it is no wonder, since the Phantom makes it clear that his life offers limited choices — a life of isolation and loneliness below or a life of ridicule and marginalization above. The Phantom reminisces about his days with Christine, and he has an uncanny sense of his own importance, which his friend dismisses as "fits of grandiosity" (140). The Phantom, for example, often says, "*Between three and four thousand human languages! And I am the Phantom of the Opera in every one of them!*" (141). So it is suitable that this collection conclude with this short story for a number of reasons — its self-reflexive tone, as well as Barthelme's own ambivalent relationship to music, order, and chaos.

While readers and the Phantom himself might gain comfort from the Phantom's fame and his own awareness of that reputation, it is small comfort for the friend and narrator of the story: "I wanted a friend with whom I could be seen abroad. With whom one could exchange country weekends, on our respective estates!" (141). The narrator and the Phantom are both selfish and self-centered, and this mundane perspective on their troubles offers a humorous take on life on the margins of society. Both are outcasts, both are bored, and both are without direction. Gone are the grand passions, the great spectacle, and the beautiful music. Barthelme takes Erik's humanizing to its logical conclusion: the Phantom here is mundane, petulant, and prone to the usual petty vices we are all prone to, in this case, however, without the grand gestures.

At this moment of greatest *ennui*, however, the narrative is interrupted by the following information:

> Gaston Leroux was tired of writing *The Phantom of the Opera*. He replaced his pen in its penholder. "I can always work on *The Phantom of the Opera* later — in the fall, perhaps. Right now, I feel like writing *The Secret of the Yellow Room*" [141].

It is a startling moment. Is the friend Leroux? Is Barthelme toying with his readers, offering a meta-narrative symbolizing the artistic process? The interruption certainly makes it clear that fictional characters are just as difficult to define, just as selfish, just as boring, and just as irritating as human beings.

Surprisingly, the story resumes, with the Phantom agreeing to have plastic surgery, a suggestion his friend made so that the two of them could go out in public more often. At the age of 65, the Phantom decides to leave the Opera House, making use of the advances in contemporary cosmetic surgery. The doctor warns him that such a change will have grave psychological consequences. His friend makes the necessary preparations anyway, only to be disappointed at the last minute — the Phantom disappears: "What vexation! Am I not slightly relieved? Can it be *he doesn't like me*?" The friend sits in front of the Opera House, waiting "until the hot meat of romance is cooled by the dull gravy of common sense once more" (143). With this brilliant adaptation, Barthelme captures much of the *Phantom's* appeal: the quest for perfection and the quest for people to be "like us" will always fail. There must be tension, and there must be subterfuge.

It is important to note that Barthelme, whom some identify as the father of postmodern fiction, chose to write a story about the Phantom. As Robert Waxman notes in his superlative essay on Barthelme:

> The interplay of these two impulses — the Apollonian search for order and Dionysian longing for freedom from conventions — informs much of Barthelme's work and is often expressed through the metaphor of music.... In its Apollonian guise, music has a tonal center, traditional chord progressions.... But music also has its Dionysian dimensions: here the dance becomes wild and frenzied as dissonance replaces consonance, tonal centers fade....

Waxman could be describing many of the variations on the Phantom theme. The interplay between the cold, rational, and domestic world and Erik's world of darkness, passion, and chaos are present throughout not only music but every version. And here in Barthelme's hands, the narrative reminds us that it, too, is constructed, created by an author, perhaps to remind us all that what we read, see, experience, is constructed in important ways. In the end, the short story reminds us that there will always be a Phantom to challenge our desires for homogeneity, the status quo, the everyday.

This book is by no means exhaustive. And with the appearance of Andrew Lloyd Webber's musical in Las Vegas, more and more people will meet Erik, Christine, and Raoul. Perhaps more people will recognize that we all wear masks, and we all must learn to look beyond the mask, to see beyond the superficial in order to listen to the music of the night, ironically to see in the darkness and appreciate the underworld that makes the world of light and love possible. Ultimately, the story of Erik and Christine is beautiful not because it is perfect but because it is flawed. Erik does not "get the girl," and Christine is torn between a life of passion, music, and the underworld and a conventional love affair with Raoul, which looks right in the light of day. Raoul, too, understands that Christine has made a choice, made a compromise, and so the "happily ever after" ending of the story is unsettling. But that is precisely what leads us to return, rethink, and for many, rewrite our own version of the story of the masked, misunderstood man.

Conclusion: The Phantom's Future

> PENGUIN
> I think you're jealous that I'm a
> genuine freak, and you have to wear
> a mask!
> BATMAN
> Maybe you're right.
> *—Batman Returns* (1992)

The interchange between the Penguin and Batman embodies the evolution of Gaston Leroux's *Phantom* to its current incarnations in several ways. First, the *Batman* film is clearly influenced by the *Phantom* myth. The Penguin's lair bears striking resemblances to Erik's habitats in numerous *Phantom* versions. Like Erik's home, the Penguin's is damp, filled with waterways, gondolas, and, of course, the ubiquitous starlet. Instead of rats, of course, this aquatic underworld has penguins, a perfect revision for the comic book villain.

Secondly, the interchange between the deformed villain and the masked hero highlights the changes the Phantom's character has undergone throughout the years. Beginning with the Leroux novel and ending with some of the contemporary novels and other entertainment forms that will be discussed in this concluding chapter, the Phantom has been transformed from a "freak of nature," as represented in the 1925 film, to a deformed "average Joe," a man who wants what all men want: a home, family, and loving wife. And while these elements were clearly highlighted in the Leroux novel, they have become more and more emphasized in subsequent versions.

The Leroux version, of course, presents Erik in a complex way. He is both deformed victim and deformed victimizer, and our sympathies towards him are not stable. At times, we feel for him in his isolation. At others, we admire his creativity and commitment to beauty, ironically a beauty he may never possess through either his physical appearance or as embodied in Christine. And at still others, we are horrified by his possessive violence.

Hollywood, perhaps embodied by the backstory politics and chaos surrounding the 1925 version, tamed Erik in many ways. He became a freak, a monster, one of the criminally insane, somehow "other." And thanks to the good will of the crowd, he was handily dispatched into the river, thereby affording Raoul and Christine the "happily ever after" ending they so deserved. But even in this botched version, Lon Chaney's performance still haunts. The film's conclusion does not satisfy, for what we remember most is the Phantom, not the domesticated couple.

The 1943 film version marks an important shift in *Phantom*'s development. Not only is the focus of the film the Christine character, but the Phantom's disfigurement is caused, not by a deformity of birth or a natural disaster, but by a deliberate act of malice in the very office of a music publisher. The very world that the Phantom has supported, loved, and lived, is the world which undoes him and maims his face.

The 1962 version also highlights the human contribution to the Phantom's suffering, with this Erik also disfigured as a result of dastardly doings in the music industry. Here, too, the focus is less on the Phantom and more on the romantic couple. Facing pressures regarding censorship and box-office sales, Hammer Films offered audiences a Mary Poppins version of the Leroux story, with the young couple being helped, not hindered by the Phantom. In this way, he was turned into a grandfatherly figure, not a romantic powerhouse.

The 1974 rock musical continues the theme of corrupt corporations and music industries, with Winslow, the Phantom, not only disfigured but imprisoned by the man who has stolen his musical score. Here the Phantom behaves as a smitten suitor, desperate to win the love of his Christine, here called Phoenix. And he is more victim than victimizer, with the evil Swan serving as the true villain of this version.

The 1983 version introduces the *Phantom* narrative to a new medium and genre, the television miniseries. Here, once again, the corrupt music industry disfigures the true artist and literally leads another artist to suicide all because a woman would not have an affair with the

Opera administrator. In the end, this Phantom also behaves humanely, ridding the world of the corrupt influences and helping the young love interest to foster their love and art.

Freddy Krueger's version transforms the Phantom into a time-walker who stalks his Christine through the centuries. He is a monster, and she is his victim. There is no Raoul, and there is no escape. The chase is eternal.

The Chinese version returns the Phantom to his role as kindly helper and victim. In this case, the Phantom has been disfigured by the oppressive and corrupt government and traditional systems of China. His attempts to bring Western music and culture are thwarted, and his attempts to love a woman of his own choosing are squelched. In the end, however, he assists a new couple and helps them find true love and culture.

Dario Argento's Phantom is one of the more unusual ones. He is not born deformed physically. Rather, he has been abandoned as a child and raised by rats. Perhaps this social group inspires his blood lust, but whatever the reason, he is one of the most brutal and beautiful of all Phantoms. In the end, his obsession kills him, but the conclusion is far from optimistic. The young couple are not entirely satisfied with their pairing and the loss of the Phantom.

Arthur Kopit's play and film version humanizes the Phantom further, providing a backstory to Erik's life. In it, Erik is an abandoned child whose father lives with him for years, without acknowledging his offspring. Erik, however, does not relinquish Christine to Raoul without a fight, but in the end the young couple are reunited at the expense of the Erik's life.

Lloyd Webber's musical leaves out the Phantom's past, but through the musical score and libretto, it is clear that Erik embodies something all of us experience — desire and passion. Through he is a mysterious figure, we can understand his motivations, as well as Christine's attraction to this "music of the night." Perhaps more than any other version, this Phantom embodies the ambivalence presented in the original Leroux novel.

The shorter versions of the narrative offer various perspectives on the Erik, with the Pinchpenny version offering a ridiculous satire which makes the Phantom just another member of the cast. In the Hirschfield version, the Phantom behaves in much the same way he always does, with little explanation for his disfigurement, but in the end, with Christine settled in with Raoul, the Phantom sets his sights on yet another young singer, thereby serving as not a man as much as a muse.

Susan Kay offers the Phantom an extensive history. Through this history, Erik's mysteriousness is emphasized. He is a genius. He is an architect. He is a musician and composer. He is a drug addict. He is a lover. In all these ways, he is extraordinary, once again.

Frederick Forsyth offers the Phantom a future through his sequel. And here, too, Erik is extraordinary, Howard Hughes-like in business and reclusiveness. We discover that despite these unusual qualities, he is, like many of us, a parent. And like any parent, he wishes to be united with his son.

Colette Gale offers more details than many Phantom aficionados would like regarding the Phantom, but once again, he is humanized. Unlike other Phantoms, hers is not omnipotent. He, too, has been victimized by a sado-masochistic villain. But once again, through Erik's intervention, but not by his hand directly, the world is rid of this evil.

Finally, Barthelme's short story returns Erik to his eccentric roots. He is a human being, but he is an odd sort. His friend suggests plastic surgery, and Erik agrees, only to disappear before the operation. The departure could represent an act of cowardice or integrity. The Phantom could fear the world, preferring life in the shadows listening to the music of the night. Or the Phantom could be choosing the life of darkness, preferring to stay as he is, without cosmetic surgery. Whatever the case, Barthelme honors the Phantom's mystery.

Throughout these versions, the Phantom themes and variations persist, and one of the most important ideas to remain is the idea regarding perception and interpretation. All the Phantoms teach us that there is more to life than meets the eye; there is the music of the night. This music could symbolize literal music, the songs that violate restrictions and promote not only order but chaos, remembrance and transcendence. But this music also symbolizes art and culture in general, worlds moved beyond the corruption of commerce and the details of the day. And while in many *Phantoms* these daylight hours and concerns have their value, most *Phantoms* want us to look beyond these delights, to see more, to listen, to perceive and to interpret differently.

In this way, this gothic romance, this mega-blockbuster musical, or this erotic novel offer reading and interpretation lessons that may make us all better readers and interpreters not just of books but of their characters and, by association, their inspiration: people. These Phantom phenomena may change the way we think about lives, about the masks that we all wear, and the real passions of our life. They all take spectacle to task, even as they are reveling in spectacle's power. Things are not what they seem, and we all need to be cautious about the judgments we make based on appearances. And this, frankly, is a refreshing message in today's overly indulgent visual culture, where everyone from pre-teens to geriatric patients are encouraged to nip, tuck, and snip away perceived imperfections. The Phantom, however, reminds us that beauty is more than skin deep, and passions may run without pornographic spectacle. There is a "music of the night" that plays, and the Phantoms remind us to listen.

Judging from the popularity of the Lloyd Webber version, as well as the numerous versions which continue to appear on Amazon.com, the *Phantom* is still succeeding and selling. The allusions to *Phantom* in *Batman* may be seen in nearly an infinite number of contemporary films and entertainments. Films such as *RoboCop* (1987) and *Darkman* (1990), for example, present well-intentioned heroes who are disfigured by their enemies and who don a mask in order to take revenge and set society right. Films such as *Batman* (1989), *Batman Returns* (1992), and *V For Vendetta* (2005) get their start from the comic book or graphic novel world, but they also borrow from the Phantom myth. Their heroes, however, are not disfigured, only disgruntled, and most tend to defend not art or the music of the night, but rather truth, justice, and either the American way, as in the case of the *Batman* sequels, or Britain, as in the case of *V for Vendetta*. Their characters, like Erik, don disguises to function in dysfunctional societies, but art is not as important in these tales.

In another trend, even characters who are not closely aligned with the Phantom narrative may exhibit Phantom-like behavior in order to elicit certain cultural responses. A case in point is the recent box-office hit, *Pirates of the Caribbean: Dead Man's Chest* (2006). In it, Davy Jones, the captain of the Flying Dutchman and a ghostly, monstrous crew, battle the hero Jack Sparrow and his friends. Like other crew members, Davy Jones's facial features have been distorted by his time at sea — he, for example, looks like an octopus. In his private moments, however, we see him tearfully playing a giant organ. And while the scene is not clearly explained in this film, it suggests, as a result of the *Phantom* myth, that there is more to this villain than meets the eye, a convenient ambiguity for a film series bent on sequels.

Truly, the Leroux novel has influenced and will continue to influence popular culture, but as is seen from the discussion of later films, plays, and novels, popular culture also continues to influence the *Phantom*. What is interesting to note as the variations shift is the narrative's ability to respond to different genres and audience expectations. Andrew Lloyd Webber's version, for example, began as a traditional stage musical, became a film, and has now morphed into a ninety-minute Vegas show. His version also led to numerous plays and novels, and it, like the 1925 performance by Lon Chaney, will perhaps influence future *Phantoms* indefinitely.

One of the most modern permutations of *Phantom* is the proliferation of promotional items. Of the 918 items available on eBay, what can only be described as an Internet yard sale, in addition to the usual DVDs, CDs, playbills, T-shirts, bracelets, cups, mugs, saucers, music boxes, teddy bears, and tote bags, there are also Barbie and Ken dolls dressed as the Phantom and Christine. And while it may be that the people purchasing these items have actually seen a production of *Phantom,* it may be safe to assume that some of them buy the merchandise just because they have heard of *Phantom* and recognize its cultural weight.

The proliferation of this symbolism clearly reflects the popularity of the narrative, but it also indicates that the image has perhaps taken on a life of its own, independent of the narrative. Of course, this Phantom merchandising phenomenon might be explained away by the rampant consumerism of the late twentieth and early twenty-first century. And there is something to that. People with cash to spare want to remember their experience with the play, the film, or the musical through some trinket, but it is very difficult to retain this argument, given the proliferation of *Phantom* paraphernalia. People who have not seen the production want to pretend they did or be a part of the *Phantom* phenomenon, or, practically speaking, cash in on the story's popularity by purchasing items now, holding them, and then selling them later at a higher price.

Perhaps, too, in this time of changing identities and flexible physical appearances, the symbol of the Phantom offers some form of nostalgic reassurance. Deformed from birth or by accident, Erik must live on, and what he does is compose beautiful music. With the introduction of Christine, however, Erik's dilemma is highlighted. He is not like everyone else, and he must address that reality. Eventually, for most Eriks, the answer is sacrifice and compassion. Through the exercise of these virtues, he is freed from his romantic obsession with Christine. In spite of changing circumstances and situations, there is something at the heart of humanity, goodness and love. It is not just about appearances. Ironically, by purchasing these items, some may remember that life is not about superficialities.

To complicate these ideas further is the narrative's ability to transform, morph, and change, to respond to the changing times, needs, and genres. It is to the narrative's credit that it has survived so many permutations, and it is still clearly an interesting story for new and established audiences throughout the world. With the advent of DVD recordings and at-home viewing, moreover, there is a greater opportunity for the story to be not only viewed but reviewed. As Frederick Wasser notes, "in show biz terminology, video may be the biggest thing that has happened to movies since sound" (qtd. in Kendrick 57). And though the technology may be new, the act of rereading, reviewing, and reinterpretation is not. In one way, the at-home viewer need not be surrounded by strangers experiencing a common film. Admittedly, a dark movie theater is very different from a darkened live theater, particularly those that offer views of other audience members through thrust or in-the-round stages, but there is still something very ritualistic and communal about watching a film with a group of strangers, judging their reactions as compared to yours.

Now, however, the at-home viewer may watch not only alone, but not even the entire film. How that affects our views of films and culture is the subject of some debate. And how it will affect our understanding of the Phantom remains to be seen.

Another technological form also presents challenges and opportunities for the Phantom narrative. As Chad Hurley, founder and CEO of YouTube, observed in 2007, "We are at an unprecedented time in the history of entertainment media. Never before has the opportunity been so great for independent writers and actors, musicians and producers to create compelling content on a par with the studios, networks, and labels. With easy and affordable access to cameras, editing software and computing power, the playing field has truly been leveled." Just at a time when more and more people are discouraged from making independent films, along comes YouTube, the Internet video-sharing website. And as Hurley also notes, "YouTube represents the first time media has become truly democratic for both the audience and the content creators." Further, YouTube is "also a network of audience members who engage content in a different way than previously possible and spread success stories by word of mouth." Consequently, people are now experiencing the *Phantom* in a new way, through a new genre, the YouTube genre.

A quick search on the website yields over 38,000 "hits," with the number growing perhaps daily. Selections include an excerpt from *The David Letterman Show* in which comedian Will Ferrell performs a song from Andrew Lloyd Webber's musical, "Music of the Night." In it, he flubs lines, and makes up his own: "My name is Jerry and I'm really lonely." He also complains about how uncomfortable the mask is. All, perhaps, in the hopes of avoiding any copyright infringement issues with Lloyd Webber, but the clip is funny, and there are many other clips which contain equally satiric commentary on the Lloyd Webber film and the Brightman clips. Other versions include homemade videos from concerts including Sarah Brightman and Antonio Banderas, Nightwish, and even a Chinese version of the Lloyd Webber music. Phantom viewers, then, get an experience of diversity of interpretations and versions from moments on YouTube, rather than months researching books, plays, and films in libraries. This immediacy is new, and once again, it is an experience that the viewer has alone. Admittedly, viewers can communicate electronically, but such communication is certainly different from the experience in a movie theater or stage, but it is more communal than a novel-reading experience. How these contexts will affect *Phantom* viewers and subsequent versions remains to be seen, but the Phantom's popularity is assured. And perhaps, more than ever, the message regarding appearances is important — things are not what they seem. Appearances are not the only means of communication. There is the "music of the night."

Notes

1. Several scholars have offered explanations for *The Phantom*'s popularity and persistence. Joan Kessler, for example, observes in her discussion *Demons of the Night: Tales of the Fantastic, Madness, and the Supernatural from Nineteenth-Century France* that the French were wild for gothic works. The Marquis de Sade based his explanation on the Revolution — the French were inured to violence and horror, so their literature had to become more gruesome. For writers like Kessler, Sade's conclusion was an oversimplification. She argues that not only the French but the entire world was interested in madness, evil, and the unconscious. Sigmund Freud's *Interpretation of Dreams* (1901) not only argued for the unconscious but also a means to analyze the images offered up by the mysterious side of human psyche.

The parallels between the Leroux Opera House and the Freudian mind have not escaped many authors. It is easy to make the connection between the conscious world and the world of the Opera House, on the one hand, and the unconscious and the dark underworld of the Phantom on the other. Slavoj Zizek, for example, read the Phantom narrative, particularly the novel, the 1925 film, and the 1990 television miniseries, from a Freudian perspective, arguing that our attraction to the Phantom is ambivalent: we are simultaneously repelled by his castration, represented by his deformed face and lack of nose, but also drawn to his power over music, Christine, the underworld, and to a great extent, the Opera House. Zizek also concludes that the appearance of monsters, hence his emphasis on the three different versions, coincides with cultural and economic changes.

Jerrold Hogle also relates monsters to cultural, psychoanalytic, and social changes, arguing that the various versions of the Phantom reflect the ways in which society disposes of undesirable elements. And while these elements may change from era to era, the fact that they are all disposed of in the same way, through oppression and repression, is not only significant but doomed. The repressed, to use the Freudian wording, always returns. These undesirable elements cannot be silenced.

2. See Jerrold Hogle's Introduction to *The Cambridge Companion to Gothic Fiction* for more details and varying perspectives on the term "gothic."

3. All further references come from *The Essential Phantom of the Opera*, edited by Leonard Wolf, and appear in the text.

4. The trade edition of the novel, the Barnes and Noble edition with a foreword by Peter Haining, offers an additional paragraph to the preface, one in which the narrator, identified as Gaston Leroux himself, thanks the opera community for their help in his research. And while this journalistic detail merely reinforces the earlier attempts at verisimilitude, the identification of the narrator as Gaston Leroux takes this attempt and makes it an attack, forcing a documentary reading of the novel and fulfilling the biographical fallacy and its tendencies in the modern reader. That is, by signing the preface with the author's name, the edition implies that there is no separation between art and reality; there is no artifice at work. And while that strategy may be worthwhile for a brief moment in the horror story's opening, it ultimately feeds into the stereotype regarding art and artists of most readers — art is based on the personal experiences of the author, not the imaginative and technical craft. Art becomes a divine, mysterious and unattainable entity, with the author being merely a conduit for the Muses. Such a conclusion trivializes the choices that authors make to create and craft their stories. Similarly, George Perry's summary of the novel in *The Complete Phantom of the Opera* makes no distinction between the narrator and Leroux.

Such conclusions perpetuate the popular but misconceived idea that the artist and the work are one and the same. The problem with this presumption, first articulated by W.K. Wimsatt in the scholarly work *The Verbal Icon* (1954), is that it perpetuates the notion that art is based on the personal experiences of the author, not the imaginative, technical, and disciplined craft of writing. And while it may seem reasonable to conclude that the artist uses personal experience, such presumptions are often misleading. Leroux's cavalier love life, for example, might lead readers to draw certain conclusions about the female characters in the novel, conclusions which are not supported by the novel but are supported by Leroux's biography.

5. Rose Theresa notes that Gounod's *Faust* was "performed more often than any other operatic work" worldwide. "It was also the opera earliest cinematographers turned to most frequently" (1).

6. Part of the problem with Raoul is that many modern audiences have grown accustomed to a model of masculinity that can only be described as machismo on steroids. It is important to remember such characters as Mary Shelley's Dr. Frankenstein, who, contrary to the Kenneth Branagh remake (1994), does not perform great physical feats. As a matter of fact, throughout the novel, he does a great deal of fainting and recuperating. Jonathan Harker in Bram Stoker's *Dracula* functions similarly, and one need only remember Leslie Howard in *Gone with the Wind*, which to a certain extent represents an important moment in modern masculine representation. The moony Leslie Howard is contrasted to the man of action, Clark Gable. There is no doubt who the film or the author, Margaret Mitchell, favors.

7. For Hogle, this moment is not so much about Raoul as it is about Christine. According to his decidedly Freudian analysis, the ecstasy that Christine experiences is one that is fraught with incestuous desires for her dead father. With the

father in the grave, these desires are expressed, and they, according to Hogle, also explain her fascination for the Phantom, literally a dead father walking (*Undergrounds* 10–11). Though his argument is compelling, and it is tempting to offer some sort of explanation for Christine's relationship with the Phantom, the text does not seem to suggest that the ecstasy is Christine's alone. It is the music that alters their consciousness, not their oedipal desires. Raoul is transported just as much as Christine, and since there is so little known about his sexual desires and family it is difficult to conclude that he, too, is having erotic fantasies regarding Daaé's father, his old music teacher. Instead, the novel once again emphasizes the power music has over the psyche and it auditors.

8. See, for example, my essay "Voices in the Dark: The Disembodied Voice in Harold Pinter's *Mountain Language*," Kaja Silverman's *The Acoustic Mirror*, and *Embodied Voices: Representing Female Vocality in Western Culture*, edited by Leslie C. Dunn and Nancy A. Jones. Catherine Clement's work on women in opera is also useful.

9. See, for example, the Hemingway short story "The Killers," as compared to the 1946 film starring Burt Lancaster and Ava Gardner. The comparison is a good one since the short story is so brief and ambiguous. The film completes the story, giving greater attention to character development and motive, which, in the end, creates yet another work of art, this time a film noir masterpiece. See John Desmond and Peter Hawkes for a discussion this and other adaptations in *Adaptation: Studying Film and Literature*.

10. See, for example, John Drinkwater's *The Life and Adventures of Carl Laemmle*.

11. In an amusing commentary on the 1925 version, the technical director, Archie Hall, lambastes the 1943 interpretation, saying that Lon Chaney embodied the role of Erik; Claude Rains's portrayal was effeminate, as evidenced by the choice of musical instruments. As we shall see later, the 1943 film is much more feminist than the 1925 version, so this commentator might have unwittingly sensed the shift and attributed it to Rains, not the script.

12. Almost as if to return the snub, the opening of *The Phantom* could only be described as decadent. As composer and organist Chauncey Haines reported:

The LA police had to assign a squad of policemen to keep the crowds back as people started arriving early in the morning to get a good view of the stars as they arrived.

The sides of the lobby were completely covered with red velvet and additional chandeliers were installed to give the audience something to think about while they waited. Dozens of posters and billboards covered the building and a special electric marquee extended the full length of the theatre with the title in gold lights [qtd. in Riley, 277].

Further, as Riley reports, the film made so much money "that it gave the Laemmles a year that was never topped in profits and box office receipts" (277).

13. Michael Blake, a make-up artist himself, offers this detailed account of the Chaney make-up:

Over the years, many writers have propagated myths about how Lon's Phantom make-up was actually accomplished. Stories range from Lon placing celluloid discs in his cheekbones (which is, of course, physically impossible), to placing wire pins in his nose to distend his nostrils. To achieve the Phantom's skull-like appearance, Lon employed the same cotton and collodion technique he used in *The Hunchback of Notre Dame* for the raised and extended cheekbones. The up-tilting of the nose was done by gluing a strip of fishskin onto the top of the nose with spirit gum, pulling it up until the desired look was achieved, and then gluing the rest of the strip of fishskin to the bridge of the nose and lower part of the forehead. Shading around the eyes with a dark liner gave the hollow-eyed look which was further emphasized with a thin line of high-light color under the lower eyelashes. The jagged teeth were made of guttapercha, accentuated by using a dark lining color on the lower lip. Lon used a skull cap with a wig sewn onto it and a fine piece of muslin on the edge of the cap. Gluing the muslin edge allowed it to blend easily with the forehead. His ears were glued back with spirit gum, completing the hideous look [*Lon Chaney* 133].

14. In her important study on female representation and traditional Hollywood narrative, Laura Mulvey identified difficulties for female spectators viewing these traditional narratives. In a word, there are few characters to identify with. Clearly this 1943 version violates the trend Mulvey outlines.

15. It is interesting to note that De Palma's graduate school teacher was named Wilford Leach, and it was during his time with this teacher that De Palma completed his first feature, *The Wedding Party* (Knapp 24).

16. Throughout the film, De Palma seems to enjoy using nearly every filmmaking technique in the business, and for this reason the film is a wonderful choice for film studies courses. In addition to De Palma's trademark use of the split screen, the film includes wipes, fishhooks, keyholes, and montage, some of which hark back to film's early years. De Palma's indebtedness to Hitchcock, too, underscores the delightful aspects of the industry: "Hitchcock made so many movies that he really covered all the good ideas. If you work in the genre, you're sort of compelled to use the best stuff that's around" (De Palma qtd. in Attanasio).

17. A version of this pairing is available on YouTube.

18. Though Wikipedia is sometimes incorrect, this story about John Kenley is supported by many performers in the central Ohio area who either worked with him or knew people who did. In a recent article on his career, Kenley hinted at the secret to his success: making theater affordable for many. As Michael Grossberg reports, "When Kenley began using Columbus's [Ohio] 4000-seat auditorium in 1959, 'they thought I was crazy,' said Kenley. 'I only charged $2 or $2.25, and that was unheard of.'" His first season in Columbus sold out.

19. See Modleski's *Loving with a Vengeance*, which highlights the ways in which popular romance media empowers female viewers.

Bibliography

Atkins, Tom. "History." *Ken Hill's Phantom of the Opera*. June 12, 2008. www.ken hillsphantomoftheopera.co.uk.

Attanasio, Paul. "Brian De Palma as Son of Hitchcock." *Washington Post*. November 4, 1984. F1.

Baker, Russell. "Abie's English Phantom." *New York Times*. January 30, 1988. Sec. 1, p. 27.

Barthelme, Donald. "The Phantom of the Opera's Friend." New York: Putnam, 1981, pp. 138–143.

Batta, Andras. *Opera: Composers, Works, Performers*. Cologne: Konemann Verlagsgesellschaft, 2000.

Bettelheim, Bruno. *The Uses of Enchantment*. New York: Vintage, 1989.

Blake, Michael. *A Thousand Faces: Lon Chaney's Unique Artistry in Motion Pictures*. New York: Vestal, 1995.

_____. *Lon Chaney: The Man Behind the Thousand Faces*. New York: Vestal Press, 1993.

"Blood Money." *Televisual*. February 4, 2003. Lexis-Nexis. 20 May 2007.

"A Book of Mysteries." *New York Times*. August 1, 1908. 426:4.

Bradshaw, Peter. "The Phantom of the Opera." *Guardian Film of the Week*. December 10, 2004; May 20, 2007. http://film.guardian.co.uk/News_Story/Critic_Review/Guardian_Film_of_the_week/0,4267,1370099,00.html.

Brustein, Robert. "The Schlepic." *The New Republic*. 198.11 (March 14, 1988): pp. 33–34.

Byrd, Max. Introduction. *The Phantom of the Opera*. New York: Signet, pp. vii–xv.

Byrne, Terry. "Phantom Writing: Frederick Forsyth's Uninspired Sequel Skimps on Story; *Phantom* Sequel is Unmasked." *Boston Herald*. November 22, 1999, p. 37.

Castanza, Philip. *The Complete Films of Jeanette MacDonald and Nelson Eddy*. Secaucus, NJ: Carol Publishing Group, 1978; 1990.

Clement, Catherine. *Opera, or the Undoing of Women*. Trans. Betsy Wing. Foreword by Susan McClary. Minneapolis: University of Minnesota Press, 1988.

"Colette Gale." May 15, 2008. http://www.colettegale.com/index_flash.html.

Conrich, Ian. "Before Sound: Universal, Silent Cinema, and the Last of the Horror-Spectaculars." *The Horror Film*. Ed. Stephen Prince. Brunswick, NJ: Rutgers University Press, 2004, pp. 40–57.

Crawford, Michael. *Parcel Arrived Safely, Tied with String: My Autobiography*. London: Century, 1999.

Crowther, Bosley. "Nelson Eddy Much in Evidence." *New York Times*. October 15, 1943; *New York Times Online*, May 20, 2007. http://movies2.nytimes.com/mem/movies/review.html?title1=Phantom%20of%20the%20Opera%2C%20The&title2=&reviewer=BOSLEY%20CROWTHER&pdate=19431015&v_id=37950.

"Culture Pulp: Writings and Comics by Mike Russell." May 15, 2008. http://homepage.mac.com/merussell/iblog/B835531044/C1592678312/E20060923191800/index.html.

Desmond, John, and Peter Hawkes. *Adaptation: Studying Film and Literature*. Boston: McGraw-Hill, 2006.

"A Detective Story." *New York Times*. March 20, 1909. 160:2.

Dolar, Mladen. "The Object Voice." In *The Gaze and Voice as Love Objects*. Eds. Renata Saleci and Slavoj Zizek. Duke University Press, 1996, pp. 7–12.

Drinkwater, John. *The Life and Adventures of Carl Laemmle*. New York: Arno Press, 1978.

Dunn, Leslie C., and Nancy Jones, eds. *Embodied Voices: Representing Female Vocality in Western Culture*. London: Cambridge University Press, 1997.

Dupont, Joan. "Enter a New *Phantom*, With Freudian Surprises." *New York Times*. March 11, 1990. Sec. 2, p. 35.

Ebert, Roger. "Andrew Lloyd Webber's *Phantom of the Opera*." Ebert.com. December 22, 2004; May 20, 2007. http://rogerebert.suntimes.com/apps/pbcs.dll/article?AID=/20041221/REVIEWS/41201007/1023.

Falstein, Bruce. *Phantom of the Opera*. Water Bearer Films, 1998.

Forsyth, Frederick. *The Phantom of Manhattan*. New York: St. Martin's Press, 1999.

Frank, Leah. "A Simpler Version of *Phantom*, with Melodrama, at Gateway." *New York Times*. July 11, 1993. LI. 15.

Freiss, Steve. "Phantom is Here." *USA Today*. June 19, 2006, p. 3D.

Gale, Colette. *Unmasqued: An Erotic Novel of the Phantom of the Opera*. New York: Signet, 2007.

Gallo, Phil. "*Phantom*: Las Vegas Spectacular." *Daily Variety*. 292.1. July 5, 2006, pp. 4–9.

"Gaston Leroux Dies." *New York Times*. April 17, 1927. 24:2.

Grossberg, Michael. "The Echoes of Applause." *The Columbus Dispatch*. April 18, 2004. D1.

Gussow, Mel. "The Phantom's Many Faces Over the Years." *New York Times*. January 31, 1988. Sec. 2.5.

Haining, Peter. Introduction. *The Gaston Leroux Bedside Companion*. London: Gollancz, 1980, pp. 1–16.

_____. Foreword. *The Phantom of the Opera*. New York: Barnes and Noble, 1985, pp. 7–24.

Hall, Ann C. "Voices in the Dark: The Disembodied Voice in *Mountain Language*." *The Pinter Review. Annual Essays 1991.* Eds. Francis Gillen and Steven H. Gale. Tampa: University of Tampa Press, 1991, pp. 17–22.

Hall, Archie. Commentary. *The Phantom of the Opera: The Ultimate Version.* DVD. Image Entertainment, 2003.

"Hammer Studios History." May 15, 2008. http://www.fortunecity.com/lavendar/judidench/339/hammer.html.

"Hays Code." May 15, 2008. http://www.classicmovies.org/articles/blhayscode.htm.

Hill, Ken. *The Phantom of the Opera.* New York: Samuel French, 1994.

Hogle, Jerrold. Introduction. *The Cambridge Companion to Gothic Fiction.* New York: Cambridge University Press, 2002.

_____. *The Undergrounds of the "Phantom of the Opera": Sublimation and the Gothic in Leroux's Novel and Its Progeny.* New York: Palgrave, 2002.

Holden, Stephen. "A New 'Phantom' from Miami Beach." Review of *The Phantom of the Opera* (1991). *New York Times.* June 8, 1991.

Honeycutt, Kirk. "Fascinated by the Phantom." *Hollywood Reporter:* May 1991 *Phantom of the Opera* Salute. S3-S20.

Hulbert, Dan. "An Early Tale of *Phantom* Spectacle, Too." *Atlanta Constitution.* August 15, 1993. N2.

Hunter, Jennifer. "In the End, Keeping or Changing Surname Continues to Be an Issue for Women." *Chicago Sun–Times.* April 13, 2005.

Hurley, Chad. *Forbes* . 179.10. May 7, 2007, pp. 68–70. EBSCO Host. Film and Television Literature Index. Ohio Dominican University, Spangler Library. May 14, 2008. http://web.ebscohost.com.ezproxy.ohiodominican.edu/ehost/detail?vid=4&hid=101&sid=344ae661–2ece–41de–ac75–8b9c6d20ecab%40 sessionmgrl07.

Hustvedt, Asti, ed. *The Decadent Reader: Fiction, Fantasy, and Perversion from Fin-de-Siècle* France. New York: Zone Books, 1998.

James, Caryn. "This Phantom Has His Lair in London, but Travels." *New York Times.* November 4, 1989.

"John Kenley." Wikipedia.

Johnson, Tom, and Deborah DelVecchio. *Hammer Films: An Exhaustive Filmography.* Jefferson, NC: McFarland, 1996.

Kay, Susan. *Phantom.* New York: Dell, 1991.

Kendrick, James. "Aspect Ratios and Joe Six-Packs: Home Theatre Enthusiasts' Battle to Legitimize the DVD Experience." *The Velvet Light Trap.* 56.1 (2005): pp. 58–70. Project Muse. Ohio Dominican University, Spangler Library. May 15, 2008. http://muse.jhu.edu.ezproxy.ohiodominican.edu/journals/the_velvet_light_trap/v056/56.1kendrick.html.

"Ken Hill Obituary." *Ken Hill's Phantom of the Opera.* June 12, 2008. Originally published for *The Times* (London), February 18, 1995. http://www.kenhills phantomoftheopera.co.uk/obit.php.

Kenley, John, and Robert Thomas Noll. *The Phantom of the Opera: The Play.* New York: Samuel French. 1988.

Kessler, Joan. Introduction. *Demons of the Night.* Chicago: University of Chicago Press, 1995, pp. xi–li.

Kinsey, Wayne. *Hammer Films: The Bray Studio Years*. Richmond: Reynolds-Hearn, 2002.

Knapp, Laurence, ed. *Brian De Palma Interviews*. Jackson: University of Mississippi Press, 2003.

Kopit, Arthur. *Phantom*. New York: Samuel French, 1992.

"The Kopit Yeston *Phantom*." *Backstage*. May 19, 1995.

Leroux, Gaston. *The Essential Phantom of the Opera*. Ed. Leonard Wolf. New York: Plume, 1996.

_____. *Missing Men*. New York: Macaulay, 1923.

_____. *The Mystery of the Yellow Room*. Cutchogue, New York: Buccaneer Books, 1993.

_____. *The Perfume of the Lady in Black*. Sawry Cambs, UK: Dedalus, 1998.

_____. *The Phantom of the Opera*. Ed. Peter Haining. New York: Barnes and Noble, 1985.

_____. "A Terrible Tale." In *The Gaston Leroux Bedside Companion*. Ed. Peter Haining. London: Victor Gollancz, 1980, pp. 17–35.

Lloyd Webber, Andrew. Interview. *Andrew Llloyd Webber's The Phantom of the Opera Companion*. London: Pavillion, 2004, pp. 8–9.

"Lloyd Webber Buys." *Washington Post*. January 12, 2000. CO3.

"Llumina Press." May 15, 2008. http://www.llumina.com/Phantom.htm.

MacQueen, Scott. "'43 *Phantom* Found New Formula for Classic Tale." *American Cinematographer*. 74. 9 (September 1993): pp. 80–85.

"The Making of *Phantom of the Paradise*." Directed by Brian De Palma. May 20, 2007. http://www.briandepalma.net/phantom/phtmint.htm.

Mulvey, Laura. *Visual Pleasure and Narrative Cinema*. New York: Routledge, 1998.

"The Nightmare on Elm Street Saga." May 20, 2007. http://www.geocities.com/hollywood/makeup/4303/nightmare.html.

"An Opera-House Phantom." *New York Times*. February 19, 1911. 6: 90.

Ouzounian, Richard. "Phantom Goes Vegas with a Tight New Show." *Toronto Star*. July 3, 2006. E03.

Perry, George, ed. *The Complete Phantom of the Opera*. New York: Henry Holt, 1987, pp. 140–167.

The Phantom Lover Official Website. May 20, 2007. http://home.clara.net/first universal/phantom-lover.htm.

The Phantom Lover (Ye Bang ge Sheng). Dir. Ronnie Yu. 1995. Mandarin Films. VHS. Tai Seng Video Marketing, 1998.

The Phantom of the Opera: The Ultimate Version. Dir. Rupert Julian. Perf. Lon Chaney, Mary Philbin. 1925. DVD. Image Entertainment, 2003.

The Phantom of the Opera. Dir. Arthur Lubin. Perf. Nelson Eddy, Susanna Foster, Claude Rains. 1943. DVD. Universal, 2001.

The Phantom of the Opera. Dir. Perf. Herbert Lom, Heather Sears, Edward de Souza. 1962. DVD. Universal, 2005.

The Phantom of the Opera. Dir. Robert Markowitz. Perf. Jane Seymour, Maximilian Schell, Michael York. 1983. VHS. Los Angeles: CBS-TV.

The Phantom of the Opera. Dir. Dwight H. Little. Perf. Robert Englund, Jill Shoelen. 1989. DVD. MGM, 2004.

The Phantom of the Opera. Dir. Tony Richardson. Perf. Burt Lancaster, Charles Dance, Teri Polo. 1990. DVD. Saban Entertainment, 2005.

The Phantom of the Opera. Dir. Dario Argento. Perf. Julian Sands, Asia Argento. 1998. DVD. Allumination, 1999.

The Phantom of the Opera. Dir. Joel Schumacher. Perf. Gerard Butler, Emily Rossum. 2004. DVD. Warner Bros. 2005.

Phantom of the Paradise. Dir. Brian De Palma. Perf. Paul Williams, William Finley, Jessica Harper. 1974. DVD. Twentieth Century Fox, 2002.

Reilly, Robert. "The Music of the Spheres, or the Metaphysics of Music." *Intercollegiate Review.* Fall 2001, pp. 12–21.

Rich, Frank. "*Phantom of the Opera.*" *New York Times.* January 27, 1998. C. 19.

Rich, Sharon. *Sweethearts: The Timeless Love Affair— On-Screen and Off— Between Jeanette MacDonald and Nelson Eddy.* New York: Dutton, 1994.

Riley, Philip J. *Phantom of the Opera: Hollywood Archives Series.* Absecon, NJ: MagicImage Filmbooks, 1999.

Robinette, Joseph, and Robert Chauls. *The Phantom of the Opera.* Woodstock, IL: Dramatic Publishing Co., 1992.

Schumacher, Joel. Interview. *Andrew Lloyd Webber's The Phantom of the Opera Companion.* London: Pavillion, 2004, pp. 48–49.

Scorsese, Martin. *Hammer Studios History.* June 12, 2008. http://www.fortunecity.com/lavendar/judidench/339/hammer.html.

Scott, A.O. "Back with a Vengeance: Music of the Night." *New York Times.* December 22, 2004. E.5.

Sharkey, Jack. *The Pinchpenny Phantom of the Opera: An Affordable Musical Comedy.* New York: Samuel French, 1988.

Showalter, Elaine. *Gender and Culture at the Fin de Siècle.* New York: Penguin, 1990.

Siegel, Ed. "The Smartest, Dullest *Phantom* Yet." *Boston Globe.* March 16, 1990, pp. 39+.

Silverman, Kaja. *The Acoustic Mirror.* Bloomington: Indiana University Press, 1998.

Skal, David J. *The Monster Show: A Cultural History of Horror.* New York: Faber and Faber, 2001.

Snelson, John. *Andrew Lloyd Webber.* New Haven: Yale University Press, 2004.

Soister, John T., with JoAnna Wioskowski. *Claude Rains: A Comprehensive Illustrated Reference.* Jefferson, North Carolina: McFarland, 1999.

Stine, R.L. *Phantom of the Auditorium.* New York: Scholastic, 1994.

"Summary." *Directed by Brian De Palma.* May 20, 2007. http://www.briandepalma.net/phantom/phantom.htm.

Terry, Clifford. "A New Phantom." *Chicago Tribune.* January 19, 1992. Sec. 13, pp. 6+.

Theresa, Rose. "From Mephistopheles to Melies: Spectacle and Narrative in Opera and Early Film." *Between Opera and Cinema.* Eds. Joe Jeongwon and Rose Theresa. New York: Routledge, 2002, pp. 1–18.

Turk, Edward Baron. "Deriding the Voice of Jeanette MacDonald: Notes on Psychoanalysis and the American Film Musical." In *Embodied Voices: Represent-*

ing Female Vocality in Western Culture. Eds. Leslie C. Dunn and Nancy A. Jones. New York: Cambridge, 1994, pp. 103–120.

Vieira, Mark A. *Hollywood Horror: From Gothic to Cosmic*. New York: Harry N. Abrams, 2003.

Waxman, Robert. "Apollo and Dionysus: Donald Barthelme's Dance of Life." *Studies in Short Fiction*. Spring 1996. Bnet. May 15, 2008. http://findarticles. com/p/articles/mi_m2455/is_/ai_20831946.

Weber, Eugen. *France: Fin de Siècle*. Cambridge, MA: Belknap Press, Harvard University Press, 1986.

Wimsatt, W.K. *The Verbal Icon*. Lexington: University of Kentucky Press, 1954.

Wolf, Leonard. Introduction. *The Essential Phantom of the Opera*. New York: New York: Plume, 1996, pp. 1–18.

Wollman, Elizabeth. *The Theatre Will Rock: A History of the Rock Musical, From Hair to Hedwig*. Ann Arbor: University of Michigan Press, 2006.

"Woman Has First Face Transplant." *BBC News*. November 30, 2005. http://news. bbc.co.uk/1/hi/health/4484728.stm.

Yu, Ronny. Interview. *Culture Pulp: Writings and Comics by Mike Russell*. May 15, 2008. http://homepage.mac.com/merussell/iblog/B835531044/C1592678 312/E20060923191800/index.html.

Zinoman, Josh. "Old and Ghostly But Still a Hoot." *New York Times*. July 1, 2005. E. PT.1.

Zizek, Slavoj. *Enjoy Your Symptom! Jacques Lacan in Hollywood and Out*. 2nd ed. New York: Routledge, 2001.

Index

Printed in the USA
CPSIA information can be obtained
at www.ICGtesting.com
CBHW020341050924
14097CB00039B/125

9 780786 442652